नीति और रामचरित

नीति और रामचरित

हिमांशु पाठक

प्रतिभा प्रतिष्ठान, नई दिल्ली

प्रकाशक : प्रतिभा प्रतिष्ठान,
1661 दखनीराय स्ट्रीट, नेताजी सुभाष मार्ग, नई दिल्ली-110002
 / संस्करण : 2017 / मूल्य : छह सौ रुपए
मुद्रक : आर-टेक ऑफसेट प्रिंटर्स, दिल्ली ISBN 978-93-80823-58-4

NEETI AUR RAMCHARIT *by* Himanshu Pathak ₹ 600.00
Published by Pratibha Pratishthan, 1661 Dakhni Rai Street,
Netaji Subhash Marg, New Delhi-110002

Dedicated

to

My Father

Late Shri Parmanand Pathak

PREFACE

There are more books written and Ph.D.s awarded for works on Tulaseedaas and the Shri Raamacharitamanas than probably on any other subject in India or probably in the world! Then, why embark upon writing another book to deal with Tulasee or his magnum-opus, Shri Ramacharitamaanas?

I had to deal with the above question before I started on this project! This project came around due to several reasons. One of the main reasons has been that I wanted to remember some selected pieces of wisdom from the Raamaayan (the Raamacharitamaanas) by Tulaseedaas. I read the Raamacharitamaanas again some years back and collected many Dohaas/ Choupaaees or Chhands that I liked and then in the second go around minimized them to 100 of them only. The number 100 came from the Hindu/Indian tradition of books from Saints like Bhartrihari: "The Bhartrihari Shatak" etc. Another main reason to write this work is our living abroad in USA and dealing with the situation that the children born to the first generation Indian-American do have access to Hindu temples but not similar exposure to our literature as we had to the great pieces of wisdom from great Hindi poets like Tulaseedaas, Kabeer, Soor, Meeraa, Raheem and others. And then worse than that is probably they will never read them here in US or like kids born in any other country outside India! The only possibility I could see is that kids over 18 years of age or even young people over 25, may read a book which is lot smaller than Raamaayan and that too in English or in semi English, i.e. in English with the option of the same material with Hindi text from Raamaayan.

Therefore, I have given here the original text in Hindi with Hindi translation, with a small dictionary of some selected difficult (that I thought) words at the end of the book. Included here are also my thoughts in the form of comments as they arose when I was reading the verses! I am sure, knowledgeable people could always express these thoughts in lesser words or could do a better or more elaborate explanation than done here. There is also a possibility that people over the age of 25 years may also find this work as useful to them depending upon their nature, interest, and life experiences.

The small dictionary is also added here because every reader of this book may not have easy access to a dictionary and even if they do carrying it everywhere they sit and read may be difficult or cumbersome!

As I mentioned above, this work is basically meant for English speaking young folks above the age of 18 years when they are college age or above and living outside India who may know a little Hindi. However this can easily benefit any one who does not understand Hindi as Hindi transliteration of the verses and their translation is also given in English! The comments here, however, are in English only. This modest work can also benefit millions of young Indian people in India who got their education in English speaking schools and may have missed exposure to the great pieces of wisdom in Hindi literature in general and the Raamacharitamaanas in particular.

However, a gentle reminder that I put together this work for "swaantah sukhaaya" i.e. for my own learning pleasure and am sure other people may also benefit who are more mature in their age than a young person of 40!

May God! Almighty bless us all! May our teachers, parents, and Gurujees bless us all without whose blessings nothing worthwhile can be learnt!

SYSTEM FOR TRANSLITERATION

No two systems of languages are there where the number of vowels and consonants are the same and are pronounced the same way! Hindi to English transliteration has the same situation. Some times with in the same language different regions of a country pronounce same words differently!

The same thing is true about Hindi which is spoken all over India and is spoken differently in the Hindi speaking states. Even in UP (Uttar Pradesh) it is spoken differently in the different parts of the state! For example the English is the same way.

With in US there are distinct pronunciations from North to South and East to West and even from with in NY city from Manhattan to Brooklyn!

Then comes the situation where kids of Indian Americans origin growing up in USA have another unique pronunciation system for Hindi alphabets. Here we have tried to cover as many situations as possible but possibly missed some. Specifically there are many sounds in Hindi Alphabet which do not exist in English usage or Roman alphabet.

Good example for this is the aspirant kh, ch, jh, t; d̲: , d̲; and ph. Therefore, the transliteration mapping is shown in the following pages. There is one alphabet 'w' which is not used much.

As it has been mentioned above, this work is basically meant for young people like Indians American and similar young people out side India in countries other than USA. This transliteration has been done with that in mind. For example every effort is made to elaborate the transliteration rules as possible. Here are some points that can be made:

- Transliteration for 'ai' is given but when 'a' and 'i' have to be pronounced distinctly, then they are showed as 'a-i'.
- 'A' at the end of a word or syllable is not written (there are very few exceptions here)
- As the rule above for 'ai', similar rule is followed for 'ou' and 'au'
- If 'a' needs to be pronounced as distinct then it is separated as '-a'
- 'A' at the beginning of a word or syllable is always pronounced.
- There are some letters for which no equivalent English sounds are used and they are like the letters like छ(chh) झ (jh) ट (t:) ठ (t:) ड (d:) ड़ (d̲:) (d;) (d̲;) and ध (dh)
- Consonants can not be pronounced without the help of vowels. Therefore, when a consonant has to be written without a vowel it is followed by another consonant with a vowel so the two joint consonants can be pronounced.

The consonant written without a vowel is called half-alphabet!

- And there is a large list of joint consonants which are represented with unique symbols in Hind. However, only very few are used in common expressions. Here are example of them which are mostly used:
  - K and sh: consonants are written together as 'ksh' and in Hindi as क्ष
  - G and y consonants are written together as 'gy' and in Hindi as ज्ञ
  - D and y consonants are written together as 'dy' and in Hindi as द्य
  - T and r consonants are written together as 'tr' and in Hindi as ट्र
  - D and v consonants are written together as 'dv' and in Hindi as द्व
  - D and r consonants are written together as 'dr' and in Hindi as द्र
  - Sh and r consonants are written together as 'sh:r' and in Hindi as श्र .

SIMPLE RULES FOR TRANSLITERATION

Devenagari Character	Sign	Roman character	Pronunciation
	अ	a	As 'a' in afford
	आ	aa	As 'a' in after
	इ	i	As 'i' in input
	ई	ee	As 'ee' in meek
	उ	u	As 'u' in full
	ऊ	oo	As 'oo' in fool

ए	e	As ‘e’ in Edward
ऐ	ai	As ‘ai’ in maitre
ओ	o	As ‘o’ in hole
औ	au	As ‘ou’ in out
अं	an	As ‘an’ Kangaroo

Consonants

Gutturals

क	k	As ‘k’ in Kangaroo
ख	kh	As ‘kh’ in Khaki
ग	g	As ‘g’ in go
घ	gh	As ‘gh’ in ghost
ङ	n	As ‘n’ in anger

Platals

च	ch	As ‘ch’ in ‘chest’
छ	chh	
ज	j	As ‘j’ in jar
झ	jh	
ञ	n	As ‘n’ in punctual

Cerebrals

ट	t:	As ‘t’ in top
ठ	t;	
ड	d:	As ‘d’ in dope
ढ	d;	
ण	n:	As ‘n’ bunt

Dentals

त	‘t’	As ‘t’ in French word

			Matron
	थ	th	As ‘th’ in theory
	द	d	As ‘th’ in weather
	ध	dh	
	न	n	As ‘n’ in new
Bilabial			
	प	p	As p in pot
	फ	ph	As ‘f’ pronounced bialabial
	ब	b	As ‘b’ in boy
	भ	bh	As ‘bh’ in ‘abhor’
	म	m	As m in mom
Semi-vowels		य	y As y in yellow
	र	r	As r in rapid
	ल	l	As l in loud
	व	v	As v value
	श	sh	As sh in shugar
Sibilants	ष	sh:	As sh in wish
	स	s	As s in signal
	ह	h	As h in help

ACKNOWLEDGEMENT

The foundation of this work was laid in the year 1962 when my eldest brother Shri Shailendra Pathak decided to read Raamaayan at night everyday when his my bhabi (his wife) was expecting her third child. My brother suggested to me that I may start marking those passages (Dohaas and Choupaaees) that I liked for my future benefit. I did that at that time but did not do much with it and probably memorized a couple of them. However, as I grew with of some these verses they sounded like 'life-savers', if I realized them in my life and actions. The verses I selected fundamentally dealt with basic human emotions and were independent of any cast, color or creed! They may be written in a language that may use the word 'a man' but they are meant for ALL humans, irrespective of gender.

The Raamacharitamaanas is filled with verses reading which one can improve one's life. I selected 100 of them, 100 in tradition of Bhartrihari Shatak, which basically deal with of them psychological aspects of life.

And finally I am unfathomably grateful to my late father, Shri Parmanandji Pathak, a great scholar, teacher and a "Bhakt" who imbibed in me a great love for Shri Raam and Shri Raamachritmaanas

अनुक्रमणिका

बालकांड • Baalkaand

बंदऊं संत असज्जन चरना। दुःखप्रद उभय बीच कछु बरना।
बिछुरत एक प्रान हरि लेहीं। मिलत एक दारुन दुःख देही॥ 1॥

Bandau sant asajjan charanaa,
Dukhaprad ubhaya beech kachhu baranaa.
Bichhurat ek praan har leheen,
Milat ek daarun dukh deheen

अर्थ : अब मैं संत और असंत दोनों के चरणों की वंदना करता हूँ, दोनों ही दुख देने वाले हैं, परंतु उनमें कुछ अंतर कहा गया है। वह अंतर है कि एक (संत) तो बिछुड़ते समय प्राण हर लेते हैं और दूसरे (असंत) मिलते हैं तब दारुण दुःख देते हैं। (अर्थात् संतों का बिछड़ना मरने के समान दुःखदायी होता है और असंतों का मिलना)।

Translation : Now I pay homage at the very feet of saints (good people) and sinners (evildoers). Both give us pain. However wise have described some difference between them. When one of them (the saints) leave us we feel death like suffering. And when the other (the evildoers) meet us they inflict deep pain on us.

Commentary :

भावाभावे पदार्थानां हर्षामर्ष विकारदा।
मलिना वासना यैषा सा संग इति कथ्यते॥
संगन्याग विदुर्मोक्ष संगत्यागादजन्मता।
संग त्वज त्वं भावानां जीवमुक्तो भवानध॥

—अन्नपूर्णोपनिषद

अर्थ : पदार्थों के होने में हर्ष और न होने में शोक रूपी विकार उत्पन्न करनेवाली जो मलिन वासना है, उसे संग कहते हैं। संग के त्याग को मोक्ष कहते हैं। संग के त्याग से जन्म का छुटकारा मिलता है। अतएव, हे अनघ! (Silent) समस्त पदार्थों में संग का त्याग करके जीवनमुक्त हो।

Translation : It is obvious that the company of sants is always praised everywhere. And when they leave us it is very painful. Sants always take us towards God! Just the opposite is true about the Asant or evildoers. Whenever we encounter them they are but trouble for everyone. They are nothing but negative about the world. They do not see any good in other people. They only make us feel as if we are not good people, even if we are. They always pick on the weaknesses of others. Therefore in order to progress in life and to go toward God one must always avoid the company of Asant (evil people) and seek the company of Sant. And as one keeps on improving oneself, ultimately one has to go beyond them to seek the path to moksh or nirvan. As Shri Ramkrishna tought Swami Vivekanand (Narendra at that time). Finally you have to go beyond all books and teachers to see God. That path you have to travel alone.

For success, respect the wise and good and do not antagonise anyone, even bad people.

———❖❖❖———

गगन चढ़इ रज पवन प्रसंगा। कीचहिं मिलइ नीच जल संगा॥
साधु असाधु सदन सुक सारीं। सुमरहिं राम देहिं गनि गारीं॥ 2॥

Gagan chad:-i raj pavan prasangaa,
Keechahin mila-i neech jal sangaa
Sadhu asaadhu sadan suk saareen,
Sumarahin Raam dehin gan gaareen

अर्थ : [संगत का प्रभाव देखिये कि] पवन के संग से धूल आकाश पर चढ़ जाती है और वही नीच (नीचे की ओर बहने वाले) जल के संग से कीचड़ में मिल जाती है। साधुओं के घर में तोता मैना राम-राम सुमिरते हैं (बोलते हैं) और असाधुओं के घर के तोता मैना गिन-गिनकर गालियाँ देते हैं।

Translation : [The influence of a company is such that] Dust flies high in the (good) company of winds and the same dust when joins the water (of low-flowing nature) it leads to mud. In the same way, a parrot (a melodeous Indian bird), in a saintly environment, at a sant's home recite, the Lord's name (Ram-Ram because that is what they hear) and in an unsaintly household they would only hear and learn to spout abusive words.

Commentary

Sant (Saints) take people to higher state of mind as Kabir has said : just meeting them removes all our sins. Meeting an Asant (bad people) all you learn from them are deplorable things no matter how good one is. When one comes in the company of bad people one learn some bad behaviour :

काजर की कोठरी में कैसो ही सयानो जाय।
एक लीक काजर की लागि है पे लागि है॥

In the company of a Sant (sainty people) one learns to rise in the worldly ways and then also to go beyond the worldly ways towards spiritualy. Slowly but surely, as one learns one rises step by step on the ladder of spirituality towards God! On the other hand in the company of fools one comes down from the ladder into the gutter of bad and deplorable sins.

A person behaves according to the company he keeps.

———❖❖❖———

निज कबित्त केहि लाग न नीका। सरस होउ अथवा अति फीका॥
जे पर भनिति सुनत हरषाही। तेबर पुरुष बहुत जग नाही॥ 3॥

Nija kabbitt kehi lag n neekaa,
Saris ho-u athava ati pheekaa
Je par bhaniti sunat harasaaheen,
Te bar purush bahut jag naaheen

अर्थ : रसीली हो या अत्यंत फीकी, अपनी कविता किसे अच्छी नहीं लगती? किंतु जो दूसरों की रचना को सुनकर हर्षित होते हैं, ऐसे उत्तम लोग जगत् में नहीं हैं।

Translation : Who does not like his (her) own poetry whether it is tasteful or extremely tasteless. In this world there are not many good people who are delighted hearing others poetic recitation.

Comment : One can notice, in formality no matter what people say, but down in their heart the poets and authors like their own creation only, by and large a very high percentage of them. They are very few who are otherwise and admire other's poems and creations or admire some one else's photograph other than their own in a group photo.

Everyone loves their own creations!

———❖❖❖———

जलुपय सरिस बिकाय, देखउ प्रीति की रीति भलि।
बिलग होइ रसु जाय कपट खटाई परत पुनि॥ 4॥

Jala pay saris bikaay,
Dekhau preet kee reet bhali
Bilag hoy ras jaaya,
Kapat: khat:aaee parat hee

अर्थ : प्रीति की सुंदर रीति देखिये कि जल भी (दूध के साथ मिलकर) दूध के समान भाव बिकता है; परंतु फिर कपटरूपी खटाई पड़ते ही पानी अलग हो जाता है (दूध फट जाता है) और स्वाद (प्रेम) जाता रहता है।

See the workings of love that even water (when mixed in milk) gets sold at the milk-rate. However when sourness of deception is put in it, the water gets seperated and the taste (love) is gone.

Comments : This is a very profound statement by the poet. Selfishness, negativity, cheat and deceit are great destroyer of not only any friendship but any group behaviour or relationship. Relations among siblings, friends, spouses, business partners etc. will not last when deception enters the relations. That is the truth—timeless truth.

If a good and well known person is your friend and you are seen in his company you are also considered a good person. And similarly when one moves in the company of bad people, he is also considered a bad person.

Love will ruin relationships and deception destroys it.

गुर के बचन प्रतीति न जेही। सपनेहुँ सुगम न सुख सिधि तेही॥ 5॥

Gur ke bachan prateet na jehee,
Sapanehun sugam na sukh sidhi tehee

अर्थ : जिसको गुरु के वचन में विश्वास नहीं है, उसे सुख और सिद्धि मिलना स्वप्न में भी सरल नहीं होती।

Translation : One who has no faith in the teachings and guidence of his (her) Guru, for him (her) to get happiness or achievements of the world beyond are not possible or easy, even in dreams.

Comments : It may not be possible (in one life time) to get the true knowledge, achievements, and happiness without a Guru's teachings and blessings. However in order to learn anything from a Guru if one does not have faith in him he (or she) will constantly doubt about the varacity of the teachings and would not follow them. And if one does not follow the Guru's teachings—would not experience what he or she was supposed to and therefore no benefit will incur in such situations.

गुशब्दस्त्वन्धकारः स्यात् रुशब्दस्तन्निरोधकः।
अन्धकारनिरोधत्वाद गुरुरित्यभिधीयते॥

'गु' शब्द का अर्थ है, अंधकार। 'रु' शब्द का अर्थ है, उसका निरोध (restrictions, obstruction)। अंधकार (ignorance) का निरोध करने से 'गुरु' कहा जाता है।

One must have faith (प्रतीति) in his Guru. No one can learn anything from a Guru without having faith in him. As said :

अश्रद्धा परमं पापं श्रद्धा पापप्रमोचिनी।

अश्रद्धा सबसे बड़ा पाप है और श्रद्धा पाप से छुटकारा दिलानेवाली है।

—वेदव्यास (महाभारत, शांतिपर्व 264/15)

श्रद्धा ही जिंदगी का सूरज है।

—महात्मा गांधी (संपूर्ण गांधी वाडमय, खंड 41, पृष्ठ 482)

न देवो विद्यते काष्ठं न पाषाणे न मृण्मये।
भावेषु विद्यते दैवस्तस्माद् भावो हि कारणम्॥

देवता न तो काष्ठ (wood) में विद्यमान रहता है, न पाषाण (stone) में और न मिट्टी की मूर्ति में। देवता भाव (श्रद्धा) में रहता है अत: श्रद्धा (faith) ही कारण है।

मौको कहाँ ढूँढ़े रे बंदे, मैं तो हूँ विश्वास में।

— कबीर

Happiness alludes them who have no faith in their Guru!

❖❖❖

पराधीन सपनेहुँ सुख नाहीं ॥ 6 ॥

Paradheen sapanehun sukh naaheen

अर्थ : दूसरों के अधीन व्यक्ति को सपने में भी सुख नहीं मिलता।

Translation : One under subjugation cannot be happy even in a dream.

Comment : One of the greatest aspect of Indian thought or Vedic thought or Hndu thought has been the 'sense of freedom'. And that sense is expressed by the couplet above. Mahatma Gandhi was once questioned repeatedly that if there is no way India could get freedom from the British rule by 'Ahimsa' or non-violence would he be willing to pick up a gun. Insisting his firm belief that he could lead India to freedom through non-violence (Ahimsa) he eventually said that if there is absolutely no way to get freedom through 'Ahimsa' he would be willing to pick up a gun. He said further—Freedom is not negotiable."

India's traditional thought and 'Shruti' (The vedas) have insisted on the freedom of the highest order, the freedom from 'Rag and Dwesh' or 'Attachment and Aversion' as the basic tool to achieve freedom from ignorance i.e. to live like a 'free' soul in this world.

Even in a dream, no one can be happy in servitude!

———❖❖❖———

जिन्हके अगुन न सगुन विवेका। जलपहिं कल्पित बचन अनेका॥
हरिमाया बस जगत् भ्रमाहीं। तिन्हहि कहत कछु अघटित नाहीं॥
बातुल भूत बिबस मतवारे। ते नहिं बोलहिं बचन बिचारे॥
जिन्ह कृत महामोह मद पाना। तिन्ह कर कहा करिअ नहिं काना॥7॥

Jinake agun na sagnun bibekaa,
Jalpahin kalpit bachan anekaa
Hari maayaa bas jagat bhramaaheen,
Tinahahi kahat kachhu aghat:it naaheen
Baatul bhoot bibas matawaare,
Te nahin bolahin bachan bichaare
Jinh krut mahaa moh mad paanaa,
Tinh kar kahaa kari-a nahin kaanaa

अर्थ : जिनको निर्गुण-सगुण का कुछ भी विवेक नहीं है, जो अनेक मनगढंत बातें बका करते हैं, जो श्री हरि की माया को वश में होकर जगत् में (जन्म-मृत्यु के चक्र में) भ्रमण करते हैं (घूमते हैं, जीते हैं) उनके लिए कुछ भी कह डालना असंभव नहीं।

अर्थ : जिन्हें वायु का रोग (सन्निपात, उन्माद आदि) हो गया हो, जो भूत के वश हो गए हैं, और जो नशे में चूर हैं, ऐसे लोग विचारकर वचन नहीं बोलते। जिन्होंने महामोह रूपी मदिरा पी रखी है, उनके कहने पर कान नहीं देना चाहिए। (ध्यान नहीं देना चाहिए)।

Translation : Those people who can not distinguish between the God or Brahma with no properties (or qualities) and the God or Brahma with qualities (and properties, e.g Avataars) utter many lies of various kinds. They are lost in this illusionary world under His control and for them nothing is unassertable.

Those who talk too much (being delirious), are possessed or are drunk and speak without due thought process, ao not pay attention to the chatterings of those who are deep in the ocean of worldly-attachments.

Comments : The poet (Tulsidas) leaves here a word of

caution with a description of people's behaviour who call themselves 'experts' or leaders in the society.

These people in the society are like half-baked bread who do not know the contents of the shastras (scriptures) properly and gossip about them mixing information with imaginary disinformation.

These people may behave and talk irrationally like a drunk or a sick person running high fever or want to show off their knowledge to impress the listeners. And therefore the best response is to ignore them and not react to them at all.

The bottomline is—one should only pay attention to real scholars and sadhus (saints) to preserve their mental energy, time and specially to avoid confusion in their mind.

Do not pay attention to: Non-Discriminating and too much worldly-attached folks!

———❖❖❖———

जे कामी लोलुप जग माहीं। कुटिल काक इव सबहि डेराहीं॥ 8॥

Je kaamee lolup jag maaheen,
Kut:il kaaka iv sabahhi deraaheen

अर्थ : जगत में जो कामी और लोभी होते हैं, वे कुटिल कौए की तरह सबसे डरते हैं।

Translation : The greedy and licentious people in this world are afraid of everybody like a malicious and crooked crow.

Comments : Whenever one has a fear of some kind, one should wonder why. If one does, one would find that somewhere in their heart they feel that they have done something wrong or thinking of doing something wrong. These fear drain people of their positive energy and deprives them of their self-worth and therefore self-confidence.

इन्द्रियाणि मनो बुद्धिरस्याधिष्ठानमुच्यते।
एतैविमोहयत्येष ज्ञानमावृत्य देहिनम्॥

इंद्रियाँ, मन और बुद्धि इसके (कामभाव) वास स्थान हैं। इनके द्वारा ज्ञान को आच्छादित (cover up) करके यह जीवात्मा को मोहित करता है।

—वेदव्यास (महाभारत, भीष्मपर्व, 27/40 अथवा गीता, 3/40)

काममूलमिदं जन्म कामः पापस्य कारणम्।
यशः क्षयकरः कामस्त्मात् तं परिवर्जयेत्॥

काम इस जन्म का मूल कारण है। काम पाप कराने में हेतु (cause) है और यश का नाशक है। अतः काम को त्याग देना चाहिए।

—नारदपुराण (पूर्वभाग, प्रथमपाद, 34/56)

कामार्त्ता हि प्रकृतिकृपणश्चेतनाचेतनेषु।

काम से पीड़ित लोग जड़-चेतन पदार्थों के संबंध में स्वभावतः विवेकशून्य हो जाया करते हैं।

—कालिदास (मेघदूत, पृ. 5)

Greedy and licentious are always in fear!

———❖❖❖———

कुपथ माँग रुज व्याकुल रोगी। बैद न देइ सुनहु मुनि जोगी॥ ९॥

Kupath maarg ruj byaakul rogee,
Bed na de-i sunahu muni jogee

अर्थ : हे योगी मुनि! सुनिये, रोग से व्याकुल रोगी यदि कुपथ्य माँगे तो वैद्य उसे नहीं देता।

Translation : O, wise Yogi and Muni! Listen: Restless due to illness if a patient requests inappropriate (harmful for him) food, a Vaidya (Ayurvedic doctor) would not prescribe that for him.

Comment : A real well wisher does not give into the request of a dear one when it is inappropriate for him depending on the local culture, the time-frame, and the situation on hand. A real wellwisher always does what is good for their dear ones in all circumstances.

A real friend always does a good for his friend. If a person is desirous of drugs and wants to be intoxicated a good friend will rather take him to a doctor for treatment than get him drugs. A well wisher will always provide his friend (or a relative) the right advice and not say what his friend wants to hear. A friend is the one who comes in when the whole world has gone out. As well stated by Vedvyas, a friend is like a father who can be completely trusted; others are just companions :

यस्मिन् मित्रे पितरीवाश्वसति।
तद् वै मित्रं संगतानीतराणि॥

—वेदव्यास (महाभारत, उद्योग पर्व 36/37)

O, King! He only is a friend who saves a person sinking in forbidden deeds; otherwise he is an enemy!

मज्जमानमकार्येषु पुरुषं विषयेषु वै।
निवारयति यो राजन् स मित्र रिपुरन्यथा॥

—भास (अभिषेक नाटक 6/22)

माया तरवर त्रिविध का, साखा, दुःख, संताप।
सीतलता सुमिनै नहीं, फल फीको तनि ताप॥

—कबीर (कबीर ग्रंथावली, पृष्ठ 34)

Worldly (maayaa) attachment engulfs every one.

तुलसी देखु सुबेषु, भूलहिं मूढ़ न चतुर नर।
सुंदर केकिहि पेखु, वचन सुधा सम असन अहि॥ 11॥

Tulasee dekh subeshu:, Bhoolahin mood; na chatur nar
Sundar kekihi pekhu, Bachan sudhaa sam asan ahee

अर्थ : तुलसीदासजी कहते हैं—सुंदर वेष देखकर मूढ़ नहीं (मूढ़ तो मूढ़ ही हैं), चतुर मनुष्य भी धोखा खा जाते हैं। सुंदर मोर को देखो, उसका वचन तो अमृत के समान है और आहार साँप है।

Translation : Tulsidas says, well-dressed appearance (i.e. perception created) confuses not only fools but smart and clever people too. For example, the beautiful peacock utters notes that are like nectar to our ears and it's food is a snack (a poisonous reptile).

Comments : It is very necessary that one acts according to their goals and objectives. As the saying goes if one who sows the seeds of an acacia (babool tree) tree then should not expect to pluck mangoes from it! Similary people are judged according to their appearance and every other thing about them. Therefore they should dress according to their nature of work. Mahatma Gandhi changed his dress completely when his work activity changed from being an attorney to a freedom fighter for India's freedom through non-violence. He wanted the people of India—largely farmers living in villages—to come along with him. That is what he professed and clad himself like the majority of the people of India. He moved from three piece suit to barely one khadhi cloth as most of the people in India at that time.

How can one expect to do good business with corporate heads if one goes to business meetings dressed like a beggar, or in any other inappropriate way. The objective is not to fool them but to make them comfortable in one's presence and keep attention in the meeting on the subject of the meeting, rather than what is one wearing.

Even wise get beguiled by well dressed!

———❖❖❖———

रिपु तेजसी अकेल अपि, लघु करि गनिअ न ताहु।
अजहुँ देत दुःख रवि ससिहि, सिर अवसेषित राहु॥ 12॥

Ripu tejasee akel api, Laghu kari gani-a na taahu
Ajahun det dukh ravi sasihi, Sir avasesh:it raahu

अर्थ : तेजस्वी शत्रु यदि अकेला भी हो तो भी उसे छोटा नहीं समझना चाहिए। जिसका सिर मात्र बचा है, वह राहु आज तक सूर्य-चंद्रमा को दुख देता है।

Translation : Never underestimate a high-spirited enemy, even if he (she) may be alone. The Rahu, Which has only head (but no body), still torments the Sun and the Moon.

Comments : Wisdom lies in never underestimating one's enemy no matter how weak or with or without a great force with him. However, when someone is known to be a resourceful, radiant, glorius, and a chivalrous person and an enemy, the wisdom lies to NEVER discount him even if he is alone or appears to be alone. Abhimanyu fought with all the great warriors alone and broke the war formation (chakravyooh) designed by the best of the Kauravas.

"One who wishes well for himself should not ignore an advancing enemy. Because scriptures have equatted an advancing enemy to a disease!"

—माघ (शिशुपालवध, 2/10)

का रस में का रोस में, अरि सों जनि पतियाय।
जैसे सीतल तप्त जल, डारत आग भुजाय॥

—वृंद (वृंद सतसई)

Never under estimate a high-spirited enemy, even if alone!

❖❖❖

भरद्वाज सुनु जाहि जब होइ बिधाता बाम।
धूरि मेरु सम जनक जम, ताहि ब्याल सम दाम॥ 13॥

Bharadwaj sunu jaahi jab, Ho-i bidhaataa baam
Dhoori meru sam janak jam, Taahi byaal sam daam

अर्थ : [यागवल्क्य कहते हैं—] हे, भारद्वाज! सुनो, विधाता जब जिसके विपरीत होते हैं, तब उसके लिये धूल सुमेरु पर्वत के समान है (भारी और कुचल डालने वाली), पिता यम के समान है (कालरूप) और रस्सी साँप के समान (काट खाने वाली) हो जाती है।

Translation : [Rishi Yagyavalkya says–] O, Bhardwaja! Listen! When the Lord's grace is missing from one's life even a pack of dust seems like a mountain (unsurmountable), the father like Yama (as deadly as the deity of death), and a rope appears like (as deadly as) a snake.

Comment : Perceptions are created by our mind. What our mind thinks depends on our life experiences, efforts (based on our nature) and lastly on God's grace. When God's grace is withdrawn from one's life downfall is inevitable and eventually one sees the whole world against them.

जाको प्रभु दारुण दुःख देही, ताकि मति पहले हरि लेही।

One can make all the efforts in the world, get all their ducks in a row but untill the God's Grace is not with him, he can never accomplish anything. According to the theory of Karma one can make only small variations in the outcome of their efforts destined by their "Karma". According to Jyotish Shastra (Astrology) when their bad period (दशा) comes people go through painful time (when the God's grace is withdrawn)!

If God's grace is missing, difficulties seem unsurmountable.

———❖❖❖———

जिन्ह के रही भावना जैसी। प्रभु मूरति तिन्ह देखी तेसी ॥ 14 ॥

Jinh ke rahee bhaavanaa jesee, Prabhu moorati tin dekhee tesee

अर्थ : (राजा जनक की धनुष यज्ञशाला में राजाओं में) जिनकी जैसी भावना थी, प्रभु (रामचंद्रजी) को उन्होंने वैसा (उसी रूप में) ही देखा।

Translation : (In Raja Janak's Dhanush Yagyashala) People perceived Lord Rama according to their own disposition (preconceived thoughts) about him.

Comments : Every individual is made up of basically three components. They are : (i) one's own nature (by birth), (ii) one's own upbringing (nurture) at home and school, and surroundings and (iii) one's own life experience. And therefore, one sees the world around them according to what one is made of—the three basic components stated above. Naturally they view religion, Dharma, and 'God' in their own individual way. Naturally many people agree on many points about anything or anybody but they donot absolutely agree on everything about anything or anybody.

रूपं रूपं प्रतिरूपो वभूव

परमात्मा ने प्रत्येक रूप के अनुरूप अपना रूप बना लिया।

— ऋग्वेद *(6/47/18)*

न तस्य प्रतिमाऽस्ति यस्य नाम महद्यशः।

महद् यश नाम वाले परमात्मा की कोई प्रतिमा (उपमा) नहीं है।

एक एव परो ह्यात्मा सर्वेषामपि देहिनाम्।
नानेव गृह्यते मूढैर्यथा ज्योतिर्यथा नभः॥

सभी देहधारियों की एक ही परम आत्मा है। मूर्खों को वही नाना प्रकार से दिखाई देता है, जैसे ज्योति और आकाश।

One's nature determines how he perceives the world!

———❖❖❖———

बैनतेय बलि जिमि चह कागू। जिमि ससु चहै नाग अरिभागू॥
जिमि चह कुसल अकारन कोही। सब संपदा चहे सिव द्रोही॥
लोभी-लोलुप कल कीरति चहई। अकलंकता कि कामी लहई॥
हरिपद बिमुख परम गति चाहा। तस तुम्हार लालचु नरनाहा॥ 15॥

Bainate-y bali jimi chah kaagoo,
Jimi sasu chahai naag ari bhaagoo
Jimi chah kusal akaaran kohee,
Sab samapadaa chahe Siv drohee
Lobhee lolup kal keerati chaha-ee
Akankalataa ki kaamee laha-ee
Haripad bimukh param gati chaahaa,
Tas tumhaar laalachu naranaahaa

अर्थ : (धनुष भंग के बाद साधु राजा असाधुओं से कहते हैं।) जैसे गरुड़ का भाग कौआ चाहे, सिंह का भाग (हिस्सा) खरगोश चाहे, बिना कारण ही क्रोध करने वाला अपना भला चाहे, शिवजी का विरोधी सब धन-संपत्ति चाहे, लोभी-लालची सुंदर कीर्ति चाहे, कामी मनुष्य निष्कलंकता चाहे तो क्या पा सकता है? और जैसे श्रीहरि के चरणों से विमुख मनुष्य परमगति (मोक्ष) चाहे, हे राजाओं! सीता के लिये तुम्हारा लालच भी वैसा ही व्यर्थ है।

Translation : If a timid bird like a crow wants to grab a piece of food (meat) belonging to Grarud, the king of birds, or if a hare (a weakling animal) would like to take away a piece of animal killed by a lion (the king of jungle), a foe of elephant, or if someone who wants his own wellbeing but gets angry for no good reason, or if a greedy who covets what belongs to others and yet wants to be renowned, if a person (licentious) yearns for a spotless reputation then is it possible? And one who is not devoted but away from the feet of Lord Vishnu, and yet wants Nirwan, O, kings! so fruitless is your covetiousness for Seeta.

Comments : There are two type of Karma—Sakaam and

Nishkaam. Of course Nishkaam karma is better than Sakaam Karma. However even if someone goes for Sakaam Karma it still behooves him not to have his expectations, inconsistent with or disproportionate to his efforts. It will be absolutely foolhardy to have expectations opposite (180° apart) to his efforts like travelling from Washington D.C. on lightway 95 North and expecting to reach South Florida very soon. Same way a couch potato having a thought to be thin and healthy can only be a thought in the mind of a fool. The example in the verses above gives example of activities and opposite outcomes.

The key is : ends and means have to be synchronised together and checked for consistency and compatibility!

As you sow, so shall you reap!

——— ❖❖❖ ———

टेढ़ जानि सब बंदइ काहू, बक्र चंद्रमा ग्रसइ न राहू ॥ 16 ॥

Ted; jaani sab banda-i kaahoo,
Bakra Chandramaa grasa-i na Raahoo

अर्थ : (श्री रामचंद्रजी ने मन-ही-मन सोचा : कहीं-कहीं सीधेपन में भी बड़ा दोष होता है।)

टेढ़ा जानकर सब लोग किसी की भी वंदना करते हैं। जैसे कि टेढ़े चंद्रमा को राहु भी नहीं ग्रसता।

Translation : People, knowing anyone to be a crook, will revere him (her), e.g. Rahu swallows a full-moon but not a crescent moon.

Comment : Perception is very important in life. Some may go to the extreme of saying that perception is the reality and there is some truth to it. Therefore some people develop an aura of toughness to ward off attacks from miscreants or even enemies. Therefore people who are tough or appear to be tough are respected in the society. Same way even people who have no positive contributions to a society or organization are also feared of or even respected (even if formally) if they have a nuisance value. To be weak or to appear weak and to be too sweet or appear to be too sweet is not very good either for the safety or welfare of any one in this world.

In every country there are people like the Mafia in U.S. So if one is a friend or a relative of any Mafioso people try to avoid crossing him. It is a safe approach. If one tries to make a friend with him there may come an occasion when there may a conflict of interest. Therefore, for most of the people the best policy would be to keep away from such a person.

It is not always good to be too sweet!

अयोध्या कांड • AYODHYA KAAND

भानु कमल कुल पोषनिहारा। बिनु जल जारि करइ सोइ छारा॥ 17॥

Bhaanu kamal kul posh:anihaaraa,
Binu jal jaari kara-i so-i chhara

अर्थ : सूर्य कमल के कुल का पालन करने वाला है पर बिना जल के वही सूर्य उसको (कमलों को) जलाकर भस्म कर देता है।

Translation : The sun is the rearer of lotus family, however, the same sun will reduce them to ashes without the presence of water.

Comment : There are several interesting points that eminate from this couplet. No one is a pure benefactor under all circumstances. How some one responds to you depends, may be, on your spouse or who your friends are or what title you hold or how rich you are. Another point that comes from this couplet is to gain a benefit of something you may need something else as well. For example great exercise regimen without balanced meals will destroy some one's health and all great meals and no exercise at all will make any one fat and sick.

No one is a pure benefactor under all circumstances.

का पूछहु तुम्ह अबहु न जाना। निजहित अनहित पसु पहिचाना॥ 18॥

Kaa poochhahu tumh abahu na jaanaa,
Nij hit anahit pasu pahachaanaa

अर्थ : (कटाक्ष के साथ ललकारती) (मंथरा बोली कैकेयी से) अरे तुमने अब भी नहीं समझा? अपने भले-बुरे को (अथवा मित्र-शत्रु को) तो पशु भी पहचान लेते हैं।

Translation : (Manthra speaks to queen Kaikeyee, in chiding tone) What are you talking? Don't you understand even now? Even an animal can discriminate between what is helpful and unhelpful (or hurtful) for it.

Comments : No one is an island in this world! Every one's life and its success is very much dependent on their parents, teachers, mentors, coaches and other well-wishers in their life. Therefore, most unlucky are those who are unable to, due to their illusions and ignorance, recognise who their real wellwishers are. Some such people may even suffer from stockhome syndrome and accept and like people who hurt and torture them. If one happens to fall in such a trap one needs to pray to the Lord and hope to get his grace soon!

Unfortunate are those who cannot recognize their well-wishers!

——❖❖❖——

को न कुसंगति पाइ नसाई। रहइ न नीच मतें चतुराई॥ 19॥

Ko na kusangati paaee nasaa-ee,
Raha-ee na neech maten chaturaa-ee

अर्थ : कुसंगति पाकर कौन नष्ट नहीं होता? नीच के मत के अनुसार चलने से चतुराई नहीं रह जाती।

Translation : [Tulsidas says] Who is not ruined by the company of evil people. Wisdom departs from one following consel of base (mean) people.

Comments : All scriptures in the world warn people to avoid bad company. Nothing destroys an individual faster than the proximity of an evil person. Hindu scriptures, at every step and poets and scholars in all their works extol the benefits of being in the company of sadhu (saint) and satsang (company of saints).

अपां प्रवाहो गांगोऽपि समुद्रं प्राप्य तद्रसः।
भवत्यवश्यं तद् विद्वान् नाश्रयेदशुभात्मकम॥

गंगा के जल प्रवाह भी समुद्र को प्राप्त कर तद्रस (like the ocean water) हो जाता है। इसलिए विद्वान् को अशुभ मन वाले व्यक्तियों का साथ नहीं करना चाहिए।

— कामंदकीयनीतिसार

कामं व्यसन वृक्षस्य मूलं दुर्जन-संगति

True it is that the company of a scoundrel is the root of a tree of adiction.

— सोमेदेव (कथासरित्सागर)

विहीनसेवी न च बुद्धिसेवी,
निहीयते कालपक्खे व चन्दो।

जो नीच पुरुषों के संग रहते हैं, ज्ञानीजनों का सत्संग नहीं करते, वे

कृष्णपक्ष के चंद्रमा के समान निरंतर हीन होते जाते हैं।

—दीघनिकाय (3/8/2) पाली

श्रेष्ठता कुसंग से डरती है। नीचता ही उसे बंधु मानकर उससे घनिष्ठ संबंध स्थापित कर देती है।

Bad company will destroy anyone!

———❖❖❖———

सोसुनि तिय रिस गयउ सुखाई। देखहु काम प्रताप बड़ाई॥
सूल कुलिस असि अँगवनिहारे। ते रतिनाथ सुमन सर मारे॥ 20॥

So suni tiy ris gaya-u sukhaa-ee,
Dekhahu kaam prataap bad;aaee
Sool kulis asi angavanihaare,
Te ratinaath suman sar maare

अर्थ : वही राजा दशरथ स्त्री का क्रोध सुनकर सूख गए। कामदेव का प्रताप और महिमा तो देखिये। जो त्रिशूल, वज्र और तलवार आदि की चोट अपने अंगों पर सहने वाले हैं, वे रतिकाम के पुष्पवाण से मारे गए।

Translation : (Tulsidas says) Behold the mighty influence of cupidity that the same (chivalerous) king was totally drained hearing the news of his wife's anger, the king who had endured Trishool (a trident), वज्र (a thunderbold like missile), and sword has been devastated by Kamadev's (a god of love, like cupid) arrows of flowers (love).

Comments : The poet has very well stressed the danger of men falling pray into the clutches of infatuation for women and loosing all their wisdom, intellect, chivalry etc. Not only kings but even great Saints like Vishwamitra became a victim of Rati (feminine attraction and fell from his spiritual efforts and penance (deep meditative state). Although some of this may also apply to women but not all as their inherent nature is different from men's.

किस व्यक्ति की दृष्टि युवती की ओर नहीं जाती? कौनसा भ्रमर लता की इच्छा नहीं करता

—हरिदास सिद्धांतवागीश (रुक्मिणीहरणम्, 3/62)

बलचंदो बलं सुरयो बलं समणब्राह्मणा,
बलं वेला समुदस्स बलातिबलं इत्थियो।

चंद्रमा बलवान है, सूर्य बलवान है, श्रमण व ब्राह्मण बलवान है, परंतु सबसे बलवान स्त्रियाँ हैं।

—जातक (लोमकस्सप जातक)

सकल छत्रपति बस किये, अपने ही बल बाल।
सबला कूँ अबला कहै, मूरख लोग जमाल॥

— जमाल (जमाल दोहावली)

Lust and infatuation for opposite sex weakens and will destroy any one !

फिर पछितैहसि अंत अभागी। मारसि गाय नहारू लागी॥ 21॥

Phir pachhitaihasi ant abhaagee,
Maarasi gaay nahaaroo laagee

अर्थ : (राजा दशरथ कैकेयी से कहते हैं) अरी अभागिनी! फिर तू अंत में पछताएगी जो तू नहारू (ताँत) के लिये गाय को मार रही है।

Translation : (King Dashrath tells queen Kaikeyee) O! In the end you will repent as you are going to kill a cow just to get a strand of cord from its veins.

Comments : We may not always realise that when we make a choice to get something we are also inherently choosing to loose something else. That is due to the reason that our focus is always on what we want to get. Obviously we always pay a price for what we do and do not do. The critical part is the price we pay. In common worldly transactions we want to pay a price that is not too much. No one is called wise when he or she pays an astronomical price for a very small gain. It behooves everyone to think dispationately of a price they may have to pay before making critical choices in their lives.

Many times people are penny wise and pound foolish! When they look at any challenge or opportunity they only do what they like to do but not what is good for them to do. Many times people limit their success by not doing what is the best for their future but do what is pleasent for them, a short sighted approach. The reason may be because what is best for them may involve very hardwork, decipline, and lot of self-control.

'Penny wise and pound foolish' get destroyed.

सहज सरल रघुबर बचन, कुमति कुटिल करि जान।
चलहिं जोंक जल वक्र गति, जद्यपि सलिलु समान॥ 22

Sahaj saral Raghubar bachan, Kumati kut:il kar jaan
Chalahin jonk jal bakra gati, Jadyapi salil samaan

अर्थ : रघुकुल में श्रेष्ठ श्री रामचंद्रजी के स्वभाव से ही सीधे वचनों को दुर्बुद्धि कैकेयी टेढ़ा ही जान रही है; जैसे यद्यपि जल समान ही होता है, परंतु जोंक उसमें टेढ़ी चाल से ही चलती है।

Translation : Though Lord Ram's words, by his very nature, are simple and straight but wicked minded Kaikeyee takes them as crooked; just as a leech always moves in crooked way in water, even though it is smooth and uniform.

Comments : It is not very easy to be objective all the time or even perfectly objective at anytime because all human being are subject to 'raag'. (attachment) and 'dwesh' (aversion) towards most of the things in life. Therefore all our analysis or processing about life are based on our individual mental capabilities and conditions. Saintly people have a more objective and positive view of the world and wicked people always take a negative view and see the world as wicked.

Truth is like a vast banyan tree. No one can see every part of it at anyone time. When one mixes with this human limitations, it is extremely difficult to get to see what the truth is. One sees only a part of the truth and if he insists that that is the way it is and no other way, it would be very ignorant on his part. It would be like the story of four blind man feeling an elephant at its leg, trunk, tail, and body and believing that that is the complete description of an elephant!

Crooked see the world crooket!

———❖❖❖———

काह न पावकु जारि सक का न समुद्र समाइ।
का न करै अबला प्रबल केहि जग कालु न खाइ॥ 23॥

Kaah na paavaku jaari sak, Kaa na samudra samaa-i
Kaa na kar abalaa prabal, Kehi jag kaalu na khaa-i

अर्थ : आग क्या नहीं जला सकती! समुद्र में क्या नहीं समा सकता! अबला कहलानेवाली प्रबल स्त्री (जाति) क्या नहीं कर सकती! और जगत् में काल किसको नहीं खाता।

Translation : What can't be burnt by fire, what an ocean can't contain, what a powerful, but so called weak, woman can't accomplish, and who will not be devoured by death.

Comments : Women are called 'Abalaa' (or weaker sex) in many places in literature and in the society because of her physically being weaker than men. However, where on one side she is called 'Abalaa' she is also called a representative of Laxmi, Durga and Kali. She is capable of blessing the society with all the great fortunes and can destroy it too. It is for the betterment of the society that women are perceived in their total perspective and they have capability to do what ever they decide to do.

निसर्गनिपुणाः स्त्रियः।
स्त्रियाँ स्वभाव से ही चतुर होती हैं।

—कालिदास (मालिवाग्निमित्र, 3/2 के पश्चात्)

शृंगारप्रमुखाश्च कामसुहृदो नार्यां जितायां जिताः

शृंगार जिनका प्रधान है, ऐसे काम के मित्रगण नारी को जीतने से जीत लिये जाते हैं।

मेधाविनश्च पुरुषाः समरेषु शूराः
स्त्रीसंन्निधो परमकापुरुषा भवति।

मेधावी तथा समर-शूर पुरुष भी स्त्री के समीप परम कायर हो जाते हैं।

Even a weak, but determined person can do anything!

——❖❖❖——

संभावित कहुँ अपजस लाहू। मरन कोटि सम दारुण दाहू ॥ 24 ॥

Sambhaavit kahun apajas laahoo,
Maran kot:i sam daarun: daahoo

अर्थ : प्रतिष्ठित पुरुष के लिए अपयश की प्राप्ति करोड़ों मृत्यु के समान भीषण संताप देनेवाली है।

Translation : Possibly, disrepute to an honourable man causes horrible mental-agony like a thousand death.

Comments : Depriving someone of their most valuable 'thing' is the highest punishment for that person. If a very beautiful rich woman is deprived of half of her wealth she will be very sad relative to the devastation she may feel if deprived of even one fourth of her beauty. Similarly depriving a health concious man of his health, a car collector of his cars, a socially respected person of his respectability etc. is as painful as death experience. In the recent history of U.S.A. threat of impeachment for President Nixon (and eventual resignation) and President Clinton's impeachment by the house of representatives was the worst that happened to them in their lives.

Character assasiantion is the worst crime against a reputated person :

संभावितस्य चाकीर्तिर्मणादतिरिच्यते।

अपकीर्ति मनुष्य के लिये मरण से भी अधिक बुरी है।

—वेदव्यास (भीष्मपर्व, 26/34, गीता 2/34)

To an honorable person, disrepute is worst than death.

———❖❖❖———

दुखित दोष गुन गनहिं न साधु। 25 ॥

Dukhit dosh: gun ganahin na saadhu

अर्थ : साधु पुरुष दुःखी मनुष्य के दोष-गुणों को नहीं गिनते।

Translation : Saintly people do not reckon (pay attention to) the faults or virtues of the grief-stricken.

Comments : It is well known that people who are depressed their capabilities to think, act, remember, analyse etc. get adversely affected. Therefore how one can call them in 'normal' condition when they are not quite themself. Therefore they deserve more of our sympathy and compassion rather than our anger, enmity or revenge. Therefore, giving people the benefit of doubt is a sign of strength and not weakness. When on one side strong people are very capable of revenge, to forgive is also a sign of strength and not weakness.

दुःखाभितप्तः शोकेन नैक्षते न श्रणोति च।

दुःख से संतप्त व्यक्ति शोक के कारण न देखता है और न सुनता है।

—अज्ञात

अभितप्तमयोऽपि मार्वदवं, भजते कैव कथा शरीरिषु।

तपाए जाने पर लोहा भी गरम हो जाता है, शरीर-धारियों की तो बात ही क्या!

—कालिदास (रघुवंश 8/43)

कोऽपि नेति बिना दुःखं सद्‌गुणगान् कुसुमं यथा
बन्धं वेधं च सहते यदा याति तदा गुणम्।

कोई भी बिना दुःख के सद्‌गुणों को प्राप्त नहीं कर सकता। जिस प्रकार फूल बंधन तथा वेध सहन करता है, तब गुण को प्राप्त करता है।

Wise do not pay attention to the faults of grief-stricken.

———❖❖❖———

माँगउँ भीख त्यागि निज धरमू। आरत काह न करइ कुकरमू॥ 26॥

Maangahun bheek tyaag nij dharamoo,
Aarat kaah na kara-i kukaramoo

अर्थ : (भरतजी कहते हैं) मैं अपना धर्म (न माँगने का क्षत्रिय धर्म) त्यागकर आपसे भीख माँगता हूँ। आर्त मनुष्य कौन सा कुकर्म नहीं करता?

Translation : (Bharat says) Abandoning my religious commitments (that a kshatriya should not beg), to you I am begging; is there ar y evil deed that a person in real-distress would not do?

Comments : Context in this example of neeti (policy) is important. In this couplet Bharat, younger (and next to Ramchandraji) to Ramchandraji is on his way to meet Shri Ram in the jungle has just reached the holy city Prayag and is praying for it's blessing for success in his efforts to get Shri Ram back to Ayodhya.

The word Dharma encompasses the whole life of a human being in vedic context. Therefore sometimes one comes across situations where clearly there are serious conflicts between two Dharmic aspects of a particular situation. Then one has to give higher priority to one Dharmic aspect with respect to the other. Here Bharat says as a Kshatriya—I am not supposed to beg. However as a Kshatriya I am also suppose to stop injustice and therefore stopping injustice is a higher priority. If I do not do that whole of the kingdom would be a looser and only my personal ego may get satisfied. And even if I ignore this I am a tortured soul (आत्मीत). I am not going to incure any Paap as an Aarta has no Dharmic requirements.

A distressed and tormented person is capable of doing anything evil.

——❖❖❖——

जग बौराइ राज पद पाए। 27 ॥

Jag bauraa-i raaj pad paa-e

अर्थ : राज पद पाने पर सारा जगत् ही पागल हो जाता है।

Translation : The whole world (any one in this world) would go crazy if they receive kingship.

Comments : If someone goes crazy it can never be justified but can be understood. Then question arises why is it necessary to understand? No matter what someone does or does not do the fact of the matter still remains that to keep one's own perspective balanced and objective it is one's own responsibility. And therefore if someone suddenly feels arrogant (crazy) due to a rise in their life and gain of power, due to money or any other thing of value to him, an observer would get totally nonplused by it. Instead one should understand such a behavior as although not good but rather not unusual in society. With this appropriate (सम्यक samyak) understanding also goes the caviate that this may happen to almost anybody in this world. People armed with such an understanding would be considered wiser rather than without it.

जो नीचो ऊँचे चढ़े, त्यों अति ही इतराय।
प्यादा से फर्जी भयो, टेढ़ो-टेढ़ो जाय॥

—रहीम

यो हि धर्मपरो राजा देवांशोऽन्यश्च रक्षसाम्।
अंशभूतो धर्मलोपी प्रजापीडाकरो भवेत्॥

जो धर्मनिष्ठ राजा है, वह देवांश कहलाता है। जो अन्य राजा हैं, वे राक्षसों के वंश से उत्पन्न धर्मलोभी तथा प्रजापीड़क कहलाते हैं।

—शुक्रनीति (1/70)

Power and money makes people egotistical.

———❖❖❖———

सब सें कठिन राज मद भाई। 28॥

Sab sen kat;in raaj mad bhaa-ee

अर्थ : (राम-सीता का लक्ष्मण से कहना) हे भाई! राज्य का मद सबसे कठिन मद है।

Translation : Intoxication of kingly power is most difficult (i.e. troublesome to that individual, difficult to that individual and difficult to remove than any other type of intoxication).

Comments : Intoxication of all kinds is considered horrible except one and that is being intoxicated in the love of God! The key characteristic of any worldly intoxication is that when one gets out of it one feels extremely pain (hangover). And when someone is intoxicated he or she may do horrible things which hurt others and consequently such hurts are visited upon the doer as karma-phala (consequences of bad deeds).

This happens during and after one gets in and out of such intoxicated situation. However to get out of intoxication due to power is an herculian task. Higher the intoxication bigger the fall and greater is the pain.

योवनं जीवनं वित्तं छाया लक्ष्मीश्च स्वामिता।
चंचलानि षडेतानी ज्ञात्वा धर्मरतो भवेत॥

यौवन, जीवन, धन, छाया, लक्ष्मी, प्रभुत्त्व—ये छह चंचल होते हैं। यह जानकर राजा को धर्मरत होना चाहिए।

—शुक्रनीति (1/138)

When one is intoxicated with power he does not listen to anyone. When one is in such a situation, his friends and other dear ones are afraid of telling him. They are afraid of loosing a friend or relative.

Hitler was intoxicated with power! Being afraid of their life, his advisor and relatives could not tell him anything other than what he wanted to hear. And if anyone dared probably lost his life.

There are many other kind of intoxicating agents (besides liquor). Relatively speaking, it is lot easier to remove their influence on an individual than the influence of egotism and arogance!

When the wine is in the wit is out.

जब शराब अंदर, तब बुद्धि बाहर।

—टामस बेकन (कैटेचिज्म, 365)

पानादर्थश्च धर्मश्च कामश्च परिहीयते।

मद्य पीने से अर्थ, धर्म और काम—तीनों नष्ट हो जाते हैं।

अहंकार-दाह-ज्वर-मूर्च्छान्धकारिता-विह्वला हि राजप्रकृतिः।

राजाओं का स्वभाव अहंकार रूप दाह-ज्वर से उत्पन्न मूर्च्छा से विवेकहीन होकर अधीरतापूर्ण हो जाता है।

—बाणभट्ट (कादंबरी, पूर्वभाग, पृष्ठ 310)

Intoxication due to worldly power is most difficult to cure!

———❖❖❖———

अरध तजहिं बुध सरबस जाता। 29॥

Aradh tajahin budh sarabas jaataa

अर्थ : बुद्धिमान लोग सर्वस्व जाता देखकर (आधे की रक्षा के लिए) आधा छोड़ दिया करते हैं।

Translation : Seeing that everything may slip away from them, the wise, let go the half (to protect the other half).

Comment : Life is not a war in which one either wins or looses. It is full of compromises that one has to make. Many times one runs into situations where someone's gain is another person's loss. If such conflicts of interests arise then the wise will choose to make compromise rather than choose to 'loose-all' or 'win-all'. That is why as described in the Mahabharat epic Duryodhan speaking on behalf of all Kaurav was wrong and Yudhishtir speaking on behalf of Pandava's was correct. Therefore wise will take an attitude of finding a compromise situation between the two extreme ends of 'win-all' or 'loose-all' positions.

Life is not a maximixation process! It is an optimisation process. When India was about to get freedom from the British Empire, they would not give freedom to India unless India accepted the partition of the country (and allow the formation of Pakistan). At that time Mahatma Gandhi and his advisors (like Nehru & others) were against it. But they had to compromise and accept British offer rather than not getting freedom at all! Similarly at the end of the second world war, Japan had to compromise. Russia and USA also had to compromise and accept division of the country into west and East Germany; even division of Berlin into East-Berlin and West-Birlin!

Let the half go, if the whole is at risk!

———❖❖❖———

बैर प्रेम नहिं दुरइ दुराएँ। 30॥

Bair prem nahin dura-i duraa-en

(रामचंद्रजी भरत से कहते हैं कि प्रेम-वश कुतर्क कर रहे हो।)

अर्थ : वैर और प्रेम छिपाए नहीं छिपते।

Translation : (Ram says to Bharat, you are arguing due to your love for me)

Inspite of one's great efforts to hide, love and enmity does not remain hidden.

Comment : As discussed in couple of pages before here are two critical points—(1) One who is intoxicated looses a sense of propriety and balance and (2) therefore may do things which are wrong, untimely, improper, unsuitable, disrespectable, unbecoming of him/her etc. etc. Here Bharat being totally drenched in his love for his elder brother has taken only one sided view of the situation and not from Shri Ram's perspective and that Shri Ram has said to Bharat that you are giving fallacious arguments. When someone deeply loves or hates another person it becomes obvious from his expressions and behaviors.

When a young couple is in love the whole world knows about it. Their looks, behavior, carring for each other etc. are obvious to an observer. Similarly, enemity between two man becomes very obvious when they are in a common environment or when one critiques the other!

न कालो दण्डमुद्यम्य शिरः कृन्तनि कस्यचित्।
कालस्य बलमेतावद् विपरीतार्थदर्शनम्॥

काल, डंडा या तलवार लेकर किसी का सिर नहीं काटता। काल का बल इतना ही है कि वह प्रत्येक वस्तु के विषय में मनुष्य की विपरीत बुद्धि कर देता है।

—वेदव्यास (महाभारत, सभापर्व, 81/11)

जब विनाश का समय आता है, जब जीवन पर संकट आता है; तब प्राणी पास पड़े हुए जाल और फंदे को भी नहीं देखता।

(पालि) — जातक ('गिज्झ जातक' तथा 'हंस जातक')

न शक्यं खलु विषमस्थैः पुरुषैरात्मबलाधानं कर्तुम्।

निस्संदेह आपत्तिग्रस्त पुरुषों को अपना बल प्रदर्शन कर पाना संभव नहीं।

— भास (उरुभंग, 1/13 के पश्चात्)

Love or enmity does not remain hidden.

———❖❖❖———

रहत न आरत के चित चेतू। 31॥

Rahat na aarat ke chit chetoo

अर्थ : आर्त (दुःखी) मनुष्य के चित्त में चेतन (विवेक) नहीं रह जाता।

Translation : A person in distress looses his (her) discriminating power (sense of reasoning).

Comment : Two words : 'Aart' and 'Vivekee' are used here. One means a 'distressed' and the other means a person with 'reasoning' capability respectively. The two do not exist together in a human being because a 'Vivekee' is a Gyani who understands that this world has pain and all mortals are bound to experience pain in their life. Some experience more than other according to their Karma in the previous lives and this life. Suffering is a feeling a person experiences who does not understand this is a play of Karma and the inevitability of pain in everyone's life. Of course an individual who could be described as an 'Aart' is not only distressed; but also desperate; he or she is desperate to do anything (lack of discrimination) to get rid of the condition which he or she blames for his pain and suffering.

A distressed person looses discrimination.

———❖❖❖———

आगम निगम प्रसिद्ध पुराना। सेवा धरम कठिन जगु जाना॥
स्वामि धरम स्वारथहिबिरोधू। बैरू अंध प्रेमहि न प्रबोधू॥ 32॥

Aagam nigam prasiddha puraanaa,
Sevaa dharama kat;in jag jaanaa
Swaami dharam swaarathahi birodhoo,
Bairoo andh premahi na prabodhoo

अर्थ : (भरतजी राजा जनक से) वेद शास्त्र और पुराणों में प्रसिद्ध है और जगत् जानता है कि सेवाधर्म बड़ा कठिन है। स्वामी धर्म में और स्वार्थ में विरोध है [दोनों एक साथ नहीं निभ सकते]। वैर अंधा होता है और प्रेम को ज्ञान नहीं रहता [मैं स्वार्थवश कहूँगा या प्रेमवश, दोनों में ही भूल होने का भय है]।

Translation : It is well recognised through Vedas, Puranas and other Shastras, and the world knows, true service is difficult to perform. True service to a master and selfishness are against each other. Enmity is blind and love is devoid of wisdom (whether I speak under the grips of selfishness or love either way I am likely to make mistakes).

Comment : Bharat (an embodiment of Dharm) and King Janak (an embodiment of Gyan and Vairagya) are in discussion. Bharat wants Shri Ram to return to Ayodhya and Janak is trying to console him in pain and suffering because Ram went to the forest for 14 years. Bharat wants to serve Ram and he is accepting that he is unable to seperate his desire to serve him and this desire has become selfish. Although to have a desire to serve is considered a very positive desire but it can also be selfish when it comes in the way of the person one wants to serve. And therefore serving selflessly is probably the world's most difficult task.

The poet has described 'enmity' as blind and 'love' as ignorant or devoid of wisdom. Anger has tremendous destructive force and when people get angry they can hurt anyone including themselves. They stop seeing things which were very obvious to them before and will see normally once the anger subsides. However, while angry with someone due to feeling of enmity they themselves shut the windows of all their reasoning capability and are virtually blind and temporarily insane (till they are overcome by the enemic feeling).

Love, however, also has power but the poet decided to call it devoid of wisdom because love is usually is not destructive, by intent, to other people. No one loves someone to harm him/her. Here the poet means a true feeling of love but not pretention of love. Pretentions, of course, can be very destructive. However, love can also hurt other due to being devoid of 'wisdom'. Here we are discussing worldly love and not love for God! A man who leaves his wife and young kids because he 'feels' he loves another woman is going to hurt his current family and friends if he leaves them and marries the other woman—his object of love.

The root cause is ignorance for all ill behavior. Either the individual is incapable of seeing the right thing, or unwilling to see the right thing due to temporary infatuation with the sense objects, i.e. objects of his love.

सेवा सबसे कठिन व्रत है।

—जयशंकर प्रसाद (कंकाल, 251)

To serve some one, is a very difficult task.

———❖❖❖———

पसु नाचत सुक पाठ प्रबीना। गुन गति नट पाठक आधीना॥ 33॥

Pasu naachat suk paat; prabeenaa,
Gun gati nat: paat;k aadheenaa

अर्थ : (भरतजी श्री रामचंद्रजी से कहते हैं) (बंदर आदि) पशु नाचते और तोते (सीखे हुए) पाठ में प्रवीण हो जाते हैं। परंतु तोते का (पाठ प्रवीणता रूप) गुण और पशु के नाचने की गति (क्रमशः) पढ़ाने वाले और नचाने वाले के अधीन है। (यहाँ पाठक का अर्थ पढ़ानेवाला लिया गया है।)

Translation : Animals dance and parrots get proficient in their lessons learnt. However, the dancing skills of an animal and the admirable characters of a parrots depends upon the dance-teacher and one who teaches the parrot respectively.

Comment : Probably, many statements can be interpreted in many ways, specially if one looks at them without context. This one is also like that.

1. In the context of the Rama Charitmanas, Tulsidas is describing what Bharat was saying to Ramchandraji, not only his elder brother but also the Lord incarnate. He means : We all are creation of the Lord of which Ram is an incarnation. Naturally we all behave according to our 'prarabdha' given to us by Him just like a parrot speaks exactly according to it's trainer or a monkey dances just as trained by its master. Whatever free will we have (which animals do not) and if we choose to take actions not conducive to take us towards him, Lord Rama is so large hearted that he will even make them appear as if they are good due to our love and affection for him.

2. If read with context it can be rightly interpreted as :

Those who do not use their own initiative, energy and brain (free will), are essentially like a parrot trained to talk by its master and the animals trained to perform tricks by its coach and keeper.

To be human we need to be as suggested by a poet :

'Let us not be dumb-driven cattle, Let us be a hero in the strife'

—H.W. Longfellow

A wise teacher can even make a nincompoop behave smartly!

❖❖❖

काक समान पाकरिपु रीती। छली मलीन कतहुँ न प्रतीती॥ 34॥

Kaak samaan paakaripu reetee,
Chhalee maleen katahun na prateetee

अर्थ : (पाकरिपु) इंद्र की रीति कौए के समान है। वह छली और मलिन-मन है, उसका कहीं किसी पर विश्वास नहीं है।

Translation : Indra's ways are like those of a crow. Deceitful and malicious, do not trust anyone anywhere.

Comment : Indra is a king and his ways are like those of deceitful and malicious people. We have always been taught not to be deceitful and malicious. On the contrary the right teachings are to be trusting, generous and forgiving. However, can one be a king and rule effectively by trusting everybody and forgiving all the time. The answer is obvious no. The teachings are right but one needs to remember that one needs to strike a balance between personal values and social (or worldly) responsibilities. However, that does not justify being deceitful and malicious. Even if a king who does not trust everybody has no reason to deceive others and be malicious. These are not 'Rajaseeya' or king like 'values' but 'tamasika' or lowly values.

In order that the world runs smoothly one has to trust some people (not everybody). A person who does not trust anyone has no friends. Real unfortunate are those people.

न विश्वसेदविश्वस्ते विश्वस्ते नातिविश्वसेत्।
विश्वासाद् भयमुत्पन्नमपि मूलानि कृन्तति॥

जो विश्वासपात्र न हो, उस पर कभी विश्वास न करें और जो विश्वासपात्र हो, उस पर भी अधिक विश्वास न करें। क्योंकि विश्वास से उत्पन्न हुआ भय मनुष्य का मूलोच्छेद कर देता है।

—वेदव्यास (महाभारत, शांतिपर्व, 138/144-45)

मर्यादातीनं न कदाचदपि विश्वसेत्।
कभी भी मर्यादा से अधिक विश्वास न करें।

— चाणक्य

नम्मिकचे गानि नडुवदेपनियु।
बिना विश्वास के कोई भी काम हो ही नहीं सकता। (तेलुगु)

— आदिभट्ल नारायणदासु (वेल्युमाट)

Deceitful and malicious do not trust anyone.

———❖❖❖———

दुचित कतहुँ परितोषु न लहहीं। 35 ॥

Duchit katahun paritosh:u na lahaheen

अर्थ : चित्त दुतरफा (संशययुक्त) हो जाने से वे कहीं संतोष नहीं पाते।

(नोट : जैसे गीता में लिखा है 'संशयात्मा विनश्यति'।)

Translation : Due to a wavering mind, people are not content any where.

Comment : Someone has said, most of the time it does not matter what decision we take as long as we take one and move on. When anyone's mind is wavering, like standing on a fork at the road and not knowing which way to go, he will be standing on the road, at the fork, till he takes a decision. When he moves forward, then he may find out if he was right or wrong and the probability is equal to or less than 50%. Good chance that he may be right. However, by a non-decision one would continue standing at the fork and would be 100% wrong! As the time passes mind becomes more and more dull and begins to loose self-confidence. Loss of self-confidence is the beginning of his destruction, as the Bhagavat Geeta says :

"Sanshayaatma vinashyatee"

i.e. a doubting person gets destroyed! How can such a person find peace and contentment anywhere in the world. Actually as doubt ends in a human mind, peace begin!

A "doubting Thomas" (one who is habitually doubtful) is never content or happy.

———❖❖❖———

**तुम्हहि बिदित सबही कर करमू। आपन मोर परम हित धरमू॥
मोहि सव भाँति भरोस तुम्हारा। तदपि कहउँ अवसर अनुसारा॥
तात तात बिनु बात हमारी। केवल गुरुकुल कृपाँ सँभारी॥
नतरु प्रजा परिजन परिवारु। हमहि सहित सबु होत खुआरू॥ 36॥**

Tumhahi bidit sabahee kar karamoo,
Aapan mor param hit dharamoo
Mohi sab bhaanti bharos tumhaaraa,
Tadapi kaha-un avasar anusaaraa
Taata taat binu baat hamaaree,
Keval gurukul krupaan sambhaaree
Nataru prajaa parijan parivaaroo,
Hamahi sahit sabu hot khuaaroo

अर्थ : तुमको सबके कर्मों (कर्तव्यों) का और अपने तथा मेरे परम हितकारी धर्म का पता है। यद्यपि मुझे तुम्हारा सब प्रकार से भरोसा है, तथापि मैं समय के अनुसार कुछ कहता हूँ।

हे तात! पिता के बिना (उनकी अनुपस्थिति में) हमारी बात केवल गुरुवंश की कृपा ने ही सँहाल रखी है, नहीं तो हमारे समेत प्रजा, कुटुंब, परिवार सभी बरबाद हो जाते।

Translation : (Shri Ramchandraji is speaking with Bharatji and the rest of the people of Ayodhya who have come to take him back, including Guru Vashishta etc.) Lord Ram tells Bharatji that he and all are quite familiar with their responsibilities and their sense about implementing them with spiritual seriousness for the ultimate good of the kingdom and the people of Ayodhya. He says that he fully knows their unparallel skills and capabilities in carrying out those responsibilities however he would like to say some things according to the place, time and the situation (देश, काल, व परिस्थित!). Lord Ram continues further to tell Bharatji and others that their family, all relatives, people of Ayodhya the kingdom and everything that is near and dear to them would have been destroyed if it was not the Guru's blessings, grace and influence that saved them all. Otherwise, if it was not the Guru Vashishta and others to save them, without their father Raja Dasharath they all would have perished without a trace!

Comments : Here Ramachandraji is emphasizing the importance of a Guru in one's life! we all need full and unconditional blessings of our Guru, who so ever he or she might be. A person who does not respect his Guru has no future in this world. As all poets, Tulsi and Kabir specially, have emphasized that one needs unequivocal support of Guru like God's blessings! As Kabir has put Guru even higher than God himself :

गुरु गोविंद दोउ खड़े, काके लागूँ पाँय।
बलिहारी गुरु आप की, गोविंद दियो बताय।।

Guru's blessings are indispensable and without them one gets destroyed.

———❖❖❖———

सेवक कर पद नयन से मुख सो साहिब होय।
तुलसी प्रीति कि रीति सुनि सुकबि सराहहिं सोइ॥
मुखिया मुख सो चाहिये, खान पान कहुँ एक।
पालइ पोषइ सकल अँग तुलसी सहित बिबेक॥ 37॥

Sevak kar pad nayan se,
Mukh so saahib hoy
Tulasee preet kee reeti suni,
Sukabi saraahahin so-i
Mukhiyaa much so chaa-hi-e
Khaan paan kahu-n ek
Paala-i possh:a-i sakal ang
Tulasee sahit bibek

अर्थ : सेवक हाथ, पैर और नेत्रों के समान और स्वामी मुख के समान होना चाहिए। तुलसीदासजी कहते हैं कि सेवक-स्वामी की ऐसी प्रीति सुनकर सुकवि उसकी सराहना करते हैं। तुलसीदास कहते हैं—(रामचंद्रजी ने कहा) मुखिया मुख के समान होना चाहिए। जो खाने-पीने को तो एक (अकेला) है, परंतु विवेकपूर्वक सब अंगों का पालन-पोषण करता है।

Translation : A servant should be like a hand, foot, and eye and the master like a mouth. Tulsidas says that when they hear of such traditions (being followed), great poets admire those people.

Tulsidasji says : A leader should be like a mouth, which is the only human organ alone for eating and drinking. However, it properly and prudently nourishes all the limbs of the body.

Comment : Here Tulsidas has stated a very critical and important value to be followed in life. It is about the art and science of being a good leader and a good follower. A good follower is one who is like the eyes, hands, and feet of a human being. They watch out the things happening in the world and implement things the brain (the leader) commands them to do. And then a leader should be like the mouth of an individual which provides appropriate nutrition to the different parts of the body. Some may get more protein, some may get more carbohydrates and then some may get more vitamins. Every part of the body does not get equal share of all neutriants but they get according to what is necessary for them.

Similarly, in a corporate world a leader should provide opportunities to his/her subordinates according to what will help them progress in their desired direction of growth which suits to their skills and temperaments. And the subordinates should do what the leader wants them to do and needs them to do.

A leader should lead unbiased to all and a follower should be totally devoted.

———❖❖❖———

आरण्य कांड • AARANYA KAAND

सेवक सुख चह मान भिकारी। व्यसनी धन सुभगति बिभिचारी।
लोभी जसु चह चार गुमानी। नभ दुहि दूध चहत ए प्रानी॥ 38॥

Sevak sukh chah maan bhikaaree,
Byasani dhan subhagati bibhichaaree
Lobhi jasu chah chaar gumaanee,
Nabh duhi doodh chahat e praanee

अर्थ : सेवक सुख चाहे, भिखारी मान चाहे, व्यसनी (जिसे जुए, शराब आदि का व्यसन हो) धन और व्यभिचारी शुभ गति चाहे, लोभी यश चाहे और अभिमानी चार फल (अर्थ, धर्म, काम, मोक्ष) चाहे तो ये सब प्राणी आकाश को दुह कर दूध लेना चाहते हैं [अर्थात् असंभव बात को संभव करना चाहते हैं]।

Translation : (Laxmanji tells Soorpanakha) If a servant wants comfort and happiness, a begger expects respect, an addict wants riches, an adulterer wants Nirvan (salvation), a greedy expects narne and fame, and an arogant expects to get the four achievements in life (Arth, Dharm, Kam, Moksha) then they are like a person who wants milk by milking the sky.

Comment : Our actions have to be commesurate with our goals and desires if we expect to achieve them. Very often we have heard people say, "You know, no matter what I eat I always gain weight." Obvious, that this is not a correct statement. For every individual there is a regimen to loose weight. It consists of a proper balance among food intake, exercise, and rest. It is not the same for all individuals and everyone has to find the balance that suits them. No one will loose weight if they eat a lot (for their size) and take absolutely no exercise. One of the main reason people are unhappy in this world is because they want or desire things in this world but they are either not doing anything to get those things or they are doing things which will produce results opposite to their coveted goals and desires.

Actions should be commensurate with goals.

———❖❖❖———

रन चढ़ि करिअ कपट चतुराई। रिपु पर कृपा परम कदराई॥ 39॥

Ran chad;i kari-a kapat: chaturaa-ee,
Ripu par krupaa param kadaraaee

अर्थ : रण में आकर कपट-चतुराई करना और शत्रु पर कृपा करना (दया दिखाना) तो बहुत बड़ी (क्षत्रीय के लिए, सबसे बड़ी) कायरता है।

Translation : (Ramchandraji tells the messangers of Khar-Dooshan)

Once getting into a battlefield, to be deceiteful, play cheap tricks, and show compassion on an enemy is utter cowardice.

Comments : There are two aspects illustrated how a Kshatriya should behave towards an enemy. Politics, including deceitful or honest has no place when in the middle of a battlefield! Only weak, fearful and coward would show behaviour like that.

Only a strong person can forgive a weak one. When a weak person tries to show forgiveness towards a strong enemy it only demonstrates his weakness. To a Kshatriya—if an enemy challenges you to a battle—to show compassion or pity or forgiveness is unmanly and against his Dharm. If an enemy is weak and challenges a Kshatriya to a battle and if the strong wants to talk him out of it is also not manly or appropriate.

Battlefield is for battle. And the only duty of a warrior in the battlefield is to fight to the finish! No matter who wins or loses and lives or dies!

When Arjun told Lord Krishna in Kurukshetra that he does not want to fight against the Kauravas because they were his cousins and on their side were his elders and even his Guru Dronacharya!
Lord Krishna advised him and convinced him why he should fight and not show weakness or to be perceived as weak by laying down his arms. All the 18 chapters of Geeta illustrate in detail the responsibilities of a warrier class or a king how they should analyze situations like a true Kshatriya king.

In a battle field, to show compassion to an every is cowardice.

———— ❖❖❖ ————

राज नीति बिनु धन बिनु धर्मा। हरिहि समर्पे बिनु सतकर्मा॥
बिद्या बिनु बिबेक उपजाएँ। श्रम फल पढ़े किए अरुपाएँ॥
संग तें जती कुमंत्र ते राजा। मान ते ज्ञान पान तें लाजा॥
प्रीति प्रनय बिनु मद ते गुनी। नासहिं बेगि नीति अससुनी॥ 40॥

Raajaneeti binu dhan binu dharmaa,
Harihi samarpe binu sat karmaa
Bidyaa bin bibek upajaa-en,
Shram phal pad;e ki-e aru paa-en
Sang ten jati kumantra te raajaa,
Maan te gyaan paan ten laajaa
Preeti pranay binu, mad te gunee,
Naasahin begi neeti as sunee

अर्थ : नीति के बिना राज्य और धर्म के बिना धन प्राप्त करने से, भगवान को समर्पण किए बिना उत्तम कर्म करने से और विवेक उत्पन्न किए बिना विद्या पढ़ने से परिणाम में श्रम ही हाथ लगता है। विषयों के संग से संन्यासी, बुरी सलाह से राजा, मान से ज्ञान और मदिरा से लज्जा, नम्रता के बिना प्रीति और मद (अहंकार) से गुणवान शीघ्र ही नष्ट हो जाते हैं, इस प्रकार नीति की मैंने सुनी है।

Translation : [Context-Soorpanakha, after Laxmanji has rejected her overtures for marriage, runs to her brother Ravan and tells him that he drinks day & night and sleeps and does not realise that his enemy is at his door].

The law and order in a state without proper policy (statecraft), accumulating riches without following Dharm, doing noble deeds but not in the name of Lord [without dedicating them to Lord Vishnu], and obtaining education, learning and knowledge without developing the reasoning faculty, giving into the physical pleasures by an ascetic or a renunciate, a king by wrong consel, wisdom due to arrogance (conceit), modesty and grace due to drinking, love without trust, and merits due to vanity get destroyed very fast. Such are the maxims given by the wise people. Ravan, a great scholar and Lord Shiva's devotee, had become debauch and given to lust. Due to this situation, his sister Soorpanakha is rebuking him and telling him to shape up or else his kingdom will be destroyed very soon.

Comments : She tells Ravan—look—if any one tries to run a kingdom by inappropriate policies, earn money unritiously (through Adharm), doing good deeds without dedicating them to God, and getting education without developing discrimination only begets him hard work and nothing else. Here the life and works of Mahatma Gandhi is a great example. His politics was fundamentally based on 'Dharm'. He was always opposed to the well known diction, "Everything is fair in Love and War." He said no! He insisted and required that the goals and methods of Satyagrah have to be based on Dharm. Ritous goals through ritous means. We all know, when people earn money through wrong methods, they either waste it themselves or through their children. Because they got it through unfair means they do not value money as much as those that have earned their money going through hard work.

Here are some other good examples of things that loose their significances if not done the right way. For example—A sanyasi is destroyed (looses respect of the people) if he is given to pleasures of life (which he is supposed to have given up when taking sanyas); a King will destroy his kingdom when he follows the wrong advice of his advisors; a wiseman looses all his respect if people feel that he is arrogant of his capabilities (instead of being humble); a drunkard looses all his grace and modesty; love has no meaning without trust and the skills and merits of a person are devalued when people know that they are vain about it.

Follow righteous policy or one would get destroyed.

———❖❖❖———

नवन नीच कै अति दुःखदाई। जिमि अंकुस धनु उरग बिलाई॥
भयदायक खल कै प्रिय बानी। जिमि अकाल के कुसुम भवानी॥ 41॥

Navan neech kai ati dukh daa-ee,
Jimi ankus dhanu urag bilaaee
Bhaya daayak khal kai priya baanee,
Jimi akaal ke kusum bhavaanee

अर्थ : नीच का झुकना (नम्रता) भी अत्यंत दुःखदायक होता है जैसे अंकुश, धनुष, साँप और बिल्ली का झुकना। हे भवानी! दुष्ट की मीठी वाणी भी (उसी प्रकार) भय देने वाली होती है जैसे बिना ऋतु के फूल।

Translation : [Context : When Ravan, adherant to selfishness and bare behavior, goes to Mareech, another demon, and bows to him, Lord Shiva is telling the story of Lord Rama to his consort Bhavani].

Bowing (politeness) of an evil person is very tormenting, e.g., the bend in an ankush (elephant-goad) bothers the elephant, and similarly troublesome are bowing of a bow, of a snake, or a cat. Sweet talk of a wicked person can be threatening just as out of season blooming of flowers.

Comment : Most of the times modesty and politeness are normally considered very good virtues of an individual. However, false modesty can be deceptive and one needs to watch for it. Lord Shiva is explaining to Parvatiji–just think about it! There has to be something fishy where a powerful man, who can order the weak, becomes modest and starts requesting them as a favour (like a weak person would).

When a vile person bows down to you (and becomes polite) it could mean lot of trouble for you. For example the instrument Ankush, hamulus used to control an elephant has a hook, so when it hits the elephant it hurts the elephant. Similarly, a bow when bends, shoots an arrow at a taget, a snake and a cat go down in a bowing posture before attacking their enemy! This is just like when you see flowers blooming in the wrong season you would know something is wrong in the environment.

Be watchful when evil people are too polite.

❖❖❖

तब मारीच हृदय अनुमाना। नवन विरोधे नहिं कल्याना॥
सस्त्री मर्मी प्रभु सठ धनी। बैद बंदि कबि भानस गुनी॥ 42॥

Tab Maarrech hrudaya anumaanaa,
Navan birodhe nahin kalyaanaa
Sastri marmee prabhu sat; dhanee,
Baid bandi kabi bhaanas gunee

अर्थ : तब मारीच ने हृदय में अनुमान किया कि शस्त्री (शस्त्रधारी), मर्मी (भेद ज़ाननेवाला), समर्थ स्वामी, दुष्ट, धनवान, वैद्य, भांड, कवि और रसोइया इन नौ व्यक्तियों से विरोध (वैर) करने में कल्याण (कुशल) नहीं होता।

Translations : [Context : when Ravan visits Mareech and bows to him]

Mareech thought to himself : It is not beneficial to oppose these nine : an armed person, one who know one's private issues, a powerful master, a wicked person, a wealthy-man, a physician, a bard (a eugolistic poet), a poet and a cook.

Comments : Here poet Tulsidas has propounded a very clever rule of thumb.

He says if you care about your own welfare then it is not very wise to antagonize the following nine, because they can very easily hurt you :

1. An armed person who can hurt you physically if you pick a fight with him.
2. A confidant who knows your secrets can hurt you by making them public,
3. A powerful master has your complete welfare in his control and can pull the plug anytime if you play 'smart' with him.
4. A wicked person, who is always looking ways to create problems for people because of his very nature.
5. Money talks, as they say! Rich people influence kings, politicians, scholars etc. People say—what is there in this

world that cannot be bought and there is lot of truth in it. And that is why one should not antagonize the rich and powerful!

6. A Vaidya (physician) as he is the only person who can help if one is physically or mentally sick.
7. A bard who can change your repute into disrepute very easily.
8. A poet whose pen is more powerful than any sword in the world, and
9. A cook who makes the meal for you. No one can be safe if a cook plays tricks with what he cooks and how he cooks! Swami Dayanandji, the well known founder of Aryasamaj, was killed by his own cook as he put poison in the meals that Swamiji ate! Many rulers in Indian history would not take their food without feeding a dog or a cat to make sure there is no poison in it!

It is not wise to antagonize key people in one's life.

सीता केरि करेहु रखबारी। बुधि बिबेक बल समय बिचारी॥ 43॥

Seeta keri karahu rakhabaaree,
Budhi bibek bal samay bichaaree

अर्थ : [रामचंद्र लक्ष्मणजी से कहते हैं] तुम बुद्धि और विवेक के द्वारा बल और समय का विचार करके सीता की रखवाली करना।

Translation : [Context : Ram chandraji is going to hunt the Golden dear at Sitaji's request and leaving Laxmanji to guard Sitaji].

Guard and protect Sitaji with wisdom and discreminating reason with due attention to timely needs and strengths involved.

Comments : When Ramchandraji is about to go to hunt the 'Golden dear' he is instructing Laxmanji how to guard Sitaji. The poet has chosen the words very carefully! Ramchandraji says to Laxmanji—I am leaving Sitaji under your protection. Please guard her, wisely and with discrimination paying due attention the needs that may arise and the delicacy of the time! Here Ramchandraji has given Laxmanji enough hints why he should not have left Sitaji behind when she asked him to go and help Ramchandraji on a false call by the deceptive dear (Mareech)! He essentially asked Laxmanji to ignore Sitaji's request, knowing that Ramchandra is the Lord himself who does not need anyone's help to protect him. He should have known that the jungle was infested with demons and Sitaji's safety could be at risk anytime.

बिनु बिबेक कीजे न कछु, तापे जो फिर होय।
वह इत्सा भगवंत की, अपने दोख न कोय॥

—दयाराम (दयाराम सतसई, दोहा 360)

The better part of valour is discretion.
विवेक वीरता का श्रेष्ठतर भाग है।

—शेक्सपियर (किंग हेनरी फोर्थ, खंड 1, 5/4)

When entrusted with a responsibility, discharge it with all at your disposal.

जुबती सास्त्र नृपहि बस नाहीं। 44 ॥

Jubatee saastra nrupahi bas naaheen

अर्थ : (स्त्री का निवास चाहे हृदय ही क्यों न हो) युवती स्त्री, शास्त्र, और राजा किसी के वश में नहीं रहते।

Translation : (Even though one may love his wife so dearly to cherish her in his heart all the time).

A young wife is in not under anyone's control like a king or scriptures (kings and scriptures wield control over people and not vice-versa).

Comments : No matter how much one may love his wife, a young wife would not be controlable by his husband or anyone else. A wife would listen to a husband with whom she has lived for a resonable length of time. When she has lived long-enough she would be able to discriminate what to listen to and under what circumstances. Shastra or scripters are there to tell people the dos and don'ts of good and appropriate behaviour. Not the other way around! People do not decide what should be written in the scripters. Same way a king tells the people or the subject what they have to do and when to do. They may seek advise from advisors and people in general but they do not have to listen to them.

One needs to be very careful in talking in front of powerful people. As the story goes, king Aurangzeb asked in his court to advise him of his shortcomings, as he wanted to improve himself. No one opened their mouth except kavi Gang. He said : "Your Majesty if no harm will befall me I may say few couplets." On King Aurangzeb's assurance he recited few couplets. Aurangazeb became furious and poet Gang was put to death.

A king, the scriptures, and a newly wed spouse can not be controlled.

——❖❖❖——

फल भारन नमि बिटप सब रहे भूमि निअराइ।
पर उपकारी पुरुष जिमि नवहिं सुसंपति पाइ॥ 45॥

Phal bhaaran nami bitap sab,
Rahe bhoomi ni-a-raa-i
Par upakaaree purush: jimi
Navahin susampati paa-i

अर्थ : फलों के बोझ से झुककर सारे वृक्ष पृथ्वी के पास आ लगे हैं। जैसे परोपकारी पुरुष बड़ी संपत्ति पाकर [विनय से] झुक जाते हैं।

Translation : The way benevolent people become even more humble when they beget some good fortunes, the tree-branches were bending down closer to the ground under the weight of their fruits.

Comments : People who are benevolent are as such very polite as they know that their capability to be benevolent is due to the grace of God! It is certainly not due to their great skills. They know it is all God's will being manifested through them. And they are modest and humble about it. The great poet Raheem, a contemporary of Tulsidas, a great benevolent person was very humble. His benevolence and humbleness is legendery.

Such a benevolent person, when receives some more good fortunes, become even more humble, just as the branches of a fruit tree bend when they beget fruits. For example an uneducated or not well educated person shows off his knowledge (or lack of it) than an scholar!

निर्जितेषु तरसा तरस्विनां।
शत्रषु प्रणतिरेव कीर्तिये॥

जब कोई पराक्रमी अपने बल से अपने शत्रुओं को जीत लेता है तो उसका प्रणाम भी उसकी कीर्ति बढ़ाता है।

—कालिदास (रघुवंश, 11/89)

मैना जो 'मै ना' कहे, दूध-भात नित खाय।
बकरी जो 'मैं-मैं' करे, उल्टी खाल खिंचाय॥

—अज्ञात

यावच्च कुर्यादन्योऽस्य कुर्याद बहुगुणं ततः।

दूसरा मनुष्य जितना उपकार करे, उससे कई गुना अधिक प्रत्युपकार स्वयं उसके प्रति करना चाहिए।

—वेदव्यास (महाभारत, आदिपर्व, 162/15)

योगिनो विविधै रूपेर्नराणामुपकारिणः।
भ्रमन्ति पृथ्वीमेतामविज्ञातस्वरूपिणः॥

लोगों का उपकार करनेवाले योगी विविध रूपों से इस पृथ्वी पर विचरण करते हैं। उनके स्वरूप ज्ञात नहीं रहते।

—विष्णुपुराण (3/15/23)

नरः प्रत्युपकारार्थी विपत्तौ लभते फलम्।

प्रत्युपकारी मनुष्य विपत्ति में ही अपने कार्य का फल प्राप्त करता है।

—भास (चारुदत्त, 4/7)

नेकी कर कुएँ में डाल।

—हिंदी लोकोक्ति

Benevolent people should be humble too.

———❖❖❖———

अवगुन मूल सूल प्रद प्रमदा सब दुःख खानि।
ताते कीन्ह निवारन मुनि मैं यह जियँ जानि॥ 46॥

Avagun mool sool prad,
Pramadaa sab dukha khaani
Tate keenh nivaaran,
Muni main yah jiyan jaani

अर्थ : [रामचंद्रजी नारद के 'मोहिनी मोहभ्रम' के समाप्ति के बाद] युवती स्त्री अवगुणों की मूल, पीड़ा देनेवाली और सब दुःखों की खान है। इसलिये हे मुनि! मैंने जी में ऐसा जानकर तुमको विवाह करने से रोका था।

Translation : [Ramchandraji tells Naradji after he is out of his illusion of Lord Vishnu's Mohini guise] (For a great renunciate like you) A young woman is the root cause of vices, is hurtful, and is the storehouse of all sufferings.

Comments : (Context : After Lord Vishnu appears as a beautiful woman to which Naradji, a renunciate, is attracted to marry, he reveals his real form and Naradji gets very upset and puts a curse on Lord Vishnu).

If the main goal of some one's life, like yours, is to worship Lord and remain renunciate, then for that man a woman is the biggest cause of trouble, pain and suffering. (Similary for a renuciate woman, a man is the biggest cause of suffering and pain.)

He explains to Naradji—You are doing all the penance so that you get moksha and you are very advanced in your goal. Why should you get involved with a woman and get drawn into this physical world and be born again and again. Being born again will be the cause of suffering once you get involved with a woman and it is a bottomless pit of sorrow and suffering. Ramchandraji says—Narad, this holds true when you get involved with any woman, but it specially gets worse when she is a very young woman. If you get married to a young woman probably she would like to have kids. If you get kids, to raise the family you will get totally immersed in the physical world (the maya) and would not be able to pursue your number one goal of achieving *moksha*. That is the reason I stopped you from marying the mohini. Even though you feel some pain, however, I have saved you from bigger and more hurtful pain and suffering.

माया तजूँ तजी नहीं जाय, फिर फिर माया मोहि लपटाय।
माया आदर माया मान, माया नहीं तहाँ ब्रह्म गियान॥

—कबीर

कंचन को माया कहते हैं, कामिनी को माया कहते हैं और भूमि को माया कहते हैं। कंचन माया नहीं और भूमि भी माया नहीं। हे शिव! मन की आशा ही माया है।

(कन्नड) —प्रभुदेव (प्रभुदेव वचनामृत, पृष्ठ 50)

A well-wisher should stop a friend on wrong path, even at personal risk.

———❖❖❖———

किषकिन्ध कांड • KISHKINDAA KAAND:

तब हनुमंत उभय दिसि की सब कथा सुनाइ।
पावक साखी देइ करि जोरी प्रीति दृढ़ाइ॥ 47॥

Tab Hanumant ubhay disi,
Kee sab kathaa sunaa-i
Paavak saakhee de-i kari,
Joree preeti drud;-i

अर्थ : तब हनुमानजी ने दोनों ओर की सब कथा अग्नि को साक्षी देकर परस्पर दृढ़ करके प्रीति जोड़ दी [अर्थात् अग्नि साक्षी देकर प्रतिज्ञापूर्वक उनकी मैत्री करवा दी]।

Translation : [Context : Hanuman, after discovering Ram and Laxman wandering near Sugreev's residence on the mountain, introduces Ram and Laxman to Sugreev so that Sugreev can help him in Sita's search.]

Then Hanuman narrated to both the side's stories about each other and with fire as their witness he firmly established their alliance for help and friendship.

Comments : Hanumanji, having realised the need of Lord Rama to find Sitaji and Sugreev's need for protection from Bali and get his wife (Taaraa) back from Bali introduces them to each other. But introduction is not enough. They need to be friends! They need to commit themselves to friendship because the very traditional value, in Indian culture was that one must help his friends. Because if one does not what kind of friend that person is.

This friendship is not a casual friendship! It is serious commitment on which one cannot go back. And therefore it has to be public and formalized. Fire is the most respected in our culture dating back to Rig-ved or even from pre-vedic times. Therefore Hanumanji established, fire as the witness, their friendship process and cement it. *Agni* is considered the most important among the basic Pancha-Tatva, five elements, of which this universe is made of. Agni and Sun are the basic life-giver and life sustainer in this world. No life is possible without them.

In those times in our culture people were left to their strong values to follow their agreements and commitments. No human witnesses or written words were necessary like these days. Now sometimes the signatories use multiple pens to sign an agreement. Verbal agreements have no meaning anymore, unfortunately!

Friendship is a serious responsibility, observe it seriously.

जे न मित्र दुःख होहिं दुखारी। तिन्हहि बिलोकत पातक भारी॥
निज दुःख गिरि सम रज करि जाना। मित्रक दुःख रज मेरु समाना॥
जिन्ह कें असि मति सहज न आई। ते सठ कत हठि करत मिताई॥
कुपथ निवारि सुपंथ चलावा। गुन प्रगटै अवगुनहि दुरावा॥ 48॥

Jen mitra dukh hohin dukharee,
Tinhahi bilokat paatak bhaaree
Nij dukh giri sạm raj kar jaanaa,
Mitrak dukh raj meru samaanaa
Jinh ken asi mati sahaj na aa-ee,
Te sat; kat hat;-i karat mitaa-ee
Kupatha nivaari supanth chalaavaa,
Gun pragat:-ai av gunahi duraavaa

अर्थ : [संदर्भ : रामचंद्र अग्नि को साक्षी मानकर सुग्रीव को मित्र बनाते हैं और बाली की कथा सुनने के बाद बाली-वध का प्रण करते हैं] जो लोग मित्र के दुःख से दुःखी नहीं होते, उन्हें देखने से ही बड़ा पाप लग जाता है। मित्र को चाहिये कि अपने पर्वत के समान दुःख को धूल के समान और मित्र के धूल के समान दुःख को सुमेरु पर्वत के समान (भारी) जानें।

जिन्हें स्वभाव से ही ऐसी बुद्धि प्राप्त नहीं है, वे मूर्ख हठ करके क्यों किसी से मित्रता करते हैं? मित्र का धर्म है कि वह मित्र को बुरे मार्ग से रोककर अच्छे मार्ग पर चलावे। उसके गुण प्रगट करे और अवगुणों को छिपावे।

Translation : [Context Ramchandraji assures Sugreev, as a friend, to kill Bali, and tells him what a friendship is.]

It is a great sin to even look at those who do not feel the suffering of a friend. One should consider his (her) sorrow, even if huge like a mountain, small like a dust particle, and should consider a friend's small sorrow, even if like a dust particle, huge like a mountain (Sumeru).

If not endowed with such wisdom by their very nature, why such fools stubornly, befriend anyone. It is a friend's duty to check his friend from going to a wrong path in life and guide him to the right one. He (she) should reveal a friends virtues (in public) and conceal his faults.

Comments : Friendship in Indian culture is a very pious relationship. Lord Krishna was a friend of Arjun—besides being a maternal uncle. Many things one cannot discuss or does not feel comfortable in discussing with relatives (even brothers) but have no problem opening upto friends.

Tulsidasji, therefore, here emphasizes that a friend is such a special personal that one must feel the hurt when he/she hears about his friend being hurt or is in somekind of pain. Tulasidas goes further to emphasize the sense of friendship that—if there breathes a man who is not affected by the pain and suffering of his friend, such a person cannot be a human but an absolutely lowly soul who should be shunned by every decent person. For decent people it is a monumental sin to even look at such a decadent soul in worldly existance! In Indian culture and tradition the correct attitude towards a friend should be like the following—

A person should consider his own pain and suffering to be like a speck of dust, even if it may be huge like a mountain. And he should feel his friend's 'speck of dust' size pain as if it is huge like mountain! He should put them on a righteous path is they go astray to an unrightous path.

He should always be on a lookout to speak well about his friends in public and tell the world his friends virtues and try to hide his friend's shortcomings! A real friend should be supportive, a good counsel, a well wisher, protector, and helper all the time.

If there are some unfortunate people who do not posses such feelings and thoughts then such fool hardy folks should not try to make friends! In the long run they hurt themselves and others whom they call friends!

प्राण परित्यागेनापि रक्षनीयाः सुहृद सवः।

प्राण देकर भी मित्र के प्राण की रक्षा करनी चाहिए।

—बालभट्ट (कादंबरी)

वैरीभूतोऽपि पश्चात् प्राक्कथितं वापि सर्वदा।
विज्ञातमपि यद् दौष्ट्यं दर्षयेत् तन्न कर्हिचित्॥

मित्र शत्रु बन जाने पर भी पहले कही गई बातों को तथा उसके दोषों को जानकर कहीं भी, कभी भी प्रकट नहीं करना चाहिए।

—शुक्रनीति (3/314)

यो च अत्थेसु जातेसु सहायो हाति सो सखा।

जो काम पड़ने पर सहायक होता है, वही मित्र है।

—दीघनिकाय (पाली) (3/8/2)

Treet your friends problem bigger than your own.

———❖❖❖———

सुर नर मुनि सब के यह रीती। स्वारथ लाभ करहिं सब प्रीती। 49 ॥

Sur nar muni sab ke yah reetee,
Swaarath laabh karahin sab preetee

अर्थ : देवता, मनुष्य और मुनि सबकी यह रीति है कि स्वार्थ के लिए सब प्रीति करते हैं।

Translation : [Context : Lord Shiv is telling Parvati that no one, including parents, a Guru, relatives, a master, or a friend, is such a benefactor of humans and the rest of the universe like Ram.

It is a very normal practice that humans, deities, saints and even sages love with selfish motives (i.e. with an agenda).

Comments : All activities and work in this universe are driven by some kind of desire to do that activity or work. No matter who may benefit from that activity but ultimately the one who does the activity is the ultimate beneficiary of the work. For example a mother feeding her baby or a father teaching his child to read and write. At the first look it seems the baby is the beneficiary of the milk feeding and the child is reaping the benefits of education. However, if we look little deeper, the mother is also a beneficiary as she gets the satisfaction of properly observing her motherly responsibility. If she does not feed the baby the baby will cry hungry and she will be called a bad mother. And of course in return for her love for the baby she gets the love from the baby. She is working for the return satisfaction and the love! Similarly, a father also gets his satisfaction and rewards in return when his child learns the lessons well and does good in school. He is happy and satisfied that his hard work has produced good returns for his child!

The same behavioral psychology is at the root of all other activities as well weather they are humans, saints, or even Gods themselves! Is it true that Saints go for constant penance or meditation to see God or get 'Moksha', a freedom from the cycle of birth and death. But that is the return they wanted for the investment in the form of "penance"

Therefore, whether it is a tangible object or an intangible object that one wants but when they embark upon a task, they are trying to 'get' that thing which is the object of their efforts, no matter how noble or abominal it may be!

मित्रं च शत्रुतामेति कस्मिंश्चित् कालपर्यये।
शस्त्रुश्च मित्रतामेति स्वार्थो हि बलवत्तर॥

कभी-कभी समय के फेर से मित्र शत्रु बन जाता है और शत्रु भी मित्र बन जाता है, क्योंकि स्वार्थ बड़ा बलवान होता है।

—वेदव्यास (महाभारत, शांतिपर्व 138/142)

All love is driven from selfish motives.

———❖❖❖———

हरित भूमि तृन संकुल समुझि परहिं नहिं पंथ।
जिमि पाखंड बाद तें, गुप्त होहिं सदग्रंथ॥ 50॥

Harit bhoomi trun sankul,
Samujhi parahin nahin panth
Jimi paakhand: baad ten
Gupta hohin sad granth

अर्थ : पृथ्वी घास से परिपूर्ण होकर हरी हो गई है जिससे रास्ते समझ में नहीं आते, जैसे कि पाखंड मत के प्रचार से सदग्रंथ (लुप्त) हो जाते हैं।

Translation : [Context Ramchandraji is projecting his human form to Laxmanji expressing his pangs of seperation from Sitaji, specially in the beautiful natural suroundings and post rainly season] The earth is green in all directions well covered with grass that the foot-ways (path ways) cannot be ascertained. It is just as criptures disappear with the spread of hypocrical 'isms'.

Comments : The pain and sufferings of Ramchandraji (here as a human husband seperated from his beloved wife) has overpowered his reasoning, so he says. He is having hard time consoling himself. It is like when the mental noise is so large that the voice of reason is getting drowned out in it. It is easier for reason to control small worries but some time it fails to do so under the lethal attack of extreme pain and suffering. Today's psychologist say that the following three pains are the most extreme to bear in life:—

* loss or death in a family
* loss of a job
* loss of a spouse {due to death/divorce or any other reason}.

Ramchandraji was going through at least two of the above, if not all the three. His father was dying due to his leaving for the 14 year stay in jungle (so he lost both his parents for at least 14 years), loss of spouse (Sitaji was kidnapped by Ravana) and he was denied the throne of Ayodhya (to help the people) by Kaikeyee!

Here the comparison of his pain is with the large growing grass (weeds) in the jungle which is so high and densely covering the walking trails so it is difficult to see the path through the jungle. This is like, in today's world, disinformation (grass) well spread in the media that it is hard to tell what is the truth and what is a lie {through the disinformation}. And therefore even high, mighty and wise people have a hard time finding the path forward and may get confused in taking decisions!

Dis-information can mis-lead even wise people.

———— ❖❖❖ ————

नाथ विषय सम मद कछु नाहीं। मुनि मन मोह करइ छन माहीं॥ 51॥

Naatha bish:ay sam mad kachhu naaheen,
Muni man moh kara-i chhan maaheen

अर्थ : [संदर्भ : सुग्रीव रामचंद्र का कार्य भूल विलासी हो गया, तब लक्ष्मणजी उसे याद दिलाते हैं और सुग्रीव कहता है]

हे नाथ! विषयों के समान और कोई मद नहीं है। यह मुनियों के मन में भी क्षण मात्र में मोह उत्पन्न कर देता है [फिर मैं तो साधारण जीव ही ठहरा]।

Translation : [Context : On being reminded by Laxmanji that he (Sugreev) has been delinquent in his commitment to look for Sitaji, Sugreev apologizes by saying]

O, Lord! There is nothing so intoxicating like the pleasures of the senses. They (the sense pleasures) can entice even saints and sages in no time. [And, I am, after all a very ordinary person].

Comments : Humans are normally tempted to enjoy life through the five sense organs—**Eyes** (to enjoy beautiful), **Ears** (to listen to pleasant things), **Nose** (to smell nice things), **Tounge** (to taste what they like), and **Skin** (to enjoy things through touch of body with another object of pleasure!)

These objects of pleasure are so powerful that not only normal human beings, who are vulnerable to pleasures of life, but even self-controlled and pleasures-trancending Swami's and Saints are also vulnerable to the temptations of life through these five senses!

There are numerous stories in Puranas and in daily life that illustrate how pleasures and temptations of beauty have led powerful saints like Narada and U.S. President like Bill Clinton loose their reputation and stature due to getting attracted to many woman.

The five senses for which even saints fall into are intoxicating i.e. put you into a mental-state where one looses the sense of reality! People love their praise that includes swamies and saints too!

Desire to hear one's praise is such a human weakness that the Rajas and Maharajas used to appoint eulogists in their courts.

Rishies, of the highest order—like Brahma rishi, Vishwamitra were tempted by the looks, praise, and fragrances of Menaka that he fell from Samadhi!

Some of the most difficult temptations to control for any one are the temptations of the mouth/tongue (eating/drinking) and physical pleasures (skin or touch) including pleasures of bed! Wars have been fought for women and kingdoms have been destroyed for them. Ramayan and Mahabharat, both the epic's central focus are women, Sitaji and Draupadi respectively. Abduction of Queen Helen in European history caused the Trojan war!

Nothing is more intoxicating then pleasures of the senses.

———❖❖❖———

पुर रखवारे देखि बहु कपि मन कीन्ह बिचार।
अति लघु रूप धरौं निसि नगर करौं पइसार॥ 52॥

Pur rakhabaare dekh bahu, Kapi man keenh bichaar
Ati laghu roop dharaun nisi, Nagar karaun pa-i-saar

अर्थ : नगर के बहुसंख्यक रखवालों को देखकर हनुमानजी ने मन में विचार किया कि अत्यंत छोटा रूप धरूँ और रात के समय शहर में प्रवेश करूँ।

Translation : [Before entering Lanka] Hanumanji, noticing lots of Rakshasas guarding the city, thought to himself that I should assume a very small size and then enter the city at night.
No point in unnecessary direct fight.

Avoid fight and keep focus on the objective(s). Here it is to find Sitaji and give her welfare information to Ramji!

Comments : Hanumanji, when he arrived at the Ravan's Fort at Lanka, he viewed the fortification and security arrangement of the Fort!

Even though defeating the guarding army or killing them all were both easy options for him but that was not his main mission! Therefore, there was no point in creating an alarm in Ravan's mind and creating a war before he even finds where Sitaji was.

His main mission was to find Sitaji and report about her welfare to Ramchandraji. He decided, therefore, he should not be observed by any one in Lanka till he discovers where Sitaji was.

Consequently, he decided to assume a very tiny form and waited till the night-fall to enter the Lanka Fort! Night time provides one more level of security, besides a tiny size, so that he can enter Lanka and find Sitaji without being noticed by anyone.

लक्ष के लिये सहज प्रवृत्तियों को भी होम कर देना होता है।

—संपूर्णानंद (स्फुट विचार, पृष्ठ 146)

Avoid all unnecessary confrontations.

———❖❖❖———

जनि जननी मानहु जियँऊना। तुम्ह ते प्रेमु राम के दूना॥ 53॥

Jani jananee maanahu jiy oo-naa,
Tumate premu raam ke doonaa

अर्थ : हे माता! मन में ग्लानि न मानिये [मन छोटा करके दुःख न कीजिए], रामचंद्र के हृदय में आपसे दूना प्रेम है [ढाढस बँधाना, अतिशयोक्ति करके]।

Translation : [Context : Hanumanji consoling Sitaji in Ashoka Vatika].

O, Mother! Do not feel small in your heart (remorseful or compuctious). Because Ramchandraji loves you twice as much as you love him. [Implying that your current situation or anything else has not changed his love for you.]

Comments : Sitaji was in Lanka for several months and was getting impatient why Ramchandraji has not come and rescued her so far. She knows Ravan is capable of any or all bad deeds, even though he has not behaved bad with her physically. Hanumanji, who knows that Ramchandraji is the very embodyment of God, the ultimate power and protector of the Universe. He tries to raise her patience by consoling her that please do not loose heart! Ramchandraji loves you much more than probably you love him. He will know on his return to Sugreev's kingdom (other side of the ocean) where you are and will get you back as soon as possible by defeating Ravan! [Here it shows how due to ignorance, people loose heart some times due to suffering or pain!]

Patience is a great virtue, specially, in difficult times.

———❖❖❖———

सुनि कपि बचन बिहसि बिहरावा। 54 ॥

Suni kapi bachan bihasi biharaavaa

अर्थ : हनुमानजी के [मार्मिक] वचन सुनकर रावण ने हँसकर बात टाल दी [बनावटी हँसी जिस में डर छुपा हुआ था]।

Translation : Hearing Hanumanji's touching words (but true and piercing) Ravan tried to ignore it by laughing it off with deprecating laughter.

Comments : [Central point here is how one behaves when ego is in conflict with fear!]

Ravan is the epitome of ego and arrogance as symbolized by his ten-heads! He realizes that Ram is the powerful person who defeated all the powerful men of the time by winning the *swayamvar* in Janakpuri and then wedding Sitaji! He is affraid that his end may be near now. Ram's ambassador, Hanuman, is so powerful that only his son Meghnath could captured him with Brahmastra [Lord Brahma's weapon], then how powerful Ram must be! Even then his ego comes in the way and tries to laugh off the truth that was delivered to him by Hanumanji! So he is unable to laugh but pretends to laugh as if Hanumanji is being illusioned!

When ego is in conflict with fear, people behave abnormally (hypocritically).

——— ❖❖❖ ———

मोह मूल बहु सूल प्रद त्यागहु तम अभिमान।
भजहु राम रघुनायक कृपा सिंधु भगवान॥ 55॥

Moh mool bahu sool prad,
Tyaagahu tam abhimaan
Bhajahu ram raghunaayak,
Krupa sindhu Bhagavan

अर्थ : मोह ही जिसका मूल है ऐसे (अज्ञान जनित), बहुत पीड़ा देने वाले, तमरूप अभिमान को त्याग दो। और रघुकुल के स्वामी, कृपा के समुद्र भगवान श्री रामचंद्रजी का भजन करो।

Translation : [Context : Hanumanji advises Ravan, as an ambassador of Ram] Give up the darkness of vanity and arrogance of which excessive attachment is the root cause and that generates lots of pain and sufferings. You can attain the light of knowledge by praying the all merciful Lord Ram! The best of the Raghu family.

Comments : Lord Rama, Maryaadaa Purushottam Ram, will always do the things the rightway. That is his greatness. So he has first sent Hanumanji as his ambassador to the Ravan's court and advised him to return Sitaji forthwith. Hanumanji explains to him (Ravan) that he is deduded and the main cause of his problems is his believe and attachment that he is the most powerful in this universe and he can do whatever he wants and get away with it. Hanumanji tells Ravan that due to attachment to his desires and believes he is totally blinded by it (ignorance) just like a fully sighted person in a total darkness! His mind is totally blinded due to the darkness of attachment and therefore ignorance.

At this point, Hanumanji says to Ravan, the only way he can get out of this delusion is by realizing that Shri Ram is not a normal human but an incarnation of Lord Vishnu—the God Himself!

Excessive attachment is the root cause of most of the human problems.

———❖❖❖———

उमा संत कइ इहइ बड़ाई। मंद करत जो करइ भलाई॥ 56॥

Umaa sant ka-ee i-ha-i bad:aa-ee
Mand karat jo karat bhalaaee

अर्थ : [शिवजी कहते हैं—] हे उमा! संत की यही बड़ाई (महिमा) है कि वे बुराई करने पर भी (बुराई करने वाली की) भलाई ही करते हैं।

Translation : Lord Shiva describes to his consort—Uma—one of the great characteristics of 'Sants' (saintly person) is that they do good to the people who even do bad things to them.

Comments : As written by Goswami Tulsidasji—The Ramcharitmanas is the story of Lord Shri Ram as being described by Lord Shiva to his consort Parvatiji.

Here Shivji is explaining to Parvatiji as to what is a key characteristic of a 'sant' or a saintly person. A sant has many good virtues but an important virtue of a Sant is that he does good to even those who may be bad to him or hurtful to him. Like Mahavir and Gautam Buddha. As Kabir has written :

संत न छाड़े संतई, कोटिक मिलहिं असंत!

That is, saintly people do not give up their virtues even if thousands of bad people may have hurt them in some shape or form.

We are all creation of God and in this life we are all here to play our roles. Our goals are to grow and be more mature. Other people, good or bad, are also like us struggling to be better from whatever state of growth they are in their lives. So we should let them grow at their rate and continue our journey without going in retrogate motion!

संत न छाड़े संतई कोटिक मिले असंत।
मलय भुजंग ही भेदिया, शीतलता न तजंत॥

—*कबीर*

Saintly people help even those who hurt them.

कह प्रभु सखा बूझिऐ काहा। कहइ कपीस सुनहु नरवाहा।
सखा नीति तुम नीकि बिचारी। मम पन सरनागत भयहारी॥ 57॥

Kah prabhu sakhaa boojhi-ai kaahaa,
Kaha-i kapees sunahu naranaahaa
Sakhaa neeti tum neeki bichaaree,
Mam pan saranaagat bhayahaaree

अर्थ : [रामचंद्रजी ने पहले मित्रों से सलाह माँगी; नीति] प्रभु श्री रामचंद्र ने कहा—हे मित्र! तुम क्या समझते हो (तुम्हारी क्या राय है)?

[फिर सब सुनने के बाद अपना निर्णय दिया] [श्री रामचंद्रजी ने कहा—] हे मित्र! तुमने नीति तो अच्छी विचारी। परंतु मेरा प्रण तो है शरणागत के भय को हर लेना।

Translation : Ramchandraji first asks his friends advice as to what he should do (Administratively right way),

Then after listening to all the advice he tells his decision that although your advice is proper but my commitment (or vow) is to always remove the fear of a person who comes to me for protection.

Comments : In this particular couplet Lord Ram is depicted as an ideal Leader. When a key decision point arrives in front of a group, the leader should consult his other leaders in the group before coming to a conclusion.

Ramchandraji is the leader of the group which includes key members like Hanumanji, Sugreev, Jamvant, Angad and others. He maintains everyone's respect.

The point in question is what is the right behavior of a leader before coming to a decision point. Suppose the group expresses an opinion which may be contrary to his own opinion. He may choose to go against the group's opinion and take an independent decision. Nevertheless, he must still seek the group's view.

In the second verse Lord Ram gives his real view. He tells everyone of his friends and followers that even though their opinion is perfect according to rules for engaging an enemy but here the case is slightly different. He says it is his policy to give protection if some one comes and request it and he makes sure to remove any element of fear from his heart and mind!

A wise leader listens to his advisors and then does what is right.

बोले राम सकोप तब भय बिनु होत न प्रीति॥
सठ सन बिनय कुटिल सन प्रीती। सहज कृपन सन सुंदर नीती॥
ममतारत सन ग्यान कहानी। अति लोभी सन बिरति बखानी॥
क्रोधिहि सम कामिहि हरि कथा। ऊसर बीज बएँ फल जथा॥ 58॥

Bole Raam sakop tab
Bhay binu hot na preet
Sat; san binay kut:il san preetee,
Sahaj krupan san sundar neetee
Mamataa rat san gyaan kahaanee,
Ati lobhee san birati bakhaanee
Krodhihi sam kaamihi hari kathaa,
Oosar beej ba-ain phal jathaa

अर्थ : तब रामचंद्रजी क्रोध सहित बोले—बिना भय के प्रीति नहीं होती। मूर्ख से विनय, कुटिल के साथ प्रीति, स्वाभाविक ही कंजूस से सुंदर नीति (उदारता का उपदेश)। ममता में फँसे हुए मनुष्य से ज्ञान की कथा, अत्यंत लोभी से वैराग्य का वर्णन, क्रोधी से शम (शांति) की बात और कामी से भगवान की कथा, इनका वैसा ही फल होता है जैसा ऊसर में बीज बोने से होता है (अर्थात् ऊसर में बीज बोने की भाँति यह सब व्यर्थ जाता है)।

Translation : Ramchandraji then, showing his angry form, said—there is no love without some fear being involved in that. To modestly request a fool, to love a crooked person, to sermonize a naturally miser person about charitable attitude, to explain Vedanta to an extremly worldly attached person, to describe "Vairagya" or complete detachment to an intensley greedy person, to discuss beauty of "sham" (or peace) with a man of anger, and to discuss God's glory to a licencious (libidinous) person will bear the same results as sowing seeds in a barren land.

Comment : This particular set of verses are reflecting very interesting aspects of human psychology!

They do not deal with the unconditional love like parents

have for their children or many times among siblings but more from relationships in general.

For example among friends, when they are affraid of loosing a freind they are afraid of how they will have good times without them. If a friend was always helpful in day-to-day life, then one may be afraid of loosing those helpful hands. Such fears always affect one's life. In the context here, the sea did not listen to Ramchandraji's requests and he waited quite a while.

However when the ocean refused to hear his requests, Lord Ram threatened to hurt it and then he appear and asks for forgiveness!

Goswami Tulsidasji goes on to state some important rules of thumb in life in dealing with people :—

Here are some actions which will never bring desired fruits—

- Making requests to wicked and crafty person to change their mind or heart according to your requests will never bring desired results.
- Loving a crooked person will not bring any love in return but he/she will only take advantage of the benefactor.
- Explaining to a miserly person why it is good to be nice to others by giving gifts or explaining that the pleasure of giving is always much more than pleasure of receiving will not help any one. Not only he will not change and remain a miser anyway, but will also dislike the advisor who tells him not to be miser.
- Explaining to one, who is deeply infatuated with women and in love with money, the wisdom of non-attachment to this world will not make any impression on him or her.
- Explaining the beauty of detachment with money and all human possessions and how it may bring one happiness, will not work.
- To a man of anger, explaining the anatomy of anger and how not to get victimised by it may only make him/her mad at the preacher,
- Narrating Lord Ram's and Lord Krishna's great stories to an

amorous person, are the things that will never bring desired results. On the contrary it may make them more upset at the preacher. Such well intended efforts are no different than trying to sow a dry pierched farm which is totally and completely barren for a while.

These are some well intended efforts not only do not produce appropriate results but frustrate the doer and discourages him/her from doing good deeds in the future.

Following an appropriate policy only can one bring expected results.

———❖❖❖———

लंका कांड • LANKAA KAAND

नाथ बयरू कीजे ताही सों। बुधि बल सकिअ जीति जाही सों॥
तुम्हहि रघुपतिहिं अंतर कैसा। खलु खद्योत दिनकरहि जैसा॥ 59॥

Naath bayaru keeje taahee son,
Budhi bal saki-a jeeti jaahee son
Tumhahi Raghupatihin antar kaisaa,
Khalu khadyot dinakarahi jaisaa

अर्थ : [मंदोदरी रावण को समझाती है] हे नाथ! बैर उसी के साथ करना चाहिए जिसको बुद्धि और बल के द्वारा जीत सके। आप में और श्री रघुनाथजी में निश्चय ही वैसा अंतर है, जैसा जुगनू और सूर्य में।

Translation : [Ravan's wife Mandodaree advises him] O! My protector, one should keep enmity with only those whom one can win with mental and physical powers. There is certainly a difference between you and Lord Ram the same way as between a fire-fly and the mighty and all shining Sun.

Comments : It has been said that no one is more unfortunate than a person who cannot realize who his/her well wishers are! Ravan, unfortunate for him, falls in that category. His wise wife advises him of a true and tested policy. The policy is, and wisdom lies in it, that never antagonize and make enemy of a powerful person, specially and specifically with a powerful person like Lord Ram who is an incarnation of Lord Vishnu himself! As well illustrated in the stories of *Panchatantra* enemies can be broadly categorised into three type:—

(i) Much weaker than you
(ii) Equal in power to you or
(iii) More powerful than you.

The way to deal with them is:—

(i) With weaker enemy—by charitable attitude and taking them under your wings.
(ii) With the ones who may be equal in power—winning them in a battle or defeating them with mind and power, and
(iii) The more powerful—can be won over by accepting their leadership and be taken under their wings!

Mandodaree, Ravan's wife, was trying to explain to him the same thing that Lord Ram is not an ordinary enemy and the whole world knows that. She explained that he is more powerful than you (Ravan)! She says that if we try to compare your power with the brightness of fire-fly then Lord Ram would be probably like brighter than thousand Suns! He is the Lord himself, his power is unfathomable.

And O Ravan! Mandodaree said, you have only one choice that would make sense—and that is to return Sitaji to Lord Ram and worship him. He will forgive you and you can peacefully live as a king of Lanka!

One should oppose only those one can win over with one's mental and physical power.

———❖❖❖———

फूलइ फरइ न बेंत, जदपि सुधा बरषहिं जलद।
मूरख हृदय न चेत, जौं गुरु मिलहिं बिरंचि सम॥ 60॥

Phoola-i phara-i na bent,
Jadapi sudhaa barash:hin jalad
Moorakh hruday na chet,
Jau-n guru milahin Biranchi sam

अर्थ : यद्यपि बादल अमृत सा जल बरसाते हैं, तो भी बेंत फलता-फूलता नहीं। इसी प्रकार चाहे ब्रह्मा के समान भी ज्ञानी गुरु मिलें तो भी मूर्ख के हृदय में चेत (ज्ञान) नहीं होता।

Translation : Bamboo plant just would not give flowers or fruits even if rains come down which would be like nectar for any crop, the same way, my friend, a fool does not learn even if he gets a Guru like Lord Brahma himself.

Comments : There are fools all over the world and of all kinds. However they have one thing in common that they have no cure! They may be behaving like fools under the star's or may be permanently unqualified and unadulterated nincompoops! Block heads do not even understand who are their well wishers and who are not. And no one can even explain to them. Some dull headed folks may gain knowledge when they find great teachers like Lord Brahma or Guru like Brahaspati! But fools are better left alone.

And then there are fools who may have learned the scriptures well but do not understand how to put them to practice. As great scholar Chanakya has said—A great scholar who does know how to deal with people is essentially a fool.

As a maxim says—One who knows not and knows not that, he is a fool—leave him. That is, there is no point explaining anything to people who are beyond analysis and reason. For example, if it rains like cats and dogs even then a Bamboo plant does not bear any flower or fruits. So there is no point in giving a fool the nectar of wisdom as it may only offend him but would not do any good to him/her.

A fool never gets wiser no matter who the Guru is!

काजु हमार तासु हित होई। रिपु सन करेहु बत कही सोई॥ 61॥

Kaaju hamaar taasu hit ho-ee,
Ripu san karehu batakaree so-ee

अर्थ : [संक्षिप्त में रामचंद्रजी की अंगद को सलाह] [मैं जानता हूँ तुम परम चतुर हो।] शत्रु से वही बातचीत करना जिससे हमारा काम हो और उसका कल्याण हो।

Translation : [Finally as the last resort to avoid war Angad is being sent as Lord Ram's ambassador to Ravan, Ramchandraji in summary instruction, says:]

[Knowing that you are wise] chat and talk with Ravan, the enemy, such that our goals are reached (to bring Sitaji home) and what is beneficial to him too.

Comments : Leadership, and a good one, lies in knowing and acknowledging the capabilities of one's friends and supporters. Lord Ram, the Maryada Purushottam, addresses Angad, son of Bali, and tells him, "You know why we came wandering into these jungles. You know that I am looking for Sitaji who has been kidnapped by Ravan. You know you are our ambassador and emissary going to Ravan's court and to request the immediate release of Sitaji. You are a smart and a capable friend who knows diplomacy and it's ways of communications. So please, you know the tasks very well and you have all the tools to accomplish the tasks very well too. Hence we send you with all our blessings and good wishes to have victory in your mission."

An ambassa should be small enough to one who does not need detailed guidance

———❖❖❖———

जरहिं पतंग मोह बस भार बहहिं खर बृंद।
ते नहिं सूर कहावहिं समुझि देखु मतिमंद॥ 62॥

Jarahin patang moh bas,
Bhaar bahahin khar brund
Te nahin soor kahaavahi-n
Samujhi dekhu mati mand

अर्थ : अरे मतिमंद! समझकर देख, पतंगे मोहवश आग में जलकर मरते हैं, गदहों के झुंड बोझ लादकर चलते हैं; पर इस कारण वे शूरवीर नहीं कहलाते।

Translation : O, Dim-witted! A moth burns itself because of its attachment and infatuation for the fire and donkeys carry lots of load on their back all their life. But because of moth's self-sacrifice or donkey's service they are not admired as great heroes.

Comments : Angad arrived in Ravan's court and tried to explain to him why he should return Sitaji hence forth. When plain simple language did not help Angad to explain to Ravan he gets little caustic in his approach.

Angad tells Ravan that he is being utterly stupid by picking a fight with Lord Ram! His stupidity is also of the highest order like that of a moth which knows that fire will burn him and he has seen other moth already burning in it. When a warrior dies in a war protecting his master or his principles, he is respected and his death is honoured and respected as a great sacrifice. But no one ever says that a moth committed a great sacrifies by dying, like a blockhead, in the fire.

Similarly when a donkey carries it's load, no one ever praises it's smartness. The donkey is not capable of anything else and hence considered a beast of burden only. You are also carring out desires like a donkey and trying to carry them out mindlessly. He warns Ravan that fighting with Ramchandraji is ultimate sign of being brain dead. He should give up and surrender to Lord Ramji!

Foolish sacrifice and unintelligent labor is not respected

———❖❖❖———

जौ अस करौं तदपि न बढ़ाई। मुएहि बधें नहि कछु मनुसाई॥
कौल कामबस कृपिन बिमूढ़ा। अति दरिद्र अजसी अति बूढ़ा॥
सदारोग बस संतत क्रोधी। विष्णु बिमुख श्रुति संत विरोधी॥
तनु पोषक निंदक अघ खानी। जीवत सव सम चौदह प्राणी॥ 63॥

Jau as karau-n tadapi na bad;aaee,
Mu-e-hi badhen nanih kachhu manusaa-ee
Kaul kaam bas krupin bimood;aa
Ati daridra ajasee ati bood;aa
Sadaa rog bas santat krodhee,
Bishnu bimukh shruti sant birodhee
Tanu poshak nindak agh khaanee
Jeevat sav sam chaudah praanee

अर्थ : अंगद रावण से कहता है : यदि ऐसा (तेरी लंका का विनाश कर सीताजी को ले जाऊँ) करूँ तो भी इसमें कोई बड़ाई नहीं है। मरे हुए को मारने में कुछ भी पुरुषत्व (बहादुरी) नहीं है। 1. वाममार्गी, 2. कामी, 3. कंजूस, 4. अत्यंत मूढ़, 5. अति दरिद्र, 6. बदनाम, 7. बहुत बूढ़ा, 8. नित्य रोगी, 9. निरंतर क्रोधयुक्त रहनेवाला, 10. भगवान विष्णु से विमुख, 11. वेद और संतों का विरोधी, 12. अपना ही शरीर पोषण करने वाला, 13. परायी निंदा करने वाला, और 14. पाप की खान (महापापी) ये चौदह प्राणी जीते-जी मुरदे के समान हैं।

Translation : Angad tells Ravan : If I do so (destroy your city Lanka and take Sitaji back) there is no glory in it. There is no chivalry (manliness) in killing a deadman. The following fourteen category of people, though alive, are no better than a corpse :

1. One on the wrong path (tantrik-cult) 2. licencious person 3. a miser 4. an idiot 5. an utterly destitute person 6. a defamed person 7. a very old person 8. one who is regularly ill 9. one who is always filled with anger 10. one who has turned against Lord Vishnu 11. a persons against Vedas and sainty people (sadhoo) 12. one who only feeds and supports oneself and no one else 13.

one who is critical of other people and 14 an extremely wicked person.

Comments : Angad as an ambasador of Lord Shri Ram, would do things which may maintain Lord Ram's stature or enhance it in the world. He is not an emissary of an ordinary person but the incarnation of Lord Vishnu himself! He tells Ravan that he is capable of killing him, destroy the whole city and everything in Lanka by himself! But that is not his exact assignment as mandated by his master Lord Shri Ram! And then again you challange me to do so, and therefore I have to tell you that not only I will not get a pat on the back by Lord Ram if I destroy the whole Lanka but no one will praise me as a great chivalrous person! Because chivalry lies fighting and destroying a strong and capable warrior in a battle field. You folks—all of you are as good as dead like a dead wood.

For example 1. A person on the wrong path in his life is already psychology aware that he is weak, 2. a licencious person knows he cannot even raise his head in a societery, 3. an idiot has no skills to stay in battlefield, 4. a destitude is constantly worried about supporting and sustaining himself and his dependents, 5. a miser is constantly busy counting his money, 6. a defamed person will not get anyone's support or moral courage to fight 7. a very old person can not even walk properly or lift an arm 8. an ill person who cannot even get up from his bed 9. an angry person who looses all reasoning and therefore all skills to fight, 10. one who has no luck in his life as he has lost the blessings of the God himself, 11. a person who is devoid of all intellect as he does not understand the wisdom of knowledge in the Vedas and teachings of Sadhus who have laid down rules to understand the rules of policy and good behaviour, 12. One who cannot support and sustain anyone financially (does not have wisdom and/or capability and is a lowly person) 13. a person who is self-righteous and critical of every one else in this world, and 14. an extremely crooked man—therefore—alone, disrespected, disliked and detested by every one is as good as a dead body and is not worth killings. And if I do kill any of you, I will only destroy my name and fame and worse, the name of Lord Shri Ram! I will never do that!

There is no chivalry in defeating a weakling.

——— ❖❖❖ ———

**तिन्हहिं ग्यान उपदेसा रावन। आपुन मंद कथा सुभ पावन॥
पर उपदेस कुसल बहुतेरे। जे आचरहि ते नर न धनेरे॥ 64॥**

Tinhahin gyaan updesaa Raavan,
Aapun mand kathaa subh paavan
Par updes kusal bahutere,
Je aacharahin te nar na ghanere

अर्थ : रावण ने उनको ज्ञान का उपदेश दिया। वह स्वयं तो नीच है, पर उसकी कथा (बातें) शुभ और पवित्र हैं। दूसरो को उपदेश देने में तो बहुत लोग निपुण होते हैं, पर ऐसे लोग अधिक नहीं हैं जो उपदेश के साथ आचरण भी करते हैं।

Translation : [After Meghnath (Ravan's son) falls in the battle field, the mother, Mandodaree, veils and others cry too, Ravan consoled them with words of real wisdom of the sages. Although he himself is a lowly person but his words are pure and pious. However, there are many people who are well versed in giving sermons to others but there are not many (only few) who practice those morals too.

Comments : Ravan is affraid and may even realize that his end is very near but his ego is of astronomical proportions (as epitomized by his ten heads and the name Dashaanan) that he tries to sermonize veiling and crying Mandodaree! Ravan had all the knowledge of the Hindu scriptures and was a devotee of Lord Shiva. Knowledge is supposed to make a person modest and humble. However if a person's phenominal amount of ego—even knowledge of all the scriptures of the world may not be able to subdue his arrogance. So is the case of Ravan. He is not only an arrogant man but a hypocrite of the fist water! He starts preaching great and virtuous things, he does not follow himself but expects others to do so.

Unfortunately there are many people in this world, specially today, who would rather sermonize than follow their own teachings.

Today on TV in US, India and in every country in the world, there are Evengelists sucking money from people by preaching. Such preachings have no value and do not benefit any one. Mahatma Gandhi is the only example of a person who practised what he preached and preached what he practised! It is extremely difficult to find people like that.

Wise walk the talk and fools just talk only.

जनि जल्पना करि सुजसि नासहि नीति सुनहि करहि छमा।
संसार मह पुरुष त्रिबिध पाटल रसाल पनस समा॥
एक सुमन प्रद एक सुमन फल एक फलइ केवल लागहीं।
एक कहहिं कहहिं करहिं अपर करहिं कहत न बागहीं॥ 65॥

Jani jalpanaa kari sujasi naasahi,
Neet sunahi karahi chhamaa
Sansaar mah poorush: tribidh,
Paat:al rasaal panas samaa
Ek suman prad ek suman phal
Ek phala-i keval laagaheen
Ek kahahin kahahin karahin apar
Karahin kahat na baagaheen

अर्थ : (रामचंद्रजी रावण से व्यंग्य में कहते हैं) व्यर्थ बकवास करके अपने सुंदर यश का नाश न करो। क्षमा करना, तुम्हें नीति सुनाता हूँ, सुनो। संसार में तीन प्रकार के पुरुष होते हैं—पाटल (गुलाब), आम, और कटहल के समान। एक फूल देते हैं (जैसे पाटल), एक फूल और फल देते हैं (जैसे आम) और एक में केवल फल ही लगते हैं। इसी प्रकार (पुरुषों में) एक कहते हैं (करते नहीं), दूसरे कहते और करते भी हैं और एक (तीसरे) करते हैं पर वाणी से कहते नहीं।

Translation : [Lord Ram tells—Ravan in a sircastic way] Please do not destroy your name and fame by this rigmarole. Please excuse me, but I shall tell you this beautiful maxim, please listen : in this world there are three kinds of peoples. They are like a rose, a mango, or like a jack fruit. The one which gives flowers only (like the rose), the one which gives flowers and fruits also (like the mango tree) and the third only gives fruits (like the jackfruit tree). Similarly among men, the one kind talk only, the other kind talk and act on it, and the third kind only act but do not talk about it.

Comments : Lord Ram tells Ravan not to give sermons to him i.e. start sermonizing in the middle of a battlefield. You have a name, he told Ravan as a strong warrior who has defeated many kings. The responsibility of a great warrior does not lie in giving great speeches and that too in the middle of a battlefield!

Ramchandraji tells Ravan that if he continues to sermonize then he will be perceived as a week person in the battle field. Of course Lord Ram wants to kill Ravan in the battlefield when he is thinking of the war only and there is nothing else on his mind.

Lord Ram continues his sircasm and tells Ravan that he may be excused for telling him a beautiful maxim and it is as follows:—

There are three kinds of people in this world with respect to what they say and what they do and they are like a plant or a tree of gulab (rose), Mango, and Jackfruit!

(i) One of them gives flowers only (but no fruits like a plant of roses),

(ii) Second one gives both flowers and fruits like a tree of mangoes.

(iii) And a third kind which give fruits and does not give flowers, e.g. a tree of jackfruits.

Similarly there are three type of people too :

(A) One kind of men talk but do not walk the talk,

(B) Second kind of men do talk but also walk the talk,

(C) And the third kind are the best! They just walk and do not talk about what they will do. They just do what they do and do not like to posture at all like the other two category! These are the best.

There are three type of people in this world. One talk (but do not walk the talk), one talk and walk the talk, and the third just walk (and do not talk at all).

———❖❖❖———

प्रभु हनुमंत कहा समुझाई। धरि बटुरूप अवधपुर जाई॥ 66 ॥

Prabhu Hanumant kahaa samujhaahee,
Dhari bat:u roop Abadh pur jaaee

अर्थ : तदनंतर प्रभु ने हनुमानजी को समझाकर कहा—तुम ब्रह्मचारी का रूप धरकर अवधपुरी को जाओ।

Translation : Lord Ram then explained and advised him to go to Avadhapuri disguised as a Brahmachari.

Comments : Here, again as expected, Lord Ram shows his wisdom and leadership by not assuming what to expect in Ayodhya i.e. the Avadhapuri. Lord Ram has been away from Ayodhya for 14 years and how can he know, as a maryadapurshottam, in what shape and form the kingdom was being run. He should know if his brother would still welcome him and how his mothers are doing. He should enter Ayodhya only when it safe to do so.

And of course a trusted devotee of him like Hanumanji is the best to do that. But no one would recognize him as Lord Ram's devotee so they may be unkind to him and therefore he should go there incognito. The society would be kind to tell the truth to a Bhramachari Brahmman so he should disguise like that!

It is better to be safe than sorry. Wise never take things for granted.

———❖❖❖———

उत्तर कांड • UTTAR KAAND

ए सब सखा सुनहु मुनि मेरे। भए समर सागर कहँ बेरे॥
मम हित लागि जन्म इन्ह हारे। भरतहु ते मोहि अधिक पिआरे॥ 67॥

E sab sakhaa sunahu muni mere,
Bha-e samara saagar kahan bere
Mam hit laagi janm inh haare,
Bharatahu te mohi adhik pi-aare

अर्थ : [फिर गुरुजी से कहा] हे मुनि! सुनिये। ये सब मेरे सखा हैं। ये संग्राम रूपी समुद्र में मेरे लिये 'बेड़े' (जहाज) के समान हुए। मेरे हित के लिए इन्होंने अपने जन्म तक हार दिए [अपने प्राणों तक को होम कर दिया]। ये मुझे भरत से भी अधिक प्रिय हैं।

Translation : [On his return to Ayodhya] Lord Ram introduced his friends to Muni Vashishtha. O, Muni! These are my friends. In a battle of Ocean they were like a ship for me. For my welfare, they were even willing to sacrifice their very lives. They are even more dearer to me than Bharat!

Comments : These couplets are taken from Uttarkand of the Shri Ramcharitmanas. Lord Ram, Laxmanji and Sitaji have already enterered Ayodhya with Hanumanji, Jamvant, Angad, Sugreev, Nishad and many others who came with him all the way from Lanka.

Lord Ram very proudly introduced his friends and colleagues to Muni Vashishthaji. He tells his Guruji that these are my friends and colleagues. They have been the greatest help to me in my time of need. In the thick of a battle they fought with me, got deadly injured but continued to fight. They have put their very lives at my disposal to help me defeat the unsurmountable army of Ravan, the king of Lanka.

They would sacrifice even their several lives and still would stand by me in the battlefield! These are only some great characteristics of these my most dear friends.

Like in the middle of an ocean when someone may be drowning and cannot come to the shore, these friends helped me as if a ship would come and rescue the man drowing in an ocean! They have saved my life. In the ocean of a battle for life or death they rescued me like a ship for a drowning man. These friends are as dear to me as my brothers [Bharat, the eldest among them and the rest].

पुंसस्त्रिवर्गो विहितः सुहृदयो ह्यनुभावितः।
न तेषु क्लिष्यमानेषु त्रिवर्गोऽर्थाय कल्पते॥

पुरुष का धर्म, अर्थ और काम त्रिवर्ग मित्रों के सुख के लिए है। यदि मित्रों को क्लेश हो तो त्रिवर्ग व्यर्थ रहा।

— भागवत (10/5/28)

स्वाभाविकं तु यन्मित्रं भाग्येनैवाभिजायते।
तदकृत्रिमसौहार्दमापत्स्वपि न मुंचति॥

स्वाभाविक मित्र भाग्य से ही मिलता है। स्वाभाविक मित्रता विपत्तियों में भी नहीं छूटती।

Appreciate a friend's help and speak well of them to others.

———❖❖❖———

बिसरे गृह सपनेहुँ सुधि नाहीं। जिमि परद्रोह संत मन नाहीं ॥ 68 ॥

Bisare gruh sapanehun sudhi naaheen,
Jimi paradroh sant mana naaheen

अर्थ : [वानरगण सब अयोध्या में इतने आनंद से हैं कि छह माह बाद भी] उन लोगों ने अपने घर भूल ही गये। [जाग्रत् की तो बात ही क्या] उन्हें स्वप्न में भी इस प्रकार घर की सुधि (याद) नहीं आती जैसे कि संत लोगों के मन में दूसरों के प्रति द्रोह नहीं आता।

Translation : [The Vaanar troops are so happy and content in Ayodhya that, even after six months...] They have forgotten all about their homes. [What of in the waking state...] Even in their dreams, the same way. They do not remember about their home, as in their huts the Saint (saints) Purush do not feel hostility towards others.

Comments : Shri Ramchandraji's all friends came to Ayodhya after winning the war at Lanka. They have been showered with welcome celebrations, have been treated and greeted by all the people and officials of Ayodhya. Lord Ram personally took care of his friends as if they are just like his family! Then how can they miss their family in their own towns and villages. This has been going on for six months! Let alone while being awake, even in their sub-conscious mind they do not miss anything back home. This is just like saintly people always think of helping others who may need help. They think of helping even those who may have hurt them. Their nature is peace! Such is Lord Ram's friendship!

Love your friends so much that they may not even miss their family if away from it.

Note: 'mana' is an exception in transliteration to get the full pronumciation of 'n' with the vowel 'a' at the end of a word

सब मम प्रिय नहिं तुम्हहि समाना। मृषा न कहहूँ मोर यह बाना॥
सब के प्रिय सेवक यह नीती। मोरें अधिक दास पर प्रीती॥ 69॥

Sab mam priy nahin tumhahi samaanaa,
Mrush:aa na kahahun mor yah baanaa
Sabake priy sevak yah neetee,
More adhik daas par preetee

अर्थ : [भाई, राज्य, संपत्ति, जानकी, अपना शरीर, घर, कुटुंब और मित्र] ये सभी मुझे प्रिय हैं, परंतु तुम्हारे समान नहीं। मैं झूठ नहीं कहता, यह मेरा स्वभाव है। सेवक सभी को प्यारे लगते हैं, यह नीति (नियम) है। [पर] मेरा तो दास पर [स्वाभाविक ही] विशेष प्रेम है।

Translation : [Context : Lord Ram is telling his followers that my brothers, kingdom, wealth, Janaki (my wife), my body, home, relatives, and friends] All these are very dear to me, but not as much as you are. I am telling you the truth, that is my true nature. As a rule, every one (Master) loves their servant. However I, by my nature, love those who serve me with a total devotion and surrender.

Comments : Lord Ram is stating to his friends and followers that everyone loves their property, their spouse, family, etc. But it is his nature that he loves his followers even more. Above and beyond what other people or things he loves, he loves his followers and helpers who serve him. It is not his thinking (Lord Ram tells followers and friends who served him in the last several years) or deleberate policy but very nature that he loves his friends and followers and servers.

Lord Ram is telling them (the friends and followers) because it may be true that every leader or every king on the earth loves those things. But it is his very nature that his heart goes out even more for his servers and supporters specially because they leave their own near and dear ones to come out of the way to serve him. Poeple who serve a leader or a king make their own life hard to make the life of their leader easier and easier!

People earn money to make their family comfortable but a person who puts his life at stake all the time to serve and protect someone else's life does even a greater sacrifice. Lord Ram is trying to impress upon his followers his heart felt gratitude who followed him to Ayodhya after putting their lives at stake in Lanka to defeat demon king Ravan!

Love those who serve you as much as you love your dearest.

——— ❖❖❖ ———

भरत अनुज सौमित्रि समेता। पठवन चले भगत कृत चेता॥ 70॥

Bharat anuj saumitra sametaa,
Pat;avan chale bhagat krut chetaa

अर्थ : भक्त की करनी याद करके भरतजी छोटे भाई शत्रुघ्नजी और लक्ष्मणजी सहित उनको पहुँचाने चले।

Translation : [Remembering the great deeds of the devotees, Bharatji, alongwith younger brothers Shatrughanji and Laxmanji, proceeds to see them off (on their journey back home).

Note : The protocol is worth noticing. Ramchandraji being the head of the kingdom did not go to see them off. He said good by to then from his court. More elaborate and respectful work is delegated to next in command—Bharatji and other brothers.

Comments : The context here is that all his followers are returning back to their home. Lord Ram says 'good-by' to them and specially he hugs Angad, the youngest among his key followers. As Ramchandraji said farewell to all the followers, his brothers Bharatji, Laxmanji, and Shatrughanji proceeded and went with them quite a ways to bid them 'good-by'! These friends and followers of Lord Ram have done so much for Ramchandraji that Bharatji thought that these followers deserved more respect than a just simple good-by from the court of Lord Shri Ram! The protocol here deserves to be noticed. Lord Ram being the head of the kingdom stayed where he was but the second, third and fourth in command at Ayodhya gave the follower high honor to see them off all the way outside to the end of the town! Here it shows also the wisdom of Bharatji that he understood this and implemented this without anyone's suggestion or signal!

Respect your friends the way you yourself.

——— ❖❖❖ ———

तुम मम सखा भरत सम भ्राता। सदा रहेऊ पुर आवन जाता॥ 71॥

Tum mam sakhaa bharat sam bhraataa,
Sadaa rahe-oo pur aavat jaataa

अर्थ : (निषाद से) तुम मेरे मित्र हो और भरत के समान भाई हो। अयोध्या में सदा आते-जाते रहना।

Translation : [To Nishad] you are my friend and a brother to me like Bharat. Keep visiting us often.

Comments : When most of Ramchandraji's friends who helped him win the war against Ravan came with him to Ayodhya are returning, he addresses Nishad, the boat man :

He tells him that he is his dear friend and as dear to him as his own brother Bharatji! Even though Nishad has to return to his family like everyone else, Ramchandraji requests Nishad to do remember him and visit him again and again to maintain the lovely relationship they had established. The pleasure does not lie in coming and staying with friends all the time but in spending some time together then staying away for some time and then meeting like that again and again! As the maxim says, "Familiarity breads contempt." We discover our love for people or some one when we are not with them rather than when we are with them!

Keep in touch with your friends.

———❖❖❖———

संत संग अपवर्ग कर कामी भवकर पंथ।
कहहि संत कवि कोबिद, श्रुति पुराण सदग्रंथ॥ 72॥

Sant sang apabarg kar,
Kaamee bhav kar panth
Kahahi sant kabi kobid,
Shruti puraan sad granth

अर्थ : संत का संग मोक्ष (भव बंधन से छूटने) का और कामी का संग जन्म-मृत्यु के बंधन में पड़ने का मार्ग है। संत, कवि और पंडित तथा वेद, पुराण आदि सभी सदग्रंथ ऐसा कहते हैं।

Translation : Company of sants (saintly people) is the path to nirvan and the company of licencious people is the path to bondage of birth and death cycle. So say the sant, poets, pándits and all the Ved, Puran and other scriptures.

Comments : Everyone has their own circle of influence or a kind of aura they carry with themselves. This is as much true about good people as it is about bad people. As true about a Godly person as about a Devilish one!

It is very difficult to find the company of saintly people. Therefore if we come across some we should try very hard to be with them as much as possible without being a distraction for them.

Company of saintly people illuminates one with spiritual knowledge. Saintly people help us see our inner beauty and find peace within us.

They help us be on the right path to knowledge. Once we do start on the right path to knowledge, there are enough attractions and distractions in this words. Saintly people may warn, ahead of time, of the impending dangers and help us stay on the path to self-knowledge and salvation, moksha, or nirvana as we may call the ultimate state of being with God himself!

Devilish folks on the other hand are just the other side of the world of knowledge. They may appear to be friendly and even helpful but their friendliness and helpfulness will only engross us more and more into attachment with the physical world at the best or even encourage us to the world of anti-social and criminal behaviour. Many many times good people get competely destroyed by the company of bad people.

Shankaracharya has said that one should not associate or live with :-

(i) fools, (ii) mean and loathsome (iii) wicked and (iv) sinful people.

वासो न संगः वह कैविधेयो, मूर्खश्च, नीचश्च, खलैश्च पापैः ।

As there is a saying that even if a most wise and skillful person goes in a room coated with soot he cannot come out without getting a blemish on himself!

Company of good people makes you good and bad people bad.

सोइ सेवक प्रियतम मम सोई। मम अनुसासन मानै जोई॥
जौं अनीति कछु भाषौं भाई। सो मोहि बरजहु भय बिसराई॥ 73॥

So-i sevak priyatam mam so-ee,
Mam anusaasan maanai jo-ee
Jau-n aneeti kachhu bhaashaun bhaaee,
To mohi barajahu bhay bisaraa-ee

अर्थ : (रामचंद्रजी कहते हैं बुलाई हुई पूरी सभा से—) वही मेरा सेवक है और वही प्रियतम है, जो मेरी आज्ञा माने। हे भाई! यदि मैं कुछ अनीति की बात कहूँ तो भय भुलाकर (बेखटके) मुझे रोक देना।

Translation : [Ramchandraji tells the members called to the meeting]. He who obeys me, really serves me well and is dear to me. O, Brother! If I say anything against the rules and policy, check me, setting aside any fear.

Comments : [After bidding farewell to all his friends Ramchandraji called a meeting of his Guru Vashishathaji and all the court personnel and the public of his kingdom.]

Now he is telling all the people under his kingdom as to what would be style of his communication process and protocols. As a king and a leader of people—he must tell every one how he plans to manage and run the affairs of the Ram-rajya and how he would like the people to be involved in it!

Lord Ram says that to run the affairs of the state he expects everyone to discharge their duties effeciently, sincerely, and deligently. While doing those work to the best of their capabilities they must remember that the work must be performed according to the rules, regulations, and discipline as laid down and expected by him. Ramchandraji says those who implement their responsibilities truely, sincerely, and to the best of their knowledge will be appreciated. However he would love and appreciate those the most that do them in the manner he wants them to be done.

Then Ramchandraji says that he is of course would be

governing the state according to the information and resources available to him. It is quite possible that, even as a great king as Ramchandraji was, even he could make a mistake, take a wrong decision or may just make a judgmental error. Therefore, he requested all the people to point out to him if such a situation arises. Understanding that people may fear to point out errors he promises them of no negative reprecusion for pointing errors in his communications or actions! That will assure checks and balances!

A good friend will correct (properly) another, when he is wrong.

———❖❖❖———

स्वारथ मीत सकल जग माहीं। सपनेहूँ प्रभु परमारथ नाहीं ॥ 74 ॥

Swaarath meet sakal jag maaheen,
Sapanehoon prabhu paramaarath naaheen

अर्थ : जगत् में सभी (भगवान और उनके सच्चे सेवकों को छोड़) स्वार्थ के मित्र हैं। हे प्रभो! उनमें सपने में भी परमार्थ का भाव नहीं है।

Translation : [O, Lord Ram!] All people in this world (except you, the Lord, and your true servants) are selfish friends! O, Lord! They do not feel philanthropic, even in their dreams.

Comments : [After Ramchandraji gave the people, gathered in his court, summarised teachings on Karm, Gyan and Bhakti yoga the people are overwhelmed with joy and love for him] As people are getting ready to leave, Lord Ram, tells them that benevolent benefactor of people is the one who would shower love, care, and help to his followers without any expectations of any return. No one in this Universe is a true or genuine philanthropist. Everyone in this world is selfish and some are selfish to the core. That goes for all relatives and friends, including parents and teachers! Lord Ram is the only exception who would help his followers every way, no matter what!

जब तक रकाबी में भात,
तब तक मेरा-तेरा साथ।

—हिंदी लोकोक्ति

रोना है तो इसका कोई नहीं किसी का,
दुनिया है और मतलब, मतलब है और अपना।

—अकबर इलाहाबादी

The devil can cite scriptures for his purpose.
अपने प्रयोजन के लिये तो शैतान भी शास्त्र उद्‌धृत कर सकता है।

—शेक्सपियर (The Merchant of Vanice, 1/3)

प्रीति की अपेक्षा प्रयोजन ने ही आज मनुष्य को सबसे अधिक ग्रस लिया है।

—विपलमित्र (परसत्ती, पृष्ठ 30)

Basically, all friendships are for selfish reasons!

———❖❖❖———

बैनतेय संकर पहिं जाहू। तात अनत पूछहु जनि काहू॥ 75॥

Bainatey sankar pahin jaahoo,
Taat anat poochhahu jani kaahoo

अर्थ : हे गरुड़! तुम शंकरजी के पास जाओ। और कहीं किसी से न पूछना।

Translation : Lord Brahma tells Garudaji] O, Garuda! Go to Lord Shankar. And do not ask (the question) to anyone else.

Comments : Lord Brahma tells Garudaji that do not ask this question to anyone on the way. Why! there may be several reasons. Here are two reasons why he said so :

- A non-discriminating mind that Garudaji was at the time, he may ask the question to another person on the way who may also be non-discrimating and ignorant. An ignorant person may give him very confusing answer and Garudaji's whole purpose will be lost.
- When someone has a wrong understanding of a subject matter, it is more difficult for that person to get the right understanding even from the right teacher like Lord Shiva, the Dakshinamurty himself. No understanding is better than wrong understanding

To get the right understanding one needs the 'right guru' for him. It is not always easy to get the right guru in one's life! Only few lucky ones succeed in their life to get a True Guru (सत्गुरु)।

ग्यान प्रकासा गुरु मिल्या, सो जानि बीसरी जाइ।
जब गोविन्द कृपा करी तब गुरु मिलिया आय॥

—कबीर (कबीर ग्रंथावली, पृष्ठ 2)

पलटू सतगुरु पाई के दास भया निरबार।
परस्वारथ के कारने, संत लिया अवतार॥

Learn the right way, the first time.

———❖❖❖———

तबहिं होई सब संसय भंगा।
जब बहु काल करिअ सतसंगा॥ 76॥

Tabahin ho-i sab sansay bhangaa,
Jab bahukaal kari-a sat sangaa

अर्थ : सब संदेहों का तभी नाश होगा, जबकि दीर्घकाल तक सत्संग किया जाए।

Translation : All doubts are destroyed only when one keeps company of saints for a long time.

Comments : Here are three key words : (i) संत (ii) सब संसय (all doubts) and (iii) बहुकाल (A long time)!

Even though we believe in re-birth, we do not bring any knowledge of the previous lives into this life (with very very few exceptions in a long time)! That is to say that knowledge and wisdom does not transmigrate.

Saints are an ocean of knowledge with the most charitable attitude to share with all the seekers who may come by to benefit from them. Not only they have taken their mind to that state where knowledge flows through their minds as waves in an ocean. That is to say that they know methods, the paths, and the pitfalls on the path of knowledge. While there are many do's to achieve the ultimate knowledge, there may be equal number of don'ts too! Avoiding them (the don'ts) may be even more important or critical than completing the 'do's' in one's life!

Saints can teach us a lot through their teachings but how they live their life can even be a greater source of knowledge! It has been stated by a great American poet—

Lives of greatman, all remind us
We can make our lives sublime
And departing leave behind us
Footprints on the sands of time

Footprints that perhaps another
Sailing over life's solemn main
Forlorn or ship racked brother
Seeing may take heart again

So lives of saints can even put a man on the right path who has been lost in the jungle of life!

The second keyword here is बहुकाला or 'long-time'. It takes time to even impart little little pieces of knowledge to anyone. We remember things contextually and therefore it will take time for saints to impart that knowledge as context arises. As one lives with saints, one would observe how they talk and interact with other people including other saints and these are great opportunities to learn. As one learns so one can start practicing the great knowledge one get, from saints. As one practices, some more questions arise and one can ask and learn more from the saints. Learning is a life long and unending process. And therefore one should stay for a long time with saints to learn the secrets of life and how to see God in self! That is the reason for the maxim: "Live and Learn!"

Only long company of sant will remove all doubts of an individual

———❖❖❖———

होइहिं कीन्ह कबहु अभिमाना। सो खौवे चह कृपा निधाना॥ 77॥

Ho-i-hin keenh kabahu abhimaanaa,
So khovai chah krupaa nidhaanaa

अर्थ : [शिवजी उमा/पार्वतीजी से कहते हैं] उसने (गरुड़) कभी अभिमान किया होगा, जिसको की कृपानिधान श्री रामजी नष्ट करना चाहते हैं।

Translation : [Lord Shiva explains to his consort Uma] Garudaji must have been arrogant some time in his life and it is that arrogance Lord Ram wants to destroy in Garudaji!

Comments : God always wants to free his devotees from ignorance and that is why he puts his devotees through various situations or experiences in life.

Here is the basic aspect of the Theory of Karm! As you sow, so you reap! If one is suffering through some bad times or enjoying some good times it is all due to what one must have done in the past lives. Among Hindus it is believed that the past we talk about could be from this life or from lives before. We cannot say, for sure, from which life's deeds we are being rewarded or punished in this life! It is for sure that we shall ultimately reap the consequences of our Karm or deeds but we have no say in the outcome of those consequences! Lord only decides the timing of the results to appear.

There are similar values in all cultures. But not the same! Many religions believe that as you sow-so you reap! However, I believe and as far as I know, only Hinduism states that one may reap the consequences of his actions either in the current life or in life or lives to follow due to rebirth.

Specifically Christianity and Islam doesn't believe in rebirth. And many times people from other religions (other than Hinduism/ Buddhism/Jainism) have difficulty understanding why an infant may die due to an accident or otherwise when it has not really committed any bad deeds or so called 'sins', if one may call bad deeds as sins. The infants or little kids are the most pure souls as we can experience in this life. They do not even know as to what is the definition of 'good' or 'bad'! So how could they die so early and due to what consequences of their actions, when they did not even get a chance to perform any real actions due to their own free will!

It is only the principles of (i) The theory of Karm and (ii) the Theory of Rebirth that can adequately explain many questions like why a child dies in a car accident!

That is why, due to love of Lord Ram for his devotee Garudaji, Lord Ram wants to destroy the ignorance in Garudaji's mind whether the doubt arose in this life or in a life before this one!

God always wants to free his devolees from ignorance.

❖❖❖

कछु तेहि ते पुनि मैं नहिं राखा। समुझइ खग खगही कै भाषा। 78॥

Kachhu tehi te puni main nahin raakhaa,
Samujha-i khag khagahee kai bhaash:aa

अर्थ : (शंकरजी उमा से कहते हैं—) फिर कुछ इस कारण भी मैंने उसको अपने पास नहीं रखा कि पक्षी पक्षी की ही बोली समझते हैं।

Translation : [Lord Shiv continues his explanation to Devi Uma, why he told Garudaji to go and listen to the Rama Katha from Kak bhushundi, a great devotee of Lord Ram]

Besides, for another reason also I did not keep him with me (and asked him to go and listen to Ramkatha from Kakbhushundi) is that same kind (birds) of people can comprehend a point their own language better than is others language.

Comments : The comprehension level of Garudaji was, very different than that of Lord Shiva and that is why he needed an exposure which will be long and comprensible at his own cultural level. This is very much true at human to human level also. Among a group of experts, a beginner not only gets lost in expounded teachings but may also get hurt due to feeling a sense of failure from such environment.

Birds of the same feather flock together.

—An English proverb

It is easier to learn some thing from people of your own cultural back ground.

——— ❖❖❖ ———

जौ अति आतप ब्याकुल होई। तरु छाया सुख जानइ सोई॥ 79॥

Jau ati aatap byaakul ho-ee,
Taru chhaayaa sukh jaana-i so-ee

अर्थ : जो धूप से अत्यंत व्याकुल होता है (हो चुका होता है), वही वृक्ष की छाया का सुख जानता है।

Translation : (जाके पैर न फटी बिवाइ, सो क्या जाने पीर पराई) That person only know the pleasure of a tree's shadow who has been extremely restless due to sunshine.

Comments : This is a very common saying in most cultures and there are many ways to say this in any culture. For example in Hindi there is another saying. One who has not had chilblains cannot feel the pain of others (who have it)! No wonder to have sympathy with others one probably has to feel similar pain himself. A boy cannot understand the pleasure or pain of being a father until he raises his own son, of course same applies for a girl. As said in English proverb :

The wearer best knows where the shoe pinches!

One dying of hunger can only appreciates
the real valve of food.

मोह न अंध कीन्ह केहि केही। को जग काम नचाव न जेही ॥ ८० ॥

Moh na andh keenh kehi kehee,
Ko jag kaam nachaava na jehee

अर्थ : (नारदजी, ब्रह्माजी और सनकादि अनेक महान् मुनि और ज्ञानी) उनमें से किन-किन को मोह ने अंधा नहीं किया? जगत् में ऐसा कौन है जिसे काम ने न नचाया हो।

Translation : [Kakbhushundi tells Garudji: Naradji, Brahmaji and Sage Sanak and his brothers] who among them have not been blinded by infatuation? Who in this world has not danced like a puppet due to lust?

Comment : There are famous stories in *Puran* about Rishi's being driven to lust by beautiful women. Rishi Vishwamitra lusted for Menaka and Rishi Narad for the Mohini!

श्वान क्षणेन निद्राति क्षणेन च प्रबुध्यते।
नृणान्तु मोहसुप्तानां प्रबोधो न चिरादपि॥

कुत्ता क्षणभर में सोता है, क्षणभर में जागता है। किंतु मोह में सोए हुए मनुष्यों का जागरण चिरकाल में नहीं होता।

— कालीपद (प्रशांत-रत्नाकर नाटक)

सततममूलमन्त्रशक्यो विषमो विषयविषास्वादमोह।

विषयरूपी विष के भोग से उत्पन्न मोह ऐसा विषम होता है कि वह जड़ी-बूटी और मंत्रों से भी नहीं उतरता।

— बालभट्ट (कादंबरी, पूर्वभाग, पृष्ठ 314)

Lust and infatuation blinds every one.

———❖❖❖———

ग्यानी तापस सूर कबि कोबिद गुन आगार।
केहि कै लोभ बिडंबना कीन्हि न एहिं संसार॥ 81॥

Gyaanee taapas soor kabi,
Kobid gun aagaar
Kehi kai lobh bid:ambanaa,
Keenhi na e-hin sansaar

अर्थ : इस संसार में ऐसा कौन ज्ञानी, तपस्वी, शूरवीर, कवि, विद्वान और गुणों का धाम है, जिसकी लोभ ने विडंबना (मिट्टी पलीद) न की हो।

Translation : In this world, is there any wise man, ascetic, valiant, poet, scholar, or abode of all virtues, whom greed has not made a subject of mockery.

Comments : Every human, leaving the Lord (भगवान, Bhagvan), is fallible and therefore one should not feel completely broken if they go through these (above) experiences or see some one else going through them. Then only they may be able to forgive themselves and therefore others.

न लुब्धो बुध्यते दोषाल्लोभान्मोहात् प्रवर्तते।

लोभी मनुष्य किसी कार्य के दोषों को नहीं समझता। वह लोभ और मोह से प्रवृत्त हो जाता है।

—वेदव्यास (महाभारत, द्रोणपर्व, 55/11)

लोभः प्रतिष्ठा पापस्य प्रसूतिलाभ एव च।
द्वेषक्रोधादिजनको लोभः पापस्य कारणम्॥

लोभ पाप का घर है। लोभ ही पाप की जन्मस्थली है और यही दोष क्रोध आदि को उत्पन्न करनेवाला है। अतः पाप का कारण लोभ है।

—बल्लाल कवि (भोज प्रसंग)

लालच हू ऐसी भली जासो पूरे आस।
चाटेहू कहुँ ओस के, मिटत काहू की प्यास॥

—वृंद (वृंद सतसई)

अतितृष्णा न कर्त्तव्या, तृष्णां नैव परित्यजेत।

लोभ तो स्वाभाविक है, किंतु अतिशय लोभ मनुष्य का सर्वनाश कर देता है।

—पंचतंत्र (मित्र संप्राप्ति, 3)

There is no greedy person who does not get mocked by the society.

———❖❖❖———

श्री मद बक्र न कीन्ह केहि प्रभुता बधिर न काहि।
मृगलोचनि के नैन सर को अस लाग न जाहि॥ 82॥

Shree mad bakra na keenh kehi,
Prabhutaa badhir na kaahi
Mrug lochani ke nain sar,
Ko as laag na jaahi

अर्थ : लक्ष्मी के मद ने किसको टेढ़ा और प्रभुता ने किसको बहरा नहीं कर दिया। ऐसा कौन है, जिसे मृगनयनी (युवती स्त्री) के नेत्रबाण न लगे हों।

Translation : Who has not deviated from a straight righteous path due to arrogance of wealth and glamour? Whom has power not rendered deaf? Is there any man who has not been affected by the arrows of loving glares of a beautiful young woman!

Comments : Kakbhushundi is continuing to explain to Garudji (the king of Birds) the typical weaknesses of a human, even best of them, as opposed to Ishwar which is beyond any such shortcoming. Here the poet has elaborated on Vedantic teaching of how a jivatma is affected by the opposites of Raga/Dwesha i.e. attachment/aversion.

अर्थ एव हि केषांचिदनर्थ भजते नृणाम्।
अर्थ श्रेयसि चासक्तो न श्रेयो विदन्ते नरः॥

कितने मनुष्यों के लिए अर्थ ही अनर्थ का कारण बन जाता है, क्योंकि अर्थ-श्रेय में आसक्त मनुष्य वास्तविक श्रेय को प्राप्त नहीं होता।

—वेदव्यास (महाभारत, वनपर्व, 2/41)

अर्थस्य पुरुषो दासो दासस्त्वर्थो न कस्यचित्।

पुरुष अर्थ का दास है। अर्थ किसी का दास नहीं है।

—वेदव्यास (महाभारत, भीष्म पर्व, 43/50)

यस्य चार्थार्थमेवार्थः स च नार्थस्य कोविदः।
रक्षेत मृतकोऽरण्ये यथा गास्तादृगेव सः॥

जिसका धन मात्र धन के लिए है, वह धन के तत्त्व को नहीं जानता। जैसे सेवक वन में गायों की रक्षा करता है, उसी प्रकार वह भी दूसरे के लिए धन का रक्षक मात्र है।

—वेदव्यास (महाभारत, वन पर्व, 33/24)

लघुता से प्रभुता मिले प्रभुता से प्रभु दूर।
चींटी ले शक्कर चली हाथि के सिर धूर॥

—अज्ञात

प्रभुता ही को सब मरैं, प्रभु को मरे न कोय।
जो कोई प्रभु को मरै, प्रभुता दासी होय॥

—मलूकदास

दूरस्थाः पर्वता रम्या वेश्या च मुखमण्डने।
युद्धस्य वार्त्ता रम्या त्रीणि रम्याणि दूरतः॥

दूरस्थ पर्वत, मुख सजा लेने पर वेश्या तथा युद्ध की वार्त्ता रम्य होते हैं। किंतु ये तीनों दूर से ही रम्य होते हैं।

—अज्ञात

All human being (at least some time) are affected (in a negative way) by wealth, power, and opposite sex. Therefore, one needs to be cautious of these enemies all the time.

———❖❖❖———

मच्छर काहि कलंक न लावा। काहि न सोक समीर डोलावा॥
चिंता साँपिनि को नहि खाया। को जग जाहि न व्यापी माया॥ 83॥

Machchhar kaahi kalank na laavaa,
kaahi na sok sameer d:olaavaa
Chintaa saanpini ke nahi khaayaa,
ko jag jaahi na byaapee maayaa

अर्थ : मत्सर (डाह) ने किसको कलंक नहीं लगाया? शोक रूपी पवन ने किसे नहीं हिला दिया? चिंता रूपी साँपिनी ने किसे नहीं खा लिया? जगत् में ऐसा कौन है, जिसे माया न व्यापी हो? [काक भुशुंडि और गरुड़जी का संवाद]

Translation : Whom has jelousy not maligned? Who has not been shaken by the winds of depression? Who has not been devoured by the snake of worries? Who is there in this world who has not been taken over by Maya or worldly attractions (or illusionary world).

[Contex Kaakbhushundi—Garud Samwad]

Comments : In this world there are all kinds of people with all kinds of (human) weaknesses. Anyone and every one who is born is bound to be affected by them even if it is of a negligible or of imperceptible amount or of a transient nature. Even when people praise others, there may be an imperceptible amount of jelousy in them saying within, 'I wish I was like that' etc. Jelousy can take hold of a person at any age—young, middle aged, or old.

Similary we all mortals have desires of some kind or another even if they are good desire. And if any one does not get fulfilled it lead one to sarrow and emotional suffering. Like powerful wind moves everyone and just as nothing will remain standing in front of a hurricane or tornado!

Why people worry? Because we all have desires to do or achieve things and we are not confident (all the time) that we will be able to. This may lead to fear of failure leading to worries about lack of success in the future.

Nothing is permanent in this transitory world. Yet people see happiness in worldly possessions or name and fame. Whether it is beauty or money or relatonships. Everyone 'wants' them—the Maaya—the worldly attractions.

Yes when mortals rise above these weaknesses then only they are considered immortal or realized souls—the souls that realise this world as all maaya and beyond that is the Lord himself!

Having worldly desires is normal, but one needs to be vigilant. Otherwise it can lead to sadness and depression

कीट मनोरथ दारु सरीरा। जेहि न लाग घुन को अस धीरा॥
सुत बित लोक ईषना तीनी। केहि कै मति इन्ह कृत न मलीनी॥ 84॥

Keet: manorath daaru sareeraa,
Jehi na laag ghun ko as dheeraa
Sut bit lok eesh:anaa teenee,
Kehi kai mati inh krut na maleenee

अर्थ : मनोरथ कीड़ा (घुन) है, शरीर लकड़ी है। ऐसा धैर्यवान कौन है, जिसके शरीर में यह कीड़ा न लगा हो? पुत्र की, धन की और लोक प्रतिष्ठा की—इन तीन प्रबल इच्छाओं ने किसकी बुद्धि को मलिन नहीं कर दिया (बिगाड़ नहीं दिया)?

Translation : If desire is like a worm and the human body is like wood, then, is there anyone so resolute who has not been affected by wood-worm. Whose mind has not been sadened (or dulled) by the three passions—desire for progeny, for money, and for worldly fame.

Comments : Examples Are : Raja Dashrath, Worldly fame Nixon—Worldly fame Mahabharat—Bhishma to Yudhishthira.

Desire is a fundamental feeling that motivates a human being to do anything in this world. These desires can be classified in many ways. Most of the mortals are driven by desire for power and prestige. The power and prestige they seek in their life in the areas which are dependet on their nature and capabilities. An educated man with a desire for money may go to the wall-street and make money or open a business of his own and try to make money. However these desires are like fire! The more effort one makes to make money like putting more wood in a fire the desire becomes stronger and stronger and the person gets more and more attached to money. The more one gets attached to money, or any desire for that matter, the more one starts worrying about it. This leads one's mind and body towards deterioration and degradation.

One of the great poets in Hindi literature, Giridhar has said very well about how worry eats one's mind and body like a wood-worm eats wood and the outcome is dust that gets scattered all around, such is the status of a person's mind who worries about anything.

One of the famous examples of attachment and worry which finally leads to the death of an individual is that of Raja Dasharath in Ramayan. Another outstanding example is that of a U.S. President—Richard Nixon. Nixon was f99ighting a Presidential election against a very weak opponent George McGovern, but he wanted to guarantee it as much as he could. That led him and his team to do illegal behavior. Therefore, inspite of his getting re-elected as a president, 2nd time, in November 1972, he was uncerimoniously removed from the office (he resigned just ahead of his impeachment)! The only president in the long history of United States of America, so disgraced.

Such is the play of Maaya (all the worldly attachments).

However, the positive form of desire is the love of God! One who goes on the path of spirituality and God, slowly and slowly but surely starts loosing worldly desires. Such people begin to detach or rather their attachments start falling off automatically.

Tulsidas, the poet, says even though there are many forms and types of desires, but none of them are stronger than one's attachment to children, money, and worldly name and fame!

Wordly desires saden and destroy human mind the way wood-worm destroys the wood.

———❖❖❖———

व्यापि रहेउ संसार महुँ माया कटक प्रचंड।
सेनापति कामादि भट, दंभ कपट पाषंड॥ 85॥

Byaapi rahe-u sansaar mahun,
Maayaa katak prachand:
Senaapati kaamaadi bhat:,
Dambha kapat: paash:a-nd:

अर्थ : माया की प्रचंड सेना संसार भर में छाई हुई है। कामादि (काम, क्रोध और लोभ) उसके सेनापति हैं और दंभ, कपट और पाखंड योद्धा हैं।

Translation : The forces of Maya (the non-permanent world and its attractions) pervade the whole cosmos. Worldly desires (specially lust), anger, and greed are its generals and vanity, deceit, and hypocrisy are the soldiers (warriors).

Comments : The poet has very interestingly given the root cause of all ills in this world. At the bottom of all worldly ills are the deep rooted worldly desires which lead one to greed and with the non-fulfillment of those greedy desires leads one to anger. However these may also manifest to an observer as vanity, deceit and hypocrisy because greedy people use these three tools to fulfill their lustful desires. It is worth comparing these lines with sloka 2-62 & 2-63 of Shrimad Bhagvat Geeta.

माया तजूँ तजी नहीं जाई, फिर फिर माया मोहिं लपटाय।
माया आदर माया मान, माया नहीं, तहाँ ब्रह्म गियान॥

—कबीर (कबीर ग्रंथावली, पृष्ठ 361)

माया दीपक नर पतंग, भ्रमि भ्रमि इवै पड़ंत।
कहै कबीर गुर ग्यान थैं, एक आध उबरंत॥

—कबीर (कबीर ग्रंथावली, पृष्ठ 113)

दैवी ह्येषा गुणमयी माया दुरत्यया।
मामेव ये प्रपद्यन्ते मायामेतां तरन्तिते॥

परमात्मा की त्रिगुणात्मक माया बड़ी दुस्तर है, जो परमात्मा की शरण में जाते हैं, वे ही इस माया को पार कर पाते हैं।

—वेदव्यास (महाभारत, भीष्मपर्व 31/14)

कंचन को माया कहते हैं, कामिनी को माया कहते हैं और भूमि को माया कहते हैं। कंचन माया नहीं और भूमि भी माया नहीं। हे शिव! मन की आशा ही माया है।

—प्रभुदेव (प्रभुदेव वचनामृत, पृष्ठ 50 कन्नड)

Attachment to the worldy things (non-permanent world) destroys human mind through the six weapons: lust, anger, greed, vanity, deceit and hypocrisy.

———❖❖❖———

नयन दोष जा कहँ जब होई। पीत बरन ससि कह सब कोई॥
नौका रूढ़ चलत जग देखा। अचल मोह बस आपुहि लेखा। 86॥

Nayan dosh: jaa kahan jab ho-ee,
Peet baran sasi kah sab ko-ee
Naukaarood; chalat jag dekhaa,
Achal moh bas aapuhi lekhaa

अर्थ : जब जिसको [कँवल आदि] नेत्र दोष होता है, तब वह चंद्रमा को पीले रंग का कहता है।

नौका पर चढ़ा हुआ मनुष्य जगत् को चलता हुआ देखता है, और अपने को अचल समझता है।

Translation : Whoever when suffers from eye disease (like jaudiced-eye) he (she) speaks of moon as yellow.

Similarly, one riding in a boat sees himself (herself) as still (is diluded) and the world moving!

Comments : The poet (Tulsidas) emphasizes and reminds that the world is relative and people perceive things only from their own capabilities and nature. Due to this reason only there are so many religions in the world with their perceptions of the Lord of the World or Ishwar.

Relate this couplet to another similar one—

One with colored glasses sees the world colored only.

❖❖❖

सहज सरल रघुबर बचन जदयपि सलिल समान।
ते सठ हठ बस संसय करहीं। निज अज्ञान राम पर धरही॥ 87॥

Te sat; hat; bas sansay karaheen,
Nij agyaan Ram par dharaheen

अर्थ : वे [भ्रमित, मोहित, मलिन बुद्धि तथा कामादि दोषों से पीड़ित व्यक्ति] मूर्ख हठ के बस होकर संदेह करते हैं और अपना अज्ञान श्री रामजी पर आरोपित करते हैं।

Translation : Those dull-wits (foolish people who are deluded and suffering from lust, worldly attachments, confusion and lowly thinking) under stuburness doubt Lord Ram and project their own ignorance on him.

Comments : The poet has been saying that the people (Jeevatma) are all affected by the Maya, the worldly attractions, even the best of sadhus and devatas. And many are so deluded that they, instead of realizing their own shortcoming and praying for the Lord's Grace, project their blame on the Lord Rama.

दश धर्मं न जानन्ति धृतराष्ट्र निबोध तान्।
मत्तः प्रमत्त उन्मत्तः श्रान्तः क्रुद्धो बुभुक्षितः॥
त्वरमाणश्च लुब्धश्च भीतः कामी च ते दश।

महाराज धृतराष्ट्र! दस प्रकार के लोग धर्म के तत्त्व को नहीं जानते। उनके नाम सुनो—नशे में मतवाला, असावधान, पागल, थका हुआ, क्रोधी, भूखा, जल्दबाज, लोभी, भयभीत और कामी।

—वेदव्यास (महाभारत, उद्योग पर्व, 33/101-102)

को वा महाअंधो मदनातुरो यः।

महाअंधा कौन है? जो कामातुर है।

—शंकराचार्य

अति हठ मत कर हठ बढ़े, बात न करिहै कोय।
ज्यौं-ज्यौं भीजे कामरी, त्यौं-त्यौं भारी होय॥

—वृंद (वृंद सतसई)

Dull-wits and fools always blame God (Lord Ram) for their problems!

———❖❖❖———

संसृत मूल सूल प्रद नाना। सकल सोक दायक अभिमाना। 88 ॥

Sansrut mool sool prad naanaa,
Sakal sok daayak abhimaanaa

अर्थ : अभिमान जन्म-मरण रूपी संसार का मूल कारण है। और अनेक प्रकार के क्लेशों तथा समस्त शोकों का देने वाला है।

Translation : [Kaakbhushundi is telling Garudji—Pride is the fundamental (root) cause for the cycle of birth and death in this world. It is the source of many mental pains and all sufferings.

Comments : Mind (मन) in human being experiences pains and pleasures of the world. However, in this non-permanent world, with the disappearance of pleasure, the mind starts feeling pain and suffering. The poet here indirectly advocates Vedant or selfless-work, the Karmayoga.

अर्थं महान्तमासाद्य विद्यामैश्वर्यमेव वा।
विचरन्त्यसन्मुद्धो यः स पंडित उच्यते॥

जो अधिक धन या अधिक विद्या या अधिक ऐश्वर्य को प्राप्त करके भी गर्वरहित व्यवहार करता है, उसी को पंडित कहा जाता है।

— वेदव्यास (महाभारत, उद्योग पर्व, 33/40)

अवंशपतितो राजा मूर्खपुत्रश्च पण्डितः।
अधनी हि धनं प्राप्य तृणवन्मन्यते जगत्॥

अकुलीन मनुष्य राजा होने पर, मूर्ख का पुत्र पंडित बनने पर तथा निर्धन धन पाकर जगत् को तृणवत् समझते हैं।

— चाणक्य नीति

सत्ता का अभिमान, संपत्ति का अभिमान, बल का अभिमान, रूप का अभिमान, विद्वत्ता का अभिमान, अनुभव का अभिमान, कर्तव्य का अभिमान, चरित्र का अभिमान—ये अभिमान के नौ प्रकार हैं। पर मुझे अभिमान नहीं है, ऐसा भास होने जैसा भयानक अभिमान दूसरा नहीं है।

— विनोबा (विचारपोथी, पृष्ठ 13)

माया तजी तो क्या भया, मान तजा नहिं जाय।
जेहि मानै मुनिवर ठगे, मान सबन को खाय॥

—अज्ञात

त्याग का अभिमान धन के अभिमान से भी ज्यादा खतरनाक है।

शिवानंद (दिव्योपदेश 1/34)

Pride must have a fall.
गर्व का पतन निश्चित है।

—Shakespear (King Richard, II 2/3)

Vanity (or false pride) is the cause of many human anguish and sufferings.

———❖❖❖———

जेहि तें कछु निज स्वारथ होई। तेहि पर ममता कर सब कोई॥ ८९॥

Jehin ten kachhu nij swaarath ho-ee,
Tehi par mamataa kar sab ko-ee

अर्थ : जिससे अपना कुछ स्वार्थ (सिद्ध) होता है, उससे सभी लोग प्रेम करते हैं।

Translation : All people bestow their love on that person from whoever their selfish motives are served.

Comments : Clearly there are two distinct aspects of the above statement by the poet.

1. The first and formost is that if everyone does that than it cannot be a totally bad thing. Society being a need based conglomerate of relationships every one needs lots of others to exist in this world. In those situations if one shows love and affection it works out better than just a transaction based relationship.

2. The second aspect is clearly about what happens when some one's selfish motives are fulfilled. If the taker (of the selfish dead) feels greatful and willing to do something in return it is a very good value and the giver would feel good and its 'givingness' may not decrease.

However, if the giver expects some favour in return, also a very average response, he/she may be disappointed when the expectations are belied. Therefore the 2nd aspect of the above statement implies that if 100% of the people bestow love due to their selfish motives, the helper/giver should not get disappointed and feel any amount of hurt if he does not get any return for his good deeds. The best is not to expect any.

'ममता' समता की विरोधी है।

—अखंडानंद (विभूतियोग, पृष्ठ 60)

यक अज हाय हुयत गुजश्तन।
दोवम सहराए हस्ती दर नवश्तन॥

तुझे सिर्फ दो बातों का स्मरण रखना उचित है।

- प्रथम यह कि तू ममत्व की बाधा को दूर कर दे।
- द्वितीय यह कि तू अस्तित्व के मैदान को पार कर जा।

—शब्सतरी (फारसी)

मित्रं च शत्रुतामेति कस्मिंश्चित् कालपर्यंते।
शत्रुश्च मित्रतामेति स्वार्थो हि बलवत्तर॥

कभी-कभी समय के फेर से मित्र शत्रु बन जाता है और शत्रु भी मित्र हो जाता है, क्योंकि स्वार्थ बड़ा बलवान है।

—वेदव्यास (महाभारत, शांति पर्व 138/142)

प्रयोजनापेक्षितया प्रभूणां, प्रायश्चलं गौरवमश्रितेषु।

प्राय: स्वामियों का अपने आश्रितों के प्रति आदरभाव अपने प्रयोजन के लिए और अस्थिर होता है।

—कालिदास (कुमारसंभव, 3/1)

कार्यार्थी भजते लोके यावत् कार्यं न सिध्यति।
उत्तीर्णं च परे पारे नौकाया: किं प्रयोजनम्॥

—अज्ञात

अपना कार्य सिद्ध होने तक ही कार्यार्थी व्यक्ति सम्मान करता है। नदी के दूसरे तीर पर नौका का क्या प्रयोजन होता है?

जब तक रकाबी में भात, तब तक तेरा मेरा साथ।

—हिंदी लोकोक्ति

रोना है तो इसका कि कोई नहीं किसी का।
दुनिया है और मतलब, मतलब है और अपना॥

—अकबर इलाहाबादी

कोणि निंदा कोणि बंदा; अमुचा स्वहिता धंधा।

कोई निंदा करे या वंदना, अपना तो स्वार्थ का धंधा है।

—मराठी लोकगीत

Every one bestows love on others for selfish reasons.

कलियुग का वर्णन

कलि मल ग्रसे धर्म सब लुप्त हुए सद ग्रंथ।
दंभिन्ह निज मति कल्पि करि, प्रगट किए बहु पंथ॥ 90॥

Kali mal grase dharm sab,
Lupta hu-e sad granth
Dambhinh nij mati kalpi kari,
Pragat: ki-e bahu panth

अर्थ : कलियुग में पापों ने सब धर्मों को ग्रस लिया। सद्ग्रंथ लुप्त हो गए और दंभियों ने अपनी बुद्धि के अनुसार कल्पना कर-कर के बहुत से पंथ प्रकट कर दिए।

Translation : In Kaliyuga all dharma (धर्म, religion being the closest word but not equivalent) have been seized by papas (bad deeds or deeds contrary to dharm). Therefore the sacred books are not visible anywhere (have disappeared). Consequently, the vain and conceited, according to their own (limited) knowledge have imagined and promulgated many religious sects.

Comments : The poet here is expressing his displeasure at the people not learning the real values from the Dharma. The original scriptures are not being taught and discussed anymore and some sort of Pseudo Dharma or religions have sprung which are being led by the vain and the conceited with limited exposure and knowledge and all kinds of imaginary (and wrong) concepts. Naturally the masses are being misguided by these pseudo-religions and sects.

पंडित वही जो गाल बजावा :

Loudest are being heard and followed. These loud leaders shout the loudest to hide their ignorance and accuse people of being unrightous (अधर्मी) if they do not listen to them and follow them. Putting guilt on people to subdue their ego is their weapon of choice.

These imposters of "Dharm-Leadership" are ignorant and illusioned. They have never tried to gain the real knowledge of Geeta or Vedas and created their immaginary religious sects full of orthodoxy and superstitious (अंधविश्वास)!

The vainglorious (having corrupted the true human-value system) have promulgated their own pseudo-value systems.

———— ❖❖❖ ————

गुर सिष बधिर अंध का लेखा। एक न सुनइ एक नहिं देखा। 91 ॥

Gur sish: badhir andh kaa lekhaa,
Ek na suna-i ek nahin dekhaa

अर्थ : कलियुग में शिष्य और गुरु में बहरे और अंधे का-सा संबंध होता है। एक (शिष्य) गुरु के उपदेश को सुनता नहीं और एक (गुरु) को दिखाई नहीं देता (उसे ज्ञान दृष्टि प्राप्त नहीं है)।

Translation : [The poet, Tulsidas, remind here of a traditional Indian story about a blind and a deaf person; one trying to help the other]. In Kaliyuga, poet says, the relationship among many Guru and their deciples, Shishyas is like that between a blind and a deaf person. The Guru is blind due to ignorance (does not posses the eyesight of knowlege) and the Shishya, the deciple is virtually deaf due to not paying any attention (listening) to his Guru, the teacher.

Comment : The reason for this situation in Kaliyuga is due to Maya.

What is the point of going to a Guru who does not have the true knowledge of "Bhrama Gyaan? It is necessary for every one to start their journey from where ever they are. One needs to go a true 'Guru' who is right for him and answer his question to the satisfaction of the student.

However, the student, on his part, has to listen and follow his Guru's teaching. He/she needs to practice and discover his own inner knowledge and improve upon it himself. No one knows everything. At some point in life, to get true knowledge, one has to go beyond any and every book. Every spoken or written word limits and therefore one needs to go beyond them to comprehend the limitless 'Brahma'!

In the Kaliyug (an eon of vices by Hindu mythology) blind try to lead the blind.

सुतमानहिं मात पिता तब लौं। अबलानन दीख नहीं जब लौं॥ 92॥

Sut maanahin maat-pitaa tab lau-n,
Ablaanan deekh naheen jab lau-n

अर्थ : पुत्र अपने माता-पिता को तभी तक मानते हैं जब तक स्त्री का मुँह नहीं दिखाई पड़ता है।

Translation : (In Kaliyuga) Sons listen to their parents only until they have a woman in their life.

Comments : [In Kaliyuga] Men get so deluded that as soon a woman comes in their life (a wife or a girlfriend) they loose their discriminating capabilities. They suddenly can not even see who their unconditional well wishers are—the parents. And once people cannot tell who their well wishers are, they listen to others conditional advice and go on wrong path in their lives.

A spouse has an awful (awsome?) in fluence on his/her counterpart. It becomes a conflict between listening to a parents grown up view or to a young view from the spouse. Then a boy also has a youthful interest in the wife that no one else can provide. A parent, specially a mother, still wants the accesibility and control like before the boy' got married or gets a girl friend! That itself results in a conflict of interest. Depending upon the personality of a boy, only very few are able to strike a balance between the wife/ girl friend and the parents!

Many times, depending upon the local culture, the parents and the grown up children live seperately. Specifically in U.S. if kids over eighteen years of age live with their parents they are considered, by and large, weird!

As well stated in the "Chanakya Neeti" as to how parents treat their ofsprings :

लालयेत् पंचवर्षाणि, दशवर्षाणि ताड्येत्।
प्राप्ते तु षोडशे वर्षे, पुत्रं मित्रवदाचरेत्॥

Human-interation protocols are very much dependent upon" देश (local culture), काल (time-frame), और परिस्थिति (situation).

Sons listen to the parents only till they beget their wives.

———❖❖❖———

गुरु नित मोहि प्रबोध दुखित देखि आचरन मम।
मोहि उपजइ अति क्रोध दंभिहि नीति कि भावई॥ 93॥

Guru nit mohi prabodh,
Dukhit dekhi aacharan mam
Mohi upajahu ati krodh,
Dambhihi neeti ki bhaava-ee

अर्थ : गुरुजी मेरा आचरण देखकर दुखित थे। वे मुझे नित्य ही भली-भाँति समझाते पर (मैं कुछ भी नहीं समझता) उलटे मुझे अत्यंत क्रोध उत्पन्न होता। दंभी को कभी नीति अच्छी लगती है?

Translation : Observing my behavior, Guruji was very sad. He would properly explain to me every day. However, (listing to him) anger would arise in me. Would a conceit ever appreciate words of wisdom and ethical cousel.

Comments : Here one needs to remember that in ancient times a teacher or Guru used to take full responsibility to educate a Shishya (शिष्य) or deciple, once they accept him as a student. Otherwise one may think why not Guruji let a non-attention paying shishya go on his way if the Shishya did not want to listen. That, probably, is the modus operandi in current times!

When one wants to learn something, from any one, one has to be polite. That is a Universal Truth! However, in the Indian traditional culture, if one wants to get true knowledge, one needs to completely follow the Guru's intructions. However if one is दंभी (arrogant) by very definition, he or she would think too high of himself or herself and would consider his Guru inadaquate for him or her. Learning can take place only when one trusts the Guru or the Teacher!

अश्रद्धा परमं पापं श्रद्धा पापप्रमोचिनी

— वेदव्यास (महाभारत शांतिपर्व, 264/15)

A conceit never appreciates words of wisdom & ethical counsel.

———❖❖❖———

अधम जाति मैं बिद्या पाए। भयउँ जथा अहि दूध पिआएँ॥ 94॥

Adham jaati main biddya paa-e,
Bhaya-un jathaa ahi doodh pi-aa-en

अर्थ : नीच जाति (प्रकृति) का मैं विद्या पाकर ऐसा हो गया जैसे दूध पिलाने से साँप।

Translation : Having gained a little knowledge (from Guruji), being of lowly nature (and thinking), I became more conceited the way a snake would become more strong and harmfull when fed on milk (by the keeper).

Comments : One can relate this to day to day life when people aquire some learning without sufficient background and preperation. In those conditions some of those people become very arrogant although all learning and knowledge is expected to make one more polite and sobber. As has been the proverb—little knowledge is a dangerous thing."

दुःखों में अज्ञान ही सबसे बड़ा दुःख है।

There is always a conflict between what is good (श्रेयस) and what one likes (प्रेयस) to do. It is only a discrimating mind that can tell the difference. One gets a discriminating mind only when one learns from a Guru under long apprentiiceship!

Little knowledge makes people more dangerous.

———❖❖❖———

जेहि से नीच बड़ाई पावा। सो प्रथमहिं हति ताहि नसावा॥
धूम अनल संभव सुनु भाई। तेहि बुझाव घन पदवी पाई॥ 95॥

Jehi te neech bad:aa-ee paavaa,
So prathamahin hati taahi nasaavaa
Dhoom anal sambhav sunu bhaaee,
Tehi bujhaav ghan padavee paaee

अर्थ : नीच मनुष्य जिससे बड़ाई पाता है, वह सबसे पहले उसी को मारकर उसी का नाश करता है। हे भाई, सुनो! आग से उत्पन्न धुँआ (भाप) मेघ की पदवी पाकर उसी अग्नि को बुझा देता है।

Translation : A lowly person will first kill and destroy the very man due to whom he acquired honor and glory! Listen, my brother! Born of fire (and heat) the smoke (water, vapour) when rises high in sky and is glorified as rain-cloud, rains to extinguish the same fire (it was born of).

Comments : Tulsidas, the poet, is emphasizing that imparting knowledge to an undeserving (अनाधिकारी) often produces bad results.

It is a very important to know that one must give anything to the deserving one and the one who wants its. In Indian tradition it is considered a 'sin' to give anything to a non-deserving one. The reason is very simple. If one breaks the policy stated here—it never brings good (or expected results). For example if a person 'Y' is trying to hurt a person 'X', then it would be fool-hardy for X to assist 'Y' in making him stronger and more powerful or more knowledgable. Specially one who is a lowly mind can never think of being greatful of anyone. Lowly people, once they gain knowlege and power, will still have a lowly thinking and will try to first hurt or eliminate that competition from whom they aquired the power. As it is a common Hindi proverb :

सीख ताको दीजिये, जाको सीख सुहाय।
सीख न दीजे बानरा, जो बया का घर जाय॥

An undeserving honoree shall dishonor the honoror first.

———❖❖❖———

सुनु खगपति अस समुझि प्रसंगा। बुध नहिं करहिं अधम कर संगा।
कबि कोबिद गावहिं अस नीती। खल सन कलह न भल नहीं प्रीती ॥ 96 ॥

Sunu khagapati as samujhi prasangaa,
Budh nahin karahin adham kar sangaa
Kabi kobid gaavahin as neetee,
Khal san kalah na bhal naheen preetee

अर्थ : [काक भुशुंडि कहते हैं] हे, पक्षिराज गरुड़जी! सुनिये, ऐसी बात समझकर बुद्धिमान लोग अधम का संग नहीं करते। कवि और पंडित ऐसी नीति कहते हैं कि दुष्ट से न कलह ही अच्छा है और न प्रेम ही।

Translation : [Kakbhushundi tells Garudji] O, king of Birds! Listen. Understanding this the wise do not keep company of the villanious people. Poets and scholars have laid this ethical policy that it is neither good to love nor to quarrel with the wicked.

Comments : This policy has been stated and supported by many wise men and poets in Indian literature.

Wise people should always avoid company of fools and seek company wise people. As very well stated by Valmiki :

शून्यमाकीर्णतामेति मृत्युरप्युत्सवायते।
आपत्सम्पदिवाभाति विद्वज्जन समागमे ॥

विद्वान् पुरुष के आने से निर्जन स्थान भी जन-संकुल (अर्थात् भरा-पूरा) हो जाता है, मृत्यु भी उत्सव जैसी हो जाती है तथा आपत्ति भी संपत्ति के समान प्रतीत होती है।

रहिमन ओछे नरन की, बैर भली ना प्रीत।
काटत चाटत स्वान की, दोउ भाँति बिपरीत।

Raheem says, it is not good to have a friendship or an enmity of low-minded people. For example, both the licking or bitting of a dog is bad.

Wise do not associate with lowly people.

———❖❖❖———

उदासीन नित रहिअ गोसाईं। खल परिहरिअ स्वान की नाईं॥ 97॥

Udaaseen nit rahi-a gosaan-een,
Khal parihari-a swaan kee naa-een

अर्थ : [दुष्टों के प्रति—] हे, गोसाईं! उनसे तो सदा उदासीन ही रहना चाहिए। दुष्टों को कुतों की तरह दूर से ही त्याग देना चाहिए।

Translation : (The poet-Tulsidas-says) Towards the villaneous people—one should always remain indifferent. One should leave (stay away from) the wicked alone as one would keep away from a dog.

Comments : The wicked can be very kind to you when they need you and can turn around and be very dangerous for even your very survival. An analog or an example can be like being close to a member of a Mafia family.

मोहजालस्य योनिर्हि मूढैरेव समागमः।
अहन्यहनि धर्मस्य योनिः साधु-समागमः॥

मूढ़ मनुष्यों से मिलना-जुलना मोहजाल की उत्पत्ति का कारण होता है। इसी प्रकार साधु-महात्माओं का संग प्रतिदिन धर्म की प्राप्ति कराने वाला है।

—वेदव्यास (महाभारत, वनपर्व 1/25)

तुलसी संगत साधु की हरे कोटि अपराध।
संगत बुरी असाधु की आठों पहर उपाधि

—तुलसीदास

निहीयति पुरसो निहीनसेवी, न च हायथ कदाचि तुल्यसेवी।
सेट्ठमुपनमं उदेति खिप्पं, तस्या अत्तनो उत्तरिं भजेथा॥

अपने से शील और प्रज्ञा से हीन व्यक्ति के संग से मनुष्य हीन हो जाता है। बराबर वाले के संग से हीन नहीं होता, ज्यों का त्यों रहता है। अपने से श्रेष्ठ संग से शीघ्र ही मनुष्य का उदय (विकास) होता है। अतः सदा श्रेष्ठ

पुरुषों का संग करना चाहिये।

(पालि-भाषा) —अंगुत्तर निकाय (3/3/6)

पूर्णमदः पूर्णमिदं पूर्णात पूर्णमुदच्यते।
पूर्णस्य पूर्णमादाय पूर्णमेवावशिष्यते॥

वह (परब्रह्म) सब प्रकार से पूर्ण है। यह जगत् भी पूर्ण है। पूर्ण से पूर्ण उत्पन्न हुआ है। पूर्ण से पूर्ण को निकाल लेने पर पूर्ण ही शेष रहता है।

—बृहदारण्यक उपनिषद (5/1/1)

There are more than 60 human emotions. Can one find a human being who has complete mastry on all those emotions? Obviously not! We are born with a spectrum of strengths and weaknesses. Even the most Gyani have some of those weakness till they achieve "nirvaan" or "moksha".

Remain indifferent towards villanes.

———❖❖❖———

सुनु प्रभु बहुत अवज्ञा किएँ। उपज क्रोध ज्ञानिन्ह के हिये॥
अनि संघरषन जौं कर कोई। अनल प्रगट चंदन ते होई॥ 98॥

Sunu prabhu bahut avagyaa ki-en,
Upaj krodh gyaaninh ke hiye
Ati sangharsh:an jaun kar ko-ee,
Anal pragat: chandan te ho-ee

अर्थ : हे प्रभो! सुनिये; बहुत अपमान करने पर ज्ञानी के हृदय में भी क्रोध उत्पन्न हो जाता है। यदि कोई चंदन की लकड़ी को बहुत अधिक रगड़े, तो उसमें भी अग्नि प्रगट हो जाएगी।

Translation : My lord! Listen; Even a sainty person would be infuriated when when excessively humiliated.

Even the Sandalwood wood (by nature a very cooling wood) if stricken excessily, the friction would generate fire in it.

Comments : The gyani or sadhu (Saintly people) are also human. Their self-control and spirituality are par-excellence or Godly. However, perfection is limited to the Lord Himself only and all mortals, no matter how achieved or elevated, are but less than perfect.

Under excessive provocations, even wise (Gyani) may get angry!

———❖❖❖———

जे असि भगति जानि परिहरहीं। केवल ज्ञान हेतु श्रम करहीं॥
ते जड़ कामधेनु गृहँ त्यागी। खोजत आकु फिरहिं पय लागी॥ 99॥

Je asi bhagati jaani pariharaheen,
Keval gyaan hetu shram karaheen
Te jad; kaamdhenu gruhan tyaagee,
Khojat aaku phirahin pay laagee

अर्थ : जो भक्ति की ऐसी महिमा जानकर भी उसे छोड़ देते हैं और केवल ज्ञान के लिए ही श्रम (साधन) करते हैं, वे मूर्ख घर पर खड़ी कामधेनु को छोड़कर दूध के लिये 'मदार' के पेड़ को खोजते फिरते हैं।

Translation : [Having described the greatness of devotion (Bhagti-yoga), kakbhushundi says] Even after having known the glory of Devotion to Ishwar, the Lord, one who strives only for knowledge (Gyana-Yoga) are like the blockheads who search for the Madaar tree (which secretes a milk like liquid) while ignoring a cow at home.

Comments : This is an interesting couplet. Figuratively and literally it holds true. Many (most) of us do not know what we already have with us (the potential to be one with Brahma or Ishwar). Knowing very well the glory Bhagti, if people ignore devottion to Lord and strive for Gyan for Gyan's sack are fools! Gyan, if one aquires should also develop devotion to God! Then most of us suddenly realize in old age that what we have been searching all our lives is either already with us or we do not need it anyway. Such is the irony of the fate!

हरि भक्तिः परा नृणां कामधेनुसमा स्मृता।
तस्यां सत्यां पिबन्त्यज्ञाः संसारगलं ह्यहो॥

भगवान् की परम भक्ति मनुष्यों के लिए कामधेनु के समान मानी गई है। उसके रहते हुए भी अज्ञानी मनुष्य संसार रूपी विष का पान करते हैं। यह कितने आश्चर्य की बात है।

—नारदपुराण (पूर्व भाग, प्रथमपाद, 4/12)

Bhakti (yoga) is the first step to all yogas!

———❖❖❖———

संत हृदय नवनीन समाना। कहा कबिन्ह परि कहै न जाना।
निज परिताप द्रवहि नवनीता। पर दुःख द्रवहिं संत सुपुनीता॥ 100॥

Sant hrudaya navaneet samaanaa,
Kahaa kabinh pari kahai na jaanaa
Nij paritaap dravahi navaneetaa,
Par dukh dravahin sant supuneetaa

अर्थ : संतों का हृदय मक्खन के समान होता है, ऐसा कवियों ने कहा है, पर उन्होंने (असली बात) कहना नहीं जाना। मक्खन तो स्वयं को ताप मिलने से पिघलता है और परम पवित्र संत दूसरों के दुःख से पिघल जाते हैं।

Translation : Poets have compared the sant's (the saints) heart with soft butter. However, they did not quite state the real point. [Although it is true that their heart is soft like butter] Butter melts when under heat (or under self distress) but sant's heart melt due to other's suffering.

Comments : Interesting point here is that softness is in the nature of both the butter as well as the saint. The saint make themself hard for their own pain and suffering but very soft for others people a selfless behaviour.

साधु चरित सुभ चरित कपासू, निरस बिसद गुनमय फल जासू।
जो सहि दुख पर छिद्र दुरावा, बंदनीय जेंहि जग जस पावा॥

—तुलसीदास (रामचरितमानस 1/1/3)

संतों का चरित कपास के चरित्र (जीवन) के समान शुभ है, जिसका फल नीरस, विशद और गुणमय होता है। (कपास का फल नीरस होता है, संत चरित्र में भी विषयासक्ति नहीं होती, इससे वह भी नीरस होता है; कपास उज्ज्वल होता है, संत का हृदय भी अज्ञान रूपी अंधकार से रहित होता है, इसलिए वह विशद (स्वच्छ) होता है; कपास में गुण होते हैं, इसी प्रकार संत का चरित्र भी सद्‌गुणों का भंडार होता है, इसलिए वह गुणमय है) कपास से कपड़ा बनने की क्रियाओं में कपास अनेक मशीनों से गुजरकर

दु:ख पाता है, पर अंततः लोगों के गुप्त स्थानों को ढकता है। उसी प्रकार संत स्वयं दु:ख सहकर दूसरों के छिद्रों (दोषों) को ढकता है। इसीलिए संतों ने जगत् में वंदनीय यश प्राप्त किया है।

Mahatma Gandhi, a real saint, suffered for everyone, Hindus, Muslims, Christians and for all the rest. Several times he went on a "fast-untill death" for peace and brotherhood between Hindus and Muslims. There are many such great example of such saints in Indian history; for example Mahaavir, Buddha and many others.

Sainty feel pain of others more than their own.

हिंदी शब्दकोश

अ

अंक *(संज्ञा पु.)* अंकवार। चिह्न, आंक, लेख, अक्षर, संख्या चिह्न—जैसे 1, 2, 3...., भाग्य, गोद।

अंग *(संज्ञा पु.)* सहायक, राजनीति के सात अंग।

अंगुल *(संज्ञा पु.)* एक हाथ का चौबीसवाँ भाग।

अंचल *(संज्ञा पु.)* आँचल, पल्ला, छोर; प्रांत या देश की सीमा के आसपास का भाग, किनारा तट।

अंचवाना *(क्रि स.)* आचमन करना।

अंचवन (संज्ञा पु.) आचमन।

अंजर *(संज्ञा पु.)* उज्ज्वल, उजला।

अंडकटाह *(संज्ञा पु.)* अंडकटाहा, ब्रह्मांड।

अंडकोस *(संज्ञा पु.)* अंडकोश। विश्व, वल्कल, सीमा, हद, फोता।

अंतर्हित *(वि.)* तिरोहित, अंतर्द्धान (अंतरध्यान), गुप्त, गायब, छिपा हुआ, अदृश्य, अलक्ष्य, लुप्त।

अंतावरी *(संज्ञा स्त्री.)* अंतड़ियाँ, आँतों का समुदाय।

अंबक *(संज्ञा पु.)* नेत्र, आँख, ताँबा, पिता।

अंबु *(संज्ञा पु.)* जल, सुगंध वाला, आम।

अंबुक *(संज्ञा पु.)* मछली, मांस।

अंबुधर *(संज्ञा पु.)* जलयुक्त मेघ।

अंभोज *(संज्ञा पु.)* कमल, चंद्रमा, कपूर।

अंवराई *(संज्ञा स्त्री.)* अमराई, आमों का बगीचा।

अकनना *(क्रि. स.)* सुनना, कर्णगोचर करना, चोरी से दूसरों की बातें सुनना।

अकना *(क्रि. स.)* उकताना।

अकल *(वि.)* जिसके अवयव न हों, अवयव रहित, अखंड, पूरा, समूचा, निर्गुण, अंगहीन, व्यर्थ। जिसका अनुमान न लगाया जा सके, परमात्मा का एक विशेषण, बिना गुण या चतुराई का, कलाहीन। (संज्ञा स्त्री.) अक्ल, अकल, बुद्धि।

अकसर *(क्रि. वि.)* प्रायः, बहुधा, अधिकतर। (प्रत्य.) (अकसर=एक+सर) अकेले, बिना किसी को साथ लिये।

अकाज *(संज्ञा पु.)* बुरा काम, हानि।

अकाजना *(क्रि. अ.)* बुरा काम होना, हानि होना, जाता रहना।

अकाजना *(क्रि. स.)* बुरा काम करना, हानि करना, विघ्न करना।

अकाजी *(वि.)* विघ्नकारी।

अकिंचन *(वि.)* जिसके पास कुछ भी न हो, निर्धन, सर्वत्यागी, साधारण या मामूली।

अंकिचन *(संज्ञा पु.)* निर्धन, गरीब।

अकुंठ *(वि.)* जो कुंठित न हो, चतुर, काम-काजी।

अकुंठ मति *(संज्ञा स्त्री.)* निर्बाध बुद्धि।

अकेल *(वि.)* अकेला, एकाकी, एकांत। (संज्ञा पु) अकेला, जिसके जोड़ का अन्य कोई न हो।

अखयवटु *(संज्ञा पु.)* अखयवट, अक्षय वट।

अग *(वि.)* अचर जीव। न चलनेवाला, टेढ़ा चलनेवाला, स्थावर, (संज्ञा पु) वृक्ष, सूर्य, साँप, पर्वत।

अगजग *(संज्ञा पु.)* अग-जग। चराचर, जगत्, संसार।

अगम *(वि.)* जहाँ कोई न जा सके, दुर्गम, पहुँच के बाहर, न चलनेवाला, चलने के अयोग्य, अगंता।

अगम *(संज्ञा पु.)* आगम। शास्त्र।

अगम्य *(वि.) न जाने योग्य, अवघट, गहन, विकट, बुद्धि के परे, अनिर्वचनीय, अकथ्य।*

अगाध *(वि.)* अथाह, गहरा।

अगोचर *(वि.)* जो गोचर न हो, इंद्रियातीत, अप्रगट, अप्रत्यक्ष, अवयक्त।

अगोचर *(संज्ञा पु.)* ब्रह्मा, वह वस्तु जो इंद्रियों का विशय न हो।

अघ *(संज्ञा पु.)* पाप, दुःख, व्यसन।

अघ *(वि.)* पापात्मा, बयरा, बदमाश, दोषी, दुष्कर्मी।

अघारी *(संज्ञा पु.)* पापों का नाश करने वाले।

अचकरी *(संज्ञा स्त्री.)* अक्खड़पन, अशिष्टता, अत्याचार।

अचगरि *(संज्ञा स्त्री.)* चपलता, ज्यादती, छेड़छाड़, शरारत।

अछत *(क्रि. वि.)* 'अछना' का कृदंत रूप जिसका प्रयोग क्रि. वि. की तरह होता है। रहते हुए, उपस्थिति में, सिवाय, अतिरिक्त, अनुपस्थित।

अज *(वि.)* जिसका जन्म न हुआ हो, स्वयंभू (संज्ञा पु.) माया, ब्रह्मा, विष्णु, दशरथ के पिता, बकरा, मेंढ़ा। अज-ईस=ब्रह्मा-महेश।

अजिन *(संज्ञा पु.)* वल्कल, चर्म, चमड़ा, खाल।

अजिर *(संज्ञा पु.)* आँगन, सहन, मैदान, हवा, वायु, शरीर, इंद्रियों का विषय, मेंढक। (वि.) शीछगामी।

अतिनर *(संज्ञा पु.)* लौकिक मनुष्य।

अदभ्र *(वि.)* बहुत ज्यादा, अपार, अनंत, महान्।

अदिन *(संज्ञा पु.)* बुरा दिन, कुसमय, संकट।

अधगो *(संज्ञा स्त्री)* नीचे की इंद्रियाँ, शिश्न या गुदा।

अधर *(संज्ञा पु.)* नीचे का ओंठ, ओंठ, आधार रहित स्थान, अंतरिक्ष, आकाश, शून्य स्थान।

अनंत *(वि.)* जिसका अंत न हो, असीम, अविनाशी, बहुत, अधिक।

अनंत *(संज्ञा पु.)* विष्णु, शेषनाग, लक्ष्मण, आकाश।

अनअहिवातु *(संज्ञा पु.)* विधवापन।

अनख *(संज्ञा पु.)* क्रोध, रोष, झुंझलाहट, दुःख, ग्लानी, (वि.) नाखून हीन।

अनट *(संज्ञा पु.)* उपद्रव, अनीति, अन्याय।

अनंदु *(संज्ञा पु.)* आनंद।

अनन्य *(वि.)* अन्य से संबंध न रखनेवाला, एक निष्ठ, एक ही में लीन।

अनपायनी *(वि.)* निष्चल, अटल।

अनवद्य *(वि.)* निर्दोष, अनिंघ।

अनामय *(वि.)* निरामय, रोगरहित, नीरोग, चंगा, तंदुरुस्त, निर्दोष, निर्विकार। (संज्ञा पु.) नीरोगता।

अनिप *(संज्ञा पु.)* नायक, सेनापति। अनि+प= सेना-स्वामी।

अनिर्वचनीय *(वि.)* अवणीरय, अकथ्य, अगम्य, अपार। (संज्ञा पु.) माया, भ्रम, अज्ञान, संसार, जगत्।

अनी *(संज्ञा स्त्री.)* अनि, सेना, समूह, नोक, सिरा, ग्लानि (आन=मयादी) नांव या जलयान का अग्रभाग।

अनीक *(संज्ञा पु.)* सेना, झुंड, (वि.) अ+नेक/नीक= जो अच्छा न हो, बुरा, खराब।

अनीठ *(वि.)* अनिष्ट, जो इष्ट न हो, अनिश्चित, अप्रिय, बुरा, खराब।

अनीह *(वि.)* इच्छा रहित।

अनुकरण *(संज्ञा पु.)* देखा-देखी काम, नकल, समान आचरण।

अनुग्रह *(संज्ञा पु.)* दूसरे का दुःख दूर करने की इच्छा, कृपा।

अनुदित *(वि.)* न कहने योग्य, निंदनीय, जो न कहा गया हो, जो उदित न हुआ हो, जो सामने न आया हो।

अनुदिन *(क्रि. वि.)* प्रतिदिन, हर रोज, नित्यप्रति, दिन-दिन।

अनुपान *(संज्ञा स्त्री.)* औषधि के साथ या ऊपर से खाई जाने वाली वस्तु।

अनुबादा *(संज्ञा पु.)* अनुबाधा। बिना बाधा के, बे-रोक-टोक। (संज्ञा पु.) जनश्रुति, अफवाह।

अनुभव *(संज्ञा पु.)* प्रत्यक्ष ज्ञान, वह ज्ञान जो साक्षात करने से प्राप्त हो, स्मृतिभिन्न ज्ञान। पजरबा। अनुभव गम्य= जो अनुभव से जानने योग्य हो।

अनुभाव *(संज्ञा पु.)* प्रभाव।

अनुभावक *(संज्ञा पु.)* प्रतीति या अनुभव (अनुभूति) करानेवाला।

अनुमोदन *(संज्ञा पु.)* समर्थन, प्रसन्नता का प्रकाशन= अनु+मोदन।

अनुसारना *(क्रि.स.)* अनुरूप आचरण करना, अनुकूल आचरण करना, आचरण करना, चलाना, अनुकरण करना।

अनुशासन *(संज्ञा पु.)* अनुशासन। आदेश, आज्ञा, हुक्म। अनुशासन देना=आज्ञा देना।

अनुहरना *(क्रि. स.)* अनुसरना, अनुसरण करना, पीछे चलना, समानता करना, अनुकरण करना, अनुकूल आचरण।

अनुहार *(संज्ञा पु.)* नकल, अनुकरण, समान, सादृश्य, अनुकूल, अनुसार।

अनूप *(वि.)* उपमा रहित, अद्वितीय, बेजोड़।

अनूप *(वि.)* जहाँ जल अधिक हो, दलदली। (संज्ञा पु.) अधिक जल वाला प्रदेश, दलदल, भैंस, ताल या तालाब, मेंढ़क, हाथी, तीतर या चकोर।

अन्हवाना *(क्रि. स.)* स्नान कराना।

अन्हाना *(क्रि. अ.)* स्नान करना।

अपडर *(संज्ञा पु.)* मिथ्या डर।

अपडरना *(क्रि. अ.)* शंकित होना, व्यथा भयभीत होना।

अपनाई *(संज्ञा स्त्री)* पराधीन।

अपनाना *(क्रि. स.)* अपने अनुकूल करना, अपने वश में करना, अपनी ओर करना, अपना बनाना।

अपबरग *(संज्ञा पु.)* अपवर्ग, मोष (चार प्रकार के—सालोक्य, सामीप्य, सारुष्य व सारुज्य।)

अपबाद *(संज्ञा पु.)* अपवाद, निंदा, विरोध, प्रतिवाद, खंडन, नियम के विपरीत नियम, पाप, कलंक, दोष।

अपभय *(संज्ञा पु.)* भय का नाश, निर्भयता, व्यर्थ का भय, अकारण भय, भय, डर।

अपभय *(वि.)* निर्भय, निडर, जो न डरे।

अपवर्ग *(संज्ञा पु.)* देखो अपबरग। मुक्ति, त्याग, दान, विशेष नियम, अपवाद।

अपान *(सर्व)* अपनी सुध। अपान बिसारना= अपनी सुध-बुध बिसारना।

अपान *(वि.)* सब दुःखों को दूर करनेवाला, ईश्वर का एक विशेषण, जो पीने योग्य न हो, अपेय।

अपान *(संज्ञा पु.)* आत्म भाव, आत्म सम्मान, आत्म ज्ञान, आपा, आत्म गौरव, सुध, होश हवास अहं अभिमान।

अपि *(अव्य.)* भी, ही, निश्चय, ठीक।

अपितु *(अव्य.) किंतु, बल्कि, और।*

अपी *(सर्व.)* स्वयं, सुद, आप, (अव्य.) अपि।

अपेल *(वि.)* जो टले नहीं, जो हटे नहीं, अटल, जिसकी अवज्ञा न की जा सके। जिसकी कोई 'अपील' न हो।

अप्रतिहत *(वि.)* जो प्रतिहत न हो, जिसका विघात न हुआ हो, अटूट, अपराजित, बिना रोक-टोक का, संपूर्ण, समग्र, अनुसरण।

अप्रतिहतगति *(संज्ञा पु.)* जिसकी गति रोकी न जा सके, निर्बाध गतिवाला।

अप्रमेय *(वि.)* बुद्धि के परे, प्रमाणों से परे, जो नापा न जा सके, अपार।

अबधू *(वि.)* अबोध, अज्ञानी, मूर्ख। (संज्ञा पु.) अवधूत, त्यागी, संन्यासी, विरागी।

अबला *(संज्ञा स्त्री.)* स्त्री, औरत, माया।

अबस *(वि.)* अवश। किसी के वश में न होनेवाला।

अबिछीन *(वि.)* जो विच्छिन्न या टूटा न हो, अविच्छिन्न, अविरल, लगातार, एकतार, अविछिन्न।

अब्याहत *(वि.)* अव्याहत। अप्रतिरुद्ध, बेरोक, अबाधित।

अभंगा *(वि.)* जो भंग न हुआ हो, अखंड, जो भंग या नष्ट न किया जा सके, सुदृढ़, मजबूत। अनडिवाइडेड। (संज्ञा पु.) एक प्रकार का पद या भजन, भंग या पराजय का अभाव।

अभाग्य *(वि.)* दुर्भाग्य, भाग्य हीनता।

अभिअंतर *(संज्ञा पु.)* अभ्यंतर। मध्य, बीच, हृदय, अंतःकरण।

अभ्यंतर *(वि.)* सुपरिचित, अतरंग, निकटतम, घनिष्टता के साथ संबंध, कुशल, भीतर का, अंदर का, भीतरी।

अभ्यंतर *(क्रि. वि.)* भीतर, अंदर।

अभिज्ञान *(संज्ञा स्त्री.)* स्मृति, स्मृति चिह्न या वस्तु, निशानी, सहदानी।

अभिमत *(वि.)* मनवांछित।

अभिराम *(संज्ञा पु.)* आनंद, सुख, मनोहर, सुंदर, मनोज, प्रिय।

अभूत *(वि.)* जो बीता न हो, अनोखा, अद्‌भुत, असत्य।

अभूतशत्रु *(संज्ञा पु.)* जिसका कोई शत्रु न हो, शत्रुहीन, अजातशत्रु।

अभेदवादी *(संज्ञा पु.)* वह जो ब्रह्म और जीव में भेद न करता हो, अर्थात एक ही समझता हो, अद्वैतवादी।

अमल *(वि.)* स्वच्छ, निर्मल। (संज्ञा पु.) शासन काल, व्यवहार।

अमात *(संज्ञा पु.)* समाना, समात।

अमाना *(क्रि.अ.)* पूरे तौर पर भर जाना, भली-भाँति समाना, समाना, अँटना, गर्व करना, फूलना इतराना। (संज्ञा पु.) अन्न की कोठरी का द्वार।

अमानी *(वि.)* जो मान न करता हो, घमंडरहित, अहंकारशून्य, निराभिमान।

अमाय *(संज्ञा पु.)* परब्रह्म।

अमाया *(वि.)* माया रहित, माया शून्य, निर्लिप्त, निष्छल, निस्वार्थ, निष्कपट।

अमोद्य *(वि.)* निष्फल न होनेवाला, अचूक। अमोघ शक्ति= शक्ति जिसका कभी व्यर्थ न हो।

अमोघ *(संज्ञा पु.)* व्यर्थ न होने का भाव, अव्यर्थ, शिव, विष्णु।

अय *(संबोधन)* यह अधिकतर 'ऐ' लिखा जाता है।

अयन *(संज्ञा पु.)* धाम, स्थान, मार्ग, राह, गमन, सूर्य का उत्तर से दक्षिण

के जाने का समय (एक अयन में तीन ऋतु, एक वर्ष में छह ऋतु, इस प्रकार दो अयन का एक वर्ष)।

अयाचक *(वि.)* जो याचक न हो, जिसे दान की जरूरत न हो, माला-माल व्यक्ति।

अयान *(संज्ञा पु.)* स्वभाव, निसर्ग, अचंचलता, स्थिरता, ठहराव, अज्ञानी, गमनाभाव। (वि.) यान हीन, बिना वाहन का। (वि.) अज्ञान अज्ञ, मूर्ख।

अयानप *(संज्ञा स्त्री.)* अज्ञानता, बेसमझी, अनजानपन।

अयानी *(संज्ञा पु.)* बेसमझ, बुद्धिहीन।

अरगजा *(संज्ञा पु.)* केसर, चंद्र और कपूर से बना सुगंधित शरीर-लेप।

अरनि *(संज्ञा स्त्री.)* अरनी। एक प्रकार की लकड़ी जिससे अग्नि उत्पन्न होती है।

अराति *(संज्ञा पु.)* शत्रु, दुश्मन, काम, क्रोध, लोभ, मोह, मद और मात्सर्य आदि मनुष्य के छह शत्रु।

अरि *(संज्ञा पु.)* शत्रु, दुश्मन। अरिहुक= शत्रु का भी।

अरुझना *(क्रि.अ.)* उलझना, फँसना, अटकना, ठहरना, अड़ना। (क्रि.स.) उलझाना, फँसाना, लड़ाना।

अरुण *(संज्ञा पु.)* लाल।

अरुणचूण *(संज्ञा पु.)* मुरगा।

अरुनारी *(वि.)* लाल रंग का, अरुण, लाल। (पु.) अरुनारा।

अर्ध्य *(वि.)* पूज्यनीय, अर्चनीय।

अर्पना *(क्रि. स.)* अरपना। अर्पित करना।

अर्बत *(संज्ञा स्त्री.)* भँवर।

अलख *(वि.)* स्थूल दृष्टि से देखने में न आने वाले।

अलान *(संज्ञा पु.)* हाथी बाँधने की काँटेदार बेड़ी या खूँटा।

अलीक *(वि.)* मिथ्या, बे-सि-पैर का, अप्रतिष्ठित।

अलीजा *(वि.)* अच्छा, बहुत अच्छा, आलीशान।

अलीह *(वि.)* मिथ्या, असत्य।

अलुझना *(क्रि. अ.)* उलझना। अलुज्झि=उलझे।

अलूला *(संज्ञा पु.)* बुलबुला, भभूका, लहर, तरंग।

अलेख *(वि.)* अलक्ष, अज्ञेय, दुर्बोध।

अलोल *(वि.)* अ+लोल। अचंचल, स्थिर।

अवकलना *(क्रि. स.)* ज्ञान होना, बुद्धि आना, समझ पड़ना, सूझना विचारों में आना।

अवकाश *(संज्ञा पु.)* विश्राम लेने का समय, अवसर, समय, स्थान, जगह, अतिरिक्त समय।

अवगावना *(क्रि अ.)* अवगाहना। नहाना, डुबकी लगाना।

अवगावना *(क्रि स.)* अवगाहना। थाहना, छानना, छानबीन करना, विचलित करना, चलाना-हिलाना, डुलाना, सोचना, विचारना, समझना, धारण करना, ग्रहण करना।

अवगाह *(संज्ञा पु.)* कठिन या गहरा स्थान, संकट की जगह।

अवघट *(वि.)* अटपट, विकट, कठिन, दुर्गट, दुर्गम।

अवज्ञा *(संज्ञा पु.)* अपमान, अनादर, आज्ञा का उल्लंघन, आज्ञा न मानना, अवहेलना, पराजय, हार।

अवटना *(क्रि स.)* मथना, आलोड़न करना, ओंटना।

अवढर *(वि.)* अकारण ही प्रसन्न होनेवाला।

अवढरदानी *(संज्ञा पु.)* मुँह माँगा दान देनेवाला, भीतर, मध्य, बीच।

अवध *(संज्ञा पु.)* कोशलदेश, अवधि, सीमा, अवध्य, न मारने योग्य।

अवधूत *(संज्ञा पु.)* साधू, योगी, संन्यासी, विनष्ट।

अवनद्य *(वि.)* दोष रहित, अनिन्द्य।

अवनिप *(संज्ञा पु.)* राजा, अवनिपाल।

अवनीष *(संज्ञा पु.)* अवनि+ईष—राजा।

अवमान *(संज्ञा पु.)* तिरस्कार, अपमान।

अवर *(वि.)* अन्य दूसरा, और, अत्यंत श्रेष्ठ, अश्रेष्ठ, अधम, नीच।

अवराधन *(संज्ञा पु.)* आराधन, पूजा, आराधना।

अवरेखना *(क्रि. स.)* (अवलेखन, आलेखन) चित्र में लिखा या रहजाना, चित्रित करना।

अवरेव *(संज्ञा पु.)* उलझन, तिरछी या वक्र चाल का, पेंच, विवाद, झगड़ा।

अवसान *(संज्ञा पु.)* अंत, समाप्ति, मरण, सायंकाल, विराम, ठहराव, सीमा।

अवसेर *(संज्ञा स्त्री)* अटकाव, उलझन, देर विलंब।

अवसेर करना *(क्रि. स.)* दुःख, चिंता, व्यग्रता, या प्रिय की प्रतीक्षा में होने वाली विकल होना।

अवसेरना *(क्रि. स.)* तंग करना, दु:ख देना।
अवस्था *(संज्ञा पु.)* चार अवस्थाएँ, जाग्रत्, स्वप्न, सुशुपित व तुरीय।
अविनय *(संज्ञा स्त्री.)* ढिठाई, उदंडता।
असंक *(वि.)* निर्भय, शंका रहित, निडर, निश्चिंत।
असन *(संज्ञा पु.)* अशन, भोजन।
असाधु *(वि.)* दुष्ट, बुरा, खल, दुर्जन, खोटा, पतित, अविनीत, अशिष्ट, जो ठीक ढंग से सिद्ध न हो, व्याकरण के विरुद्ध।
असाधु *(संज्ञा पु.)* असाधु। भ्रष्ट या पतित साधु, असज्जन।
असि *(संज्ञा स्त्री.)* तलवार, खड्ग।
अस्मित *(वि.)* बिनाखिला, अविकसित।
अस्मिता *(संज्ञा स्त्री.)* अहंकार, सांख्य में मोह और वेदांत में हृदयग्रंथि कहते हैं, योग शास्त्र में पाँच क्लेशों में से एक, द्रक, द्रष्टा और दर्शन को एक मानना या पुरुष (आत्मा) और बुद्धि में अभेद मानना।
अहंता *(संज्ञा स्त्री.)* अहंकार, घमंड, गर्व।
अह *(संज्ञा पु.)* दिन, सूर्य, दिन का अभिमानी देवता।
अहना *(क्रि. अ.)* वर्तमान रहाना, होना।
अहनिसि *(क्रि. वि.)* अहर्निश। रात-दिन, सदा, नित्य।
अहमिति *(संज्ञा स्त्री.)* अहिमिति। अहम्मति। अज्ञान, अविद्या, अहंकार।
अहर *(संज्ञा पु.)* रूढ़ संख्या, छीपियों के रंग का मिट्टी का बरतन।
अहिबात *(संज्ञा पु.)* अहिवात। सुहाग, सौभाग्य।
अहिराजा *(संज्ञा पु.)* शेषनाग।
अहोर-बहोर *(संज्ञा पु.)* फिरि-फिर, बार-बार।
अहोर-बहोर *(संज्ञा पु.)* विवाह की एक रीति।

आ

आंक *(संज्ञा पु.)* चिह्न, निशान, निश्चित सिद्धांत, दृढ़ निश्चय।
आँब *(संज्ञा पु.)* आँम।
आइ *(संज्ञा स्त्री.)* आयु, जीवन। आइ खुटानी= आयु समाप्त या पूरी होना।
आकु *(संज्ञा पु.)* अक। अर्क, अकवन या मदार का पेड़।

आकुल *(वि.)* व्यग्र, विव्हल, कातर, संकुल, व्याप्त।

आगर *(संज्ञा पु.)* धाम, घर, छप्पर, गृह, खान, समूह, कोष, निधि, (वि.) बुद्धि निधान, श्रेष्ट, उत्तम, चतुर।

आतप *(संज्ञा पु.)* धूप, ज्वर, सूर्य का प्रकाश।

आतपत्र *(संज्ञा पु.)* छाता।

आतमबादी *(संज्ञा पु.)* आत्म तत्त्व के मर्मज्ञ, आत्मवादी, अहंभाव रखनेवाला।

आत्मवंचक *(संज्ञा पु.)* अपने आप को ठगनेवाला, अपनी हानि स्वयं करनेवाला, अज्ञानी।

आत्महन *(वि.)* आत्मघाती, अविश्वासी, जो अपनी भलाई के प्रति उदासीन हो या उसकी उपेक्षा करे।

आदर्श *(संज्ञा पु.)* दर्पण, शीशा, वह जिससे ग्रंथ का अभिप्राय झलक जाए, टीका, व्याख्या, वह जिसके रूप और गुण आदि का अनुकरण किया जाए, नमूना।

आन *(संज्ञा स्त्री.)* मर्यादा, शपथ, घोषणा, ढंग, तर्ज, क्षण, लमहा, अकड़, प्रतिज्ञा। (वि.) दूसरा, और।

आनन *(संज्ञा पु.)* मुँह, चेहरा।

आना *(क्रि. स.)* बुलाने वाले के पास पहुँचाना, प्राप्त होना, उत्पन्न होना, आमदनी होन, फलफूल लगना।

आनि *(संज्ञा स्त्री.)* आन।

आभीर *(संज्ञा पु.) अहीर, ग्वाले।*

आमिष *(संज्ञा पु.)* मांस, गोश्त, भोग्य वस्तु, लालच।

आयत *(वि.)* लंबा-चौड़ा, विशाल, विस्त्रत। आयत उर=विशाल वक्षस्थल।

आयतन *(संज्ञा पु.)* मकान, गृह, विश्राम स्थान।

आयसु *(संज्ञा स्त्री.)* आज्ञा, आदेश।

आयुध *(संज्ञा पु.)* भुजाओं में धारण करने वाले शस्त्र।

आरति हर *(संज्ञा पु.)* दुःख को हरनेवाला।

आराति *(संज्ञा पु.)* शत्रु। आराती।

अ.रेसु *(संज्ञा स्त्री.)* आरेस। डाह, जलन, ईर्ष्या।

आरौ *(संज्ञा पु.)* शब्द, आवाज, आरव।

आल-बाल *(संज्ञा पु.)* आलवाल। वृक्षों के नीचे का थाँवला, थाला।

आशुतोष *(संज्ञा पु.)* जल्द तोषित हो जानेवाला। आशु+तोष।

आस *(संज्ञा पु.)* दिशा, आशा, उम्मीद।

इ

इमि *(क्रि.वि.)* इस प्रकार, इस तरह, ऐसे।

इव *(अव्य.)* किसी के समान, सदृश्य, तुल्य, भाँति, नाईं, जैसे।

इति *(अव्य.)* समाप्ति सूचक अवयय। (संज्ञा स्त्री.) समाप्ति, पूर्णता।

ई

ईति *(संज्ञा स्त्री.)* खेति को हानि पहुँचाने वाले छह उपद्रवः 1. अति वर्षा, 2. सूखा, 3. चूहे, 4. तोते, 5. टिड्डियाँ, 6. सेना की चढ़ाई (युद्ध)। ईति का भय= तरह-तरह की विपदा, प्राकृतिक या मानवीय, बाधा, दुःख।

ईश्वर *(संज्ञा पु.)* योगशास्त्र के अनुसार क्लेश, कर्म, विपाक (कर्मफल) तथा आशय से पृथक, परमेश्वर, स्वामी, मालिक।

ईषना *(संज्ञा स्त्री.)* अबलवती इच्छा। त्रिबिध ईषना= पुत्र, धन और मान की प्रबल अभिलाशा।

उ

उअना *(क्रि. अ.)* उगना, उदित होना।

उच्चाटन *(संज्ञा पु.)* किसी मिली या संयक्त वस्तु से पृथक करना, उखाड़, नोच-खसोट, चित्त को हटाना, विरक्ति, खिन्नता, उदासीनता।

उछाऊ *(संज्ञा पु.)* उछाह। उत्साह, उमंग, प्रसन्नता।

उडु *(संज्ञा पु.)* तारा, नक्षत्र, पक्षी, चिड़िया, केवट।

उडुगन *(संज्ञा पु.)* नक्षत्र।

उतंग *(वि.)* ऊँचा, बुलंद।

उतकरष *(संज्ञा पु.)* उत्कर्ष। बड़ाई, प्रशंसा, समृद्धि, मूल्य, भाव या महत्त्व का बढ़ना।

उताइल *(संज्ञा पु.)* उतायल। उतावला।

उतान *(वि.)* उत्तान। सीधा, चित्त (पीठ जमीन पर और मुँह ऊपर की ओर)।

उत्पल *(संज्ञा पु.)* कमल, नील कमाल।

उपधान *(संज्ञा पु.)* तकिया, विशेषता, प्रेम, प्रणय।

उपनय *(संज्ञा पु.)* समीप ले जाने का कार्य, बालक को गुरु के पास ले जाने की क्रिया, उपनयन संस्कार।

उपबरहन *(संज्ञा पु.)* तकिया।

उपरना *(संज्ञा पु.)* ऊपर ओढ़ने का वस्त्र, चादर, दुपट्टा।

उपल *(संज्ञा पु.)* पत्थर, बरफ का ओला, रत्न, बादल।

उपारना *(क्रि स.)* उखाड़ना।

उपाधि-उपाधी *(संज्ञा स्त्री.)* और को और बताने का छल कपट, उपद्रव, उत्पात, प्रतिष्ठासूचक शब्द, खिताब।

उबरा *(वि.)* फालतू, बचा, बचा हुआ।

उभय *(वि.)* दोनों, युगल।

उयना *(क्रि. अ.)* उदय होना।

उरग *(संज्ञा पु.)* साँप, सर्प।

उरगाद *(संज्ञा पु.)* गरुड़।

उरगारि *(संज्ञा पु.)* उरगारी। गरुड़।

उसाँस *(संज्ञा पु.)* लंबी साँस, कष्ट या रंज में साँस खींचान।

ऊ

ऊना *(वि.)* कम, थोड़ा, तुच्छ, नाचीज। (संज्ञा पु.) दु:ख, रंज, मन का खराब होना, (संज्ञा स्त्री.) ग्लानि। (संज्ञा पु.) एक प्रकार की छोटी तलवार जो कि स्त्रियों के व्यवहार के लिये बनती थी।

ऊसर *(संज्ञा पु.)* नोनी (सूखी, बंजर) भूमि जिसमें अन्न उत्पन्न न हो।

ऋ

ऋतु *(संज्ञा स्त्री.)* वर्ष की छः ऋतुएँ—वसंत, ग्रीष्म, वर्षा, शरद, हेमंत, शिशिर। वसंत चैत्र और वैशाख में आती हैं, मार्च-अप्रैल में। ग्रीष्म ज्येष्ट और आषाढ़ में आती हैं, मई-जून में। वर्षा श्रावण और भाद्रपद में आती हैं, जुलाई-अगस्त में। शरद क्वार और कार्तिक में आती हैं, सितंबर-अक्तूबर में। हेमंत अघहन और पूस में आती हैं, नवंबर-दिसंबर में। शिशिर माघ और फाल्गुन में आती है, जनवरी-फरवरी में।

ऋक्ष *(संज्ञा पु.)* भालू, नक्षत्र, मेष, वृक्ष, आदि राशि।

ऋक्षराज *(संज्ञा पु.)* भालुपति, ऋक्षपति, जामवंत, नक्षत्रों के राजा, चंद्रमा।

ए

एतादृस *(वि.)* इसके सदृश्य।

ओ

ओधे *(संज्ञा पु.)* स्वामी, मालिक।

क

कंक *(संज्ञा पु.)* (संज्ञा स्त्री., कंका, कंकी) चील, कोंच पक्षी, बकुला, बगुला।

कंज *(संज्ञा पु.)* कमल, ब्रह्मा, अमृत, केश, सिर के बाल।

कंटक *(संज्ञा पु.)* कंट। काँटा, सुई की नोंक, विघ्न, रोमांच, ऐसा काम या बात जिससे किसी को परेशानी हो। न्यूसेंस।

कंडु *(संज्ञा स्त्री.)* कंडू। खुजली, खाज।

कंद *(संज्ञा पु.)* बिना रेशे की गूदेदार जड़, जैसे सकरकंद। सुखकंदा= सुख का मूल कारण।

कंदर *(संज्ञा पु.)* पर्वत की गुफा।

कंध *(संज्ञा पु.)* डाली, कंधा।

कंधर *(संज्ञा पु.)* गरदन, ग्रीवा, बादल, मोथा।

कच *(संज्ञा पु.)* बाल, बादल, दबने या कुचले जाने का शब्द, अंगरखे का पल्ला।

कटक *(संज्ञा स्त्री.)* सेना, फौज, स-दलबल चलने की तैयारी।

कड़िहार *(संज्ञा पु.)* कर्णधार, निकालनेवाला, उद्धारक, पार लगानेवाला, केवट।

कत *(अव्य.)* क्यों, किसलिए, काहे को। (वि.) कितना, अधिक।

कतहुँ *(अव्य.)* कहीं-कहीं, किसी जगह, किस ओर।

कदराई *(संज्ञा स्त्री.)* कायरता।

कदराना *(क्रि. अ.)* डरना, भयभीत होना।

कनिका *(संज्ञा पु.)* कणिका। कण, किसी वस्तु का छोटा टुकड़ा।

कनी *(संज्ञा स्त्री.)* कण, छोटा टुकड़ा, हीरे का टुकड़ा, चावल का दाना, वर्षा की बूँद, कन्या, बालिका।

कपिंदा *(संज्ञा पु.)* कपींद्र। बानरों में श्रेष्ट, बानरों के राजा, हनुमान, सुग्रीव, जामवंत।

कबाड़ *(संज्ञा पु.)* काम में न आने वाली चीज।

कबार *(संज्ञा पु.)* धंधा, व्यवसाय।

कमठ *(संज्ञा पु.)* कच्छप, कछुआ, साधुओं का तुंबा, बाँस।

कर *(प्रत्य.)* का।

कर *(संज्ञा पु.)* हाथ, हाथी की सूँड, किरण, ओला, टैक्स। (वि.) करनेवाला।

करु *(संज्ञा पु.)* कड़आ। कड़वा, कटु, तीता, अप्रिय।

करज *(संज्ञा पु.)* नख, नाखून, उँगली, अँगुलि।

करतल *(संज्ञा पु.)* हतेली।

करबदर *(संज्ञा पु.)* हथेली पर बैर।

करबर *(संज्ञा स्त्री.)* करवर। विपत्ति, संकट, आफत, आपत्ति।

करबाल *(संज्ञा स्त्री.)* तलवार, नख, नाखून।

करष *(संज्ञा पु.)* कर्ष। विरोध, खिंचाव, तनाव, द्वेष, लड़ाई का जोश।

कराल *(वि.)* बड़े-बड़े दाँतवाला, भयानक, डरावना।

करि *(संज्ञा पु.)* हाथी।

करुणा *(संज्ञा स्त्री.)* दया। करुणा-कंद-=करुणा के मूल।

कर्ष *(संज्ञा पु.)* खींचान, जोतना, वह भार या दबाव जिससे अनिष्ट की संभावना हो।

कल *(वि.)* मधुर, सुंदर, कोमल, (संज्ञा पु.) अव्यक्त मधुर ध्वनि, (संज्ञा स्त्री.) सुख, चैन, आराम, ओर, बल, पुरजे वाली मशीन।

कलबल *(वि.)* तोतला। (संज्ञा पु.) उपाय, दाँवपेंच, जुगत, हल्लागुल्ला, शोरगुल।

कलमलाना *(क्रि. अ.)* हिलना-डुलना, कुलबुलाना।

कलि *(संज्ञा स्त्री.)* कलह, झगड़ा, पाप, क्लेश, संग्राम, युद्ध, कलियुग। (वि.) श्याम, काला।

कलिल *(वि.)* मिश्रित, मिला हुआ, गहन, घना, दुर्गम। (संज्ञा पु.) कीचड़, समूह ढेर।

कवन *(सर्व.)* कौन।

कहँ *(प्रत्य.)* के लिए (क्रि.वि.) कहाँ। जैसे: कहँ लगि= कहाँ तक।

कह *(वि.)* क्या।

कहरना *(क्रि. अ.)* कराहना।

काँखा-सोती *(संज्ञा स्त्री.)* दुपट्टे को दाहिने कंधे के नीचे से ले जाकर बाएँ कंधे पर डालना।

काँजी *(संज्ञा स्त्री.)* खटाई।

काक *(संज्ञा पु.)* कौआ।

काकरुक *(संज्ञा पु.)* जोरू का गुलाम, स्त्री भक्त।

काका *(संज्ञा पु.)* कौआ, चाचा।

काकु *(संज्ञा पु.)* ताना, व्यंय, वक्रोक्ति अलंकार का एक भेद।

काकुवाद *(संज्ञा पु.)* गिड़गिड़ा कर कही हुई बात।

काकूक्ति *(संज्ञा पु.)* काकुवाद।

काचा *(वि.)* कच्चा, कमजोर, कच्चे दिल का, कायर, डरपोक।

काछा *(संज्ञा पु.)* स्वाँग करने वालों के पहने कपड़े।

काछे *(क्रि. वि.)* पास, निकट, नजदीक।

काढ़ा *(संज्ञा पु.)* औषधियों को पानी औटाकर या उबाल कर बनाया हुआ शरबत, जोशांदा

कादर *(वि.)* व्याकुल, अधीर, भयभीत, आर्त्त, दुखित।

कामरि *(संज्ञा पु.)* काम+अरि। शिव।

कामरूप *(संज्ञा पु.)* कामरूपत्व, मन माना रूप धारण कर सकने वाला।

कामरूपी *(संज्ञा पु.)* मायावी।

कामाशन *(संज्ञा पु.)* इच्छानुसार भोजन।

कारण *(संज्ञा पु.)* सबब, वजह, साधन, हेतु, निमित्त, प्रयोजन।

कारुनीक *(वि.)* कारुणिक। करुनामय, (संज्ञा पु.) करुणा करनेवाला।

कालकूट *(संज्ञा पु.)* एक प्रकार का तीव्र विष, काला बच्छ नाग।

किंकर *(संज्ञा पु.)* दास। (संज्ञा स्त्री.) किंकरी।

किधौं *(अव्य.)* अथवा, वा, या तो, न जाने, शायद।

किमपि *(अव्य.)* कोई भी, कुछ भी। किम+अपि= (क्या, कौन सा) + (भी, ही, निश्चय)।

किरिच *(संज्ञा स्त्री.)* कड़ी वस्तु का छोटा नुकीला टुकड़ा।

किरीट *(संज्ञा पु.)* मुकुट।

किसलय *(संज्ञा पु.)* किशल, किसल, किशलय। कोमल नया पत्ता, कल्ला। (संज्ञा फ.) पलास।

की *(अव्य.)* क्या (या, या) , यातो।

कीर *(संज्ञा पु.)* तोता।

कीस *(संज्ञा पु.)* कीश। वानर, चिड़िया, सूर्य, गर्भ की थैली।

कुंचित *(वि.)* टेढ़ा, वक्र, घुँघराले।

कुंजर *(संज्ञा पु.)* हाथी, बाल।

कुंठ *(वि.)* सुस्त, जो चोखा या तीक्ष्ण न हो, गुठला, भोथरा, बुथरी धार का, ढीला, कुंद, मूर्ख, स्थूल बुद्धि का, कुंदजेहन, आलसी, सुस्त, कमजोर, निर्बल।

कुंठक *(वि.)* बुद्धिहीन, नासमझ।

कुंठा *(संज्ञा स्त्री.)* खीज, चिढ़, निरालापन, मन की गाँठ, मानसिक ग्रंथि, मूर्खता, निकम्मापन।

कुंठित *(वि.)* जिसकी धार चोखी या तीक्ष्ण न हो, कुंद, गुठला, विकृत, परिवर्तित, मूर्ख, जड़।

कुंत (*संज्ञा पु.*) भाला, बरछी, जूँ, अनख।

कुंद (*संज्ञा पु.*) कमल, कनेर का पेड़, खराब।

कुंभ (*संज्ञा पु.*) हाथी के मस्तक का ऊपरी भाग, घड़ा।

कुंभज (*संज्ञा पु.*) घटसंभव। घड़े से उत्पन्न, अगस्त मुनि।

कुजोगी (*वि.*) असंयमी, विषयी।

कुटिलकेस (*संज्ञा पु.*) घुँघराले बाल।

कुठाहर (*संज्ञा पु.*) कुठौर। बुरी जगह पर, बुरा स्थान, बे-मौका।

कुधर (*संज्ञा पु.*) पहाड़, पर्वत, शेषनाग।

कुबलय (*संज्ञा पु.*) कमल।

कुबामा (*संज्ञा स्त्री.*) खोटी, बुरी स्त्री।

कुमुद (*संज्ञा पु.*) लाल कमल, चाँदी, विष्णु।

कुरंग (*संज्ञा पु.*) बादामी या तामड़े रंग का हिरन, हिरन, मृग। (वि.) बदरंग, बुरे रंग का।

कुररी (*संज्ञा स्त्री.*) कौंच पक्षी की मादा, टिटिहरी।

कुरी (*संज्ञा स्त्री.*) खंड, विभाग, टुकड़ा।

कुरी (*संज्ञा पु.*) वंश, घराना, खानदान।

कुलगुर (*संज्ञा पु.*) पूर्वज, बड़े, कुलगुरु, वंश या खानदान का गुरु।

कुलिस (*संज्ञा पु.*) वज्र, कलिश।

कुसुमित (*वि.*) फूला हुआ, पुष्पित।

कूज (*संज्ञा स्त्री.*) ध्वनि, शब्द, आवाज़, शब्द करने की क्रिया।

कूजना (*क्रि. अ.*) आवाज, शब्द या ध्वनि करना।

कूट (*संज्ञा पु.*) पहाड़ की ऊँची चोटी, सींग, राशी, ढेर, छल, धोखा, गुप्त रहस्य, वह हास्य या व्यंग्य जिसका अर्थ गूढ़ हो, वह पद जिसका अर्थ जल्दी स्पष्ट न हो।

कूल (*संज्ञा पु.*) तट, किनारा, नहर, तालाब, (अव्य.) समीप, पास, निकट। कूल द्रुम = नदी के तट के वृक्ष।

कृतकृत्य (*वि.*) कृतकत्य। कृतार्थ। जिसका कार्य पूर्ण रूप से हो चुका हो, सफल मनोरथ।

कृतजुग (*संज्ञा पु.*) सतयुग।

कृतग्य (*संज्ञा पु.*) कर्म (रहस्य) के ज्ञाता।

कृतांत (*संज्ञा पु.*) यमराज, मृत्यु, समाप्त करनेवाला, पाप, देवता, शनिवार।

कृतांत *(संज्ञा पु.)* काल, कृति का अंत, क्रतांत भक्षक= काल भक्षक।

कृतार्थ *(संज्ञा पु.)* जो अपना काम बन जाने के कारण बहुत प्रसन्न या संतुष्ट हो।

कृपा-कटाक्ष *(संज्ञा पु.)* कृपा की तिरछी दृष्टि।

कृपायतन *(संज्ञा पु.)* कृपा + आयतन= कृपा के धाम, कृपानिधि, अत्यंत दयालु।

कृसानु *(संज्ञा पु.)* कृशानु, अग्नि, चीता।

केतु *(संज्ञा पु.)* ध्वजा, पताका, ज्ञान, दीप्ति, चमक, नवग्रहों में से एक, पुच्छल तारा।

केर *(प्रत्य.)* का (संबंध सूचक)। (क्रि.वि.) की तरह, के समान।

केरि *(प्रत्य.)* केरी, की। केलि (संज्ञा स्त्री.) क्रीड़ा, रति, हंसि।

केहरि *(संज्ञा पु.)* केसरी, शेर।

कैरव *(संज्ञा पु.)* कुमुद, सफेद कमल, शत्रु, जुआरी।

कोंछ *(संज्ञा पु.)* गोद, ओढ़नी के आँचल का छोर।

कोक *(संज्ञा पु.)* चकवा, सुरखाब, (संज्ञा पु.) विष्णु, भड़िया, मेंढक। (संज्ञा स्त्री.) कोकी।

कोटर *(संज्ञा पु.)* पेड़ का खोखला भाग, वृक्ष गाहवर, दुर्ग की रक्षा के लिए लगाया हुआ जंगल।

कोठी *(संज्ञा पु.)* धाम, घर।

कोतल *(संज्ञा पु.)* बिना सवार का घोड़ा।

कोदंड *(संज्ञा पु.)* धनुष, कमान, भौंह।

कोपर *(संज्ञा पु.)* परात। (संज्ञा पु.) डाल का पका आम, टपका।

कोरी *(वि.)* नवीन, अछूती।

कोसलाधीश *(संज्ञा पु.)* कोसल+अधीश। कोशल के महाराजा, राम।

कोह *(संज्ञा पु.)* क्रोध, गुस्सा।

कोहबर *(संज्ञा पु.)* वह घर जहाँ विवाह के अवसर पर कुल देवता स्थापित किए जाते हैं।

कौल *(संज्ञा पु.)* उत्तम कुल का, वाम मार्गी, कमल, कटोरा।

क्रम *(संज्ञा पु.)* वस्तु या कार्यों का आग-पीछे होने का नियम। क्रम-क्रम से=धीरे- धीरे, शनै-शनै।

क्रिया *(संज्ञा स्त्री.)* चार प्रकार की क्रिया, यज्ञ क्रिया, श्रद्धा क्रिया, योग क्रिया व ज्ञान क्रिया।

क्षुब्ध *(वि.)* चंचल, व्याकुल, क्रुद्ध, कुपित, रेस्टलेस।

ख

खग *(संज्ञा पु.)* पक्षी, बांण, ग्रह, देवता, सूर्य, चंद्रमा, वायु।

खचना *(क्रि. अ.)* जड़ा जाना, अंकित होना, रमजाना। (संज्ञा पु.) शोक, चिंता, व्याकुलता, भय, डर।

खर *(संज्ञा पु.)* गधा, खच्चर, तिनका। (वि.) सख्त, तेज, अशुभ।

खरदूषण *(संज्ञा पु.)* रावण के दो भाई, खर और दूषण। (वि.) बहुत दोषों वाला।

खरभर *(संज्ञा पु.)* रौला, शोर, गुल-गपाड़ा, हलचल, गड़बड़।

खरभरना, खरभराना *(क्रि. अ.)* खलबलाना, घबराना, क्षुब्ध होना।

खर्पर *(संज्ञा पु.)* भिक्षा माँगने का खप्पर, खोपड़ा, काली का रुधिर पान का पात्र, धूर्त, चोर।

खर्ब *(वि.)* छोटा, लघु, तुच्छ।

खलु *(क्रि. वि.)* निश्चय ही। (अव्य.) मत, नहीं।

खसना *(क्रि. अ.)* अपने स्थान से हटना, खसकना, गिरना।

खाँगी *(संज्ञा पु.)* घाटा, कमी, त्रुटि।

खिसिआना *(क्रि. अ.)* शरमाना, लज्जित होना, रिसिआना, क्रुद्ध होना।

खीस *(वि.)* नष्ट, बरबाद, (संज्ञा स्त्री.) खीज, अप्रसन्नता, क्रोध, लज्जा, ।

खीस *(संज्ञा स्त्री.)* ओंठ के बाहर निकले दाँत, जैसे खीस निपोरना, खीस काढ़ना, दीन होकर कुछ माँगना, मर जाना।

खीस *(संज्ञा स्त्री.)* खिसिआना भाव, लज्जा, शरम: जैसे खीस मिटाना।

खुनिस *(संज्ञा स्त्री.)* खुनस। गुस्सा, क्रोध, अप्रसन्नता।

खेत *(संज्ञा पु.)* रणभूमि, अन्न उपजाने की भूमि।

खोरि *(संज्ञा स्त्री.)* ऐब, दोष, बुराई, सँकरी गली, खोट।

खौर *(संज्ञा स्त्री.)* चंदन का आड़ा तिलक, त्रिपुंड।

ग

गंभीर *(वि.)* घना, गभीर, बहुत गहरा, गूढ़ अर्थ वाला, विकट, भारी।

गंजन *(संज्ञा पु.)* अवज्ञा, तिरस्कार, पीड़ा, कष्ट, मारने या नष्ट करनेवाला।

गंजना *(क्रि. स.)* निरादर करना, चूर-चूर करना, नष्ट करना, पूर्णतया परास्त करना। मद गंजा=गर्व चूर्ण किया हुआ।

गंजय *(वि.)* जो गंज/गंजन करने योग्य हो। (संज्ञा फ.) नाश करनेवाला।

गँवई *(संज्ञा स्त्री.)* छोटा गाँव।

गँवहियाँ *(संज्ञा पु.)* अथिति, मेहमान।

गच *(संज्ञा पु.)* फर्श, चूने-सीमेंट का बना पक्का फर्श, नरम वस्तु में कड़ी या पेनी चीज के घुसने का शब्द।

गजमुक्ता *(संज्ञा स्त्री.)* काल्पनिक मोति जो कि हाथी के मस्तक से निकलता है।

गजाली *(संज्ञा स्त्री.)* हाथियों की कतार।

गथ *(संज्ञा पु.)* दाम, पूँजी, जमा, माल, गिरोह, झुंड।

गद *(संज्ञा पु.)* रोग, विष।

गनकन्ह *(संज्ञा पु.)* ज्योतिषी।

गनकन्ह *(वि.)* गणना करनेवाला।

गम *(संज्ञा पु.)* मार्ग, रास्ता, गमन, सहवास।

गरल *(संज्ञा स्त्री.)* विष, जहर, सर्प का विष, पूला, घास का मुट्ठा।

गरीस *(वि.)* भारी, गहरा।

गरुआ *(वि.)* गरु, भारी, वजनी, गौरवशाली, शांत, धीर।

गर्द *(संज्ञा स्त्री.)* धूल, राख, खाक।

गयन्दु *(संज्ञा पु.)* पकड़ा या कैद हाथी।

गलित *(वि.)* गला हुआ, गिरा हुआ, परिपक्व, चूआ हुआ।

गहन *(वि.)* गंभीर, गहरा, अथाह, वन का गुप्त स्थान, दुःख, जल पकड़ने का भाव।

गहबर *(वि.)* सघन, दुर्गम।

गहरु *(संज्ञा स्त्री.)* विलंब, देर।

गह-गहे *(क्रि. वि.)* बड़ी प्रसन्नता से, बड़े धूम-धाम से।

गारुड़ी *(संज्ञा पु.)* मंत्र द्वारा साँप का विष उतारने वाला।

गिरा *(संज्ञा स्त्री.)* वाणी, जिव्हा, भाषा, बोली, कविता, सरस्वती।

गिलना *(क्रि. स.)* निगलना, मन में रखना। मति गिलई= चाहे निगल जाए।

गुंजा *(संज्ञा स्त्री.)* घुँघची।

गुड़ी *(संज्ञा स्त्री.)* पतंग, गोली, कपट की गांस (बैर, बंधन)।

गुणानुवाद *(संज्ञा पु.)* गुणकथन, प्रशंसा, तारीफ, बड़ाई।

गुदरना *(क्रि. स.)* (गुजर + ना) *त्याग करना, अलग करना, छोड़ना।*

गुनउ *(संज्ञा पु.)* एक गुण।

गुरनारी *(संज्ञा स्त्री.)* बड़ी-बूढ़ी महिला।

गो *(संज्ञा स्त्री.)* इंद्रियाँ, किरण, वाणी, दिशा, पृथ्वी, दृष्टि, गाय, बकरी इत्यादि दूध देने वाले चौपाए।

गोचर *(वि.)* जो इंद्रियों से पहचाना जा सके, गायों द्वारा चरा हुआ, रहनेवाला, विचरने वाला, पृथ्वी पर रहने या विचरनेवाला।

गोचर *(संज्ञा पु.)* वह विषय जिसका ज्ञान इंद्रियों से हो सके, चरागाह, देश, प्रांत।

गोतीत *(वि.)* जो इंद्रियों से न जाना जा सके, अगोचर। गिरा गोतीत= जो कहा न जा सके।

गोना *(क्रि. स.)* छिपाना।

गोप्यमपि *(संज्ञा पु.)* अत्यंत गोपनीय रहस्य।

गोमाय *(संज्ञा पु.)* गीदड़।

गोरोचन *(संज्ञा पु.)* गो के पित्त में से निकलने वाला एक प्रकार का पीला द्रव्य।

गोविंद *(संज्ञा पु.)* वेदांतवेत्ता, तत्त्वज्ञ, बृहस्पति, श्रीकृष्ण, वेद वाक्यों द्वारा जानने योग्य।

ग्रीवा *(संज्ञा पु.)* गरदन।

घ

घटसंभव *(संज्ञा पु.)* घड़े से उत्पन्न, अगस्त मुनि।

घटाटोप *(संज्ञा पु.)* चारों ओर से घिरी बादलों की घटा, गाड़ी या पालकी को ढकने का परदा।

घमोई *(संज्ञा स्त्री.)* लकड़ी (बाँस) की कीड़ा, बाँस में लगनेवाला रोग।

घाटारोह *(संज्ञा पु.)* नदी के घाटों को रोक देना, घाट से आने-जाने न देना।

घालना *(क्रि. स.)* डालना, रखना, फकिना, चलाना, छोड़ना, कर डालना, बिगाड़ना, मार डालना। (संज्ञा पु.) पासंग (तोल बराबर करने के लिए तराजू के पलड़े पर रखा बोझ)।

घुनाच्छर *(वि.)* घुणाक्षर। बिना उद्योग के ही प्राप्त।

घुनाच्छर-न्याय *(संज्ञा पु.)* घुणाक्षर-न्याय। संयोगवश कोई कार्य हो जाना, ऐसी रचना जो अनजाने में हो जाए: जैसे कि घुन के खाते-खाते लकड़ी में अक्षर बन जाते हैं।

घुर्मित *(वि.)* घूमता हुआ, चक्कर खाता हुआ।

घ्रान *(संज्ञा स्त्री.)* घ्राण। नासिका, नाक, सूँघने की शक्ति, गंध, सुगंध।

च

चंचरीक *(संज्ञा पु.)* भौंरा।

चँदवा *(संज्ञा पु.)* कपड़े फूल आदि का छोटा मंडप।

चँदोवे *(संज्ञा पु.)* मंडप जैसी सजावट।

चंद्रहास *(संज्ञा पु.)* तलवार, रावण की तलवार का नाम।

चक्षण *(संज्ञा पु.)* कृपादृष्टि, अनुग्रह, कथन, मदिरा के ऊपर खाने की चाट।

चतुरसम *(संज्ञा पु.)* चतुस्सम। एक सुगंधित द्रव्य जो चार चीजों से बनता है—चंदन, केसर, कस्तूरी, और कपूर।

चर्म *(संज्ञा पु.)* ढाल।

चवहाना *(क्रि. स.)* टपकाना।

चहुँ *(संज्ञा पु.)* चार, चारों।

चहुं ओर *(संज्ञा स्त्री.)* चारों ओर।

चहुँहट्ट *(संज्ञा पु.)* चौराहा।

चाड़ *(संज्ञा स्त्री.)* गहरी चाह, चाव, प्रेम।

चाड़सरना *(क्रि. अ.)* इच्छा पूरी होना।

चातक *(संज्ञा पु.)* वर्षा काल में बोलने वाला एक पक्षी, पपीहा।

चाप *(संज्ञा पु.)* दबाव, पैर की आवाज या ध्वनि। कमान, (संज्ञा पु.) धनुष, कमान।

चामुंडा (*संज्ञा स्त्री.*) भैरवी, देवी का एक नाम।

चार (*वि.*) दो का दुगना। (संज्ञा पु.) आचरण, रीति, रसम, दास, सेवक, गति, चाल, बंधन, कारागार, गुप्तचर, जासूस।

चितेरा (*संज्ञा पु.*) चित्रकार।

चूड़ाकर्म (*संज्ञा पु.*) चूड़ाकरण, बच्चों का मुंडन संस्कार।

चोप (*संज्ञा पु.*) चाह, इच्छा, जोश, उत्साह, उमंग, शौक, रुचि।

चोपना (*क्रि. अ.*) मोहित होना।

चौतनी (*संज्ञा स्त्री.*) चौकोर टोपी।

चौहट्ट (*संज्ञा पु.*) चौहट्टा। बाजार का चौक।

छ

छई (*संज्ञा स्त्री.*) क्षई। क्षय रोग, जिसे क्षय रोग हो, क्षीण होनेवाला, नष्ट होनेवाला।

छजना (*क्रि अ.*) छाजना, शोभा देना, उपयुक्त जान पड़ना, फबना, ठीक जँचना।

छड़ना (*क्रि. स.*) अलग होना, अनाज को भूसी से अलग करना।

छत (*संज्ञा पु.*) घाव, चुना मिट्टी, गारे इत्यादि से बनाया घर के ऊपर का फर्श।

छत्र (*वि.*) आवृत्त, आच्छादित, लुप्त। मायाछत्र=माया से ढका हुआ।

छमा (*संज्ञा स्त्री.*) क्षमा। पमाईपृथ्वी, धरती, अवनि।

छर (*वि.*) घटने वाला, क्रम से कम होने वाला, (क्षर) नष्ट होनेवाला, छल।

छरे (*वि.*) चुने।

छीजना (*क्रि. स.*) घटना, कम होना।

छुद्धित (*वि.*) क्षुधित। छुधित, भूखा।

छेदना (*क्रि. स.*) काटना, छेद करना।

छोह (*संज्ञा पु.*) क्षोभ, स्नेह, कृपा।

ज

जंबुक *(संज्ञा पु.)* गीदड़, सियार, शृंगाल, जामुन (बड़ा)।

जच्छ *(संज्ञा पु.)* यक्षक, यक्ष लोग।

जच्छपति *(संज्ञा पु.)* कुबेर।

जथा *(क्रि. वि.)* यथा, जिस तरह, जैसे।

जथारथ *(अव्य.)* यथार्थ, ठीक उचित, सत्य, जैसा है वैसा।

जन *(संज्ञा पु.)* दास, अनुयायी, अनुचर, लोग, समूह, लोक।

जनाना *(क्रि. अ.)* दिखाना, दर्शाना, जाहिर करना।

जनि *(अव्य.)* न, नहीं, मत, (संज्ञा स्त्री.) नारी, स्त्री, माता, पुत्र-वधू, जन्म, जन्मभूमि, पत्नी।

जमना *(क्रि. अ.)* उगना, उपजना, फूटना, तरल का ठोस होना, सुचारु रूप से संपादित होना, जैसे 'काम जमना'।

जमनिका *(संज्ञा स्त्री.)* परदा (जैसे किसी नाटक में)।

जमी *(वि.)* इंद्रियनिग्रही, विरक्त।

जम्बुक *(संज्ञा पु.)* गीदड़।

जरठ *(वि.)* कठिन, कर्कश, जीर्ण। (संज्ञा पु.) बुढ़ापा।

जरनि *(संज्ञा स्त्री.)* दिल की जलन, जलने की पीड़ा।

जरि *(संज्ञा स्त्री)* जड़, जड़ी।

जरी *(वि.)* वृद्ध, बुडढा।

जल गंभीर *(संज्ञा पु.)* गहरा पानी।

जलज *(वि.)* जल में उत्पन्न होनेवाला, जो जल में उत्पन्न हों।

जलज *(संज्ञा पु.)* कमल, शंख, मछली, मोती, चौलाई, बादल।

जलजाभ *(संज्ञा पु.)* कमल।

जलसीकर *(संज्ञा स्त्री.)* जल की बूँद।

जवास *(संज्ञा पु.)* एक काँटेदार पौधा जो औषधि के काम में आता है।

जाचक *(संज्ञा पु.)* याचक।

जातरूप *(संज्ञा पु.)* स्वर्ण, सोना।

जातु *(अव्य.)* कदाचित

जातुधान *(संज्ञा पु.)* राक्षस, निशाचर।

जान *(संज्ञा पु.)* यान, रथ। (संज्ञा स्त्री.) ज्ञान, जानकारी, परिचय, खयाल, अनुमान।

जानपन *(संज्ञा पु.)* समझदारी।

जानु *(संज्ञा पु.)* घुटना। जाँघ।

जाम *(संज्ञा पु.)* पहर, प्रहर, दिन का – भाग= 3 घंटे।

जामना *(क्रि. अ.)* जमना। उगना, जन्मना, उत्पन्न होना।

जामा *(संज्ञा पु.)* पोशाक, पहरावा।

जामिनी *(संज्ञा स्त्री.)* यामिनी। रात।

जामी *(संज्ञा पु.)* पिता। (जनमना या जमना का रूप)।

जाल *(संज्ञा पु.)* बुने हुए या गुँथे हुए डोरों का समूह, जारा या जाला (जैसे मकडीका), अहंकार, फरेब, धोखा।

जिआना *(क्रि. स.)* जिलाना। पालना, जीवित रहने में सहायता करना।

जिनस *(संज्ञा स्त्री.)* जाति।

जीन *(संज्ञा पु.)* घोडे की गद्दी या सैंडल, एक प्रकार का मोटा कपड़ा।

जीव *(संज्ञा पु.)* जो श्वास लेता हो, चार प्रकार के जीवः अंडज, स्वदेश, जरायुज, और उीद्वज।

जुग *(संज्ञा पु.)* दो, जोड़ा, युग।

जुझारा *(वि.)* जुझार, लड़ाका, वीर, सूरमा, युद्ध।

जूथ *(संज्ञा पु.) यूथ। झुंड, समूह, सेना, फौज। जूथप+जूथ=झुंड के झुंड।*

जेहि *(सर्व.)* जिस, जिसको, जिसे।

जोगवना *(क्रि. स.)* किसी वस्तु को हिफाजत से रखना, संचित करना, आदर करना, कुछ खयाल न करना, जाने देना।

जोना *(क्रि. स.)* देखना।

जोटा *(संज्ञा पु.)* जोड़ा, युगल।

जोश *(संज्ञा पु.)* उत्साह, उफान, मनोवेग।

जोष *(संज्ञा पु.)* प्रेम, प्रीति, सुख। (संज्ञा स्त्री.) स्त्री, नारी।

जोषित *(संज्ञा स्त्री.)* स्त्री। दारु जोषित= लकड़ी की स्त्री, कठपुतली।

जोहार *(संज्ञा स्त्री.)* अभिवादन। नमस्कार, प्रणाम इत्यादि।

जोहारना *(क्रि. अ.)* अभिवादन करना। नमस्कार, प्रणाम इत्यादि करना।

झ

झटिति *(क्रि. वि.)* झटित। झट से, तत्काल, तुरंत, बिना समझे-बूझे।

झष *(संज्ञा पु.)* मगर, मछली, ताप, गरमी।

झार *(संज्ञा स्त्री.)* झाल, दाह, जलन। (संज्ञा पु.) समूह, झुंड, प्रयत्न। (वि.) केवल, एकमात्र, निपट, कुल, सब, संपूर्ण।

झारि *(संज्ञा स्त्री.)* झार।

झारी *(संज्ञा स्त्री.)* झार। झाड़ी, टोंटीदार बरतन, झरना।

झीनी *(वि. स्त्री.)* महीन।

झूठ *(संज्ञा पु.)* झूठ। वह कथन जो वास्तविक स्थिति के विपरीत हो, वह बात जो यथार्थ न हो। असत्य, सत्य का उलटा। झूठ प्राय: विचारित भाषण माना जाता है। (वि.) झूठ बोलने वाला व्यक्ति, झूठा।

झोटिंग *(संज्ञा पु.)* झोंटे वाला, जटाधारी।

ट

टहल *(संज्ञा स्त्री.)* सेवा (काम), सेवा-सुश्रूषा, नौकरी-चाकरी।

टिट्टिभ *(संज्ञा स्त्री.)* टिटिहरी पक्षी जो कि आकाश की तरफ पैर करके सोता है।

टेका *(संज्ञा स्त्री.)* टेक। सहारा, ढासना, आश्रय, अवलंब, चबूतरा, टीला, अड़, हठ, दृढ़ संकल्प, गीत या पट का वह टुकड़ा जो बारंबार गाया जाता है, स्थायी, आधार।

ठ

ठकुर सुहाती *(संज्ञा स्त्री.)* खुशामद, चापलूसी।

ठगाना *(क्रि. अ.)* ठगा जाना। ठगे से रह जाना= स्तंभित रह जाना, चकित होना, आश्चर्य से स्तब्ध होना।

ठटना (*क्रि. स.*) ठहराना, निश्चित करना, सजाना, (राग) छेड़ना, अड़ना।

ठवनि (*संज्ञा स्त्री.*) बैठक, स्थिति, बैठने या खड़े होने का ढंग, आसन।

ड

डंबर (*संज्ञा पु.*) आयोजन, आडंबर, ढकोसला, विस्तार, एक प्रकार का चंदोबा।

डसाना (*क्रि. स.*) बिछाना।

डाँस (*संज्ञा पु.*) बड़ा मच्छर।

डाढ़ा (*संज्ञा स्त्री.*) अग्नि, दावानल, जलन, ताप।

डाबर (*संज्ञा पु.*) नीची जमीन, गड़ही, पोखरी, हाथ धोने का पात्र, चिलमची।

डीठना (*क्रि. अ.*) दिखाई देना, दृष्टि में आना।

डोडो (*संज्ञा स्त्री.*) एक चिड़िया जो अब नहीं पाई जाती।

डोल (*संज्ञा पु.*) कुँए से पानी खींचने का एक लोहे का बरतन, हिंडोला, झूलना, पालना, डोली, पालकी, शिविका, धार्मिक उत्सवों में निकलने वाली चौकियाँ या विमान, कंप, खलबली, हलचल।

ढ

ढिंग (*क्रि. वि.*) ढिग। समीप, पास, निकट, किनारा। (संज्ञा स्त्री.) पास, सामीप्य, तट, किनारा, कपड़े का कोर, किनारा, हाशिया।

ढिठाई (*संज्ञा स्त्री.*) ढिढाई। अनुचित साहस, धृष्टता, ढीठ होना।

त

तकना (*क्रि. अ.*) देखना, ताक में रहना, आश्रय लेना। तकहु= आश्रय लो, या छिप जाओ।

तग्य (वि.) तत्त्व ज्ञानी। तग्य बिरागी= तत्त्व ज्ञानी एवं विरागी।

तड़ागा (संज्ञा स्त्री.) तालाब, सरोवर, ताल।

तनय (संज्ञा पु.) पुत्र।

तनया (संज्ञा स्त्री.) पुत्री।

तपपुंज (संज्ञा पु.) तपोमूर्ति।

तमकना (क्रि. अ.) क्रोध का आवेश दिखलाना, क्रोध के कारण उछल पड़ना।

तमरसु (संज्ञा पु.) तमरस, कमल।

तमीचर (संज्ञा पु.) निशाचर।

तरकना (क्रि. अ.) उछलना, कूदना, झपटना। (तर्क) तर्क करना, सोच विचार- करना, अनुमान करना।

तरजना (क्रि. अ.) तर्जना। धमकाना, डाटना।

तरनतारण (संज्ञा पु.) स्वयं तरे हुए एवं दूसरों को तारने वाले, उद्धार, निस्तार, मोक्ष।

तरल (वि.) चंचल, बहने वाला, द्रव्य, क्षणभंगुर, चमकीला, कोमल। लिक्विड। तरल त्रिसूल=चमकता हुआ त्रिशूल।

तरु (संज्ञा पु.) वृक्ष, पेड।

तलफना (क्रि. अ.) पड़पना, छटपटाना, व्याकुल होना, बैचेन होना।

ताटंक (संज्ञा पु.) ताडंक। कर्णफूल।

ताड़ना (क्रि. स.) डाँटना, पीटना।

तात (वि.) ताता। तपा हुआ, गरम, उष्ण।

तामजान (संज्ञा पु.) एक प्रकार की छोटी खुली पालकी।

तामरस (संज्ञा पु.) कमल, सोना, ताँबा, धतूरा, सारस।

ताल (संज्ञा पु.) ताड़ का पेड़, करतल, हथेली, करतल ध्वनि, ताली, नृत्य और संगीत में समय या गति का परिमाण।

तिजारी (संज्ञा पु.) तिजरा। तीसरे दिन चढ़ने वाला ज्वर।

तिर्यक (वि.) तिरछा, आड़ा, टेढ़ा, पशु-पक्षी।

तिष्टना (क्रि. स.) बनाना, रचना।

तीछी (वि.) तेज नोकवाला, तीक्ष्ण, तेज, उग्र, तीव्र, प्रचंड।

तुराइ (क्रि. वि.) आतुरता के साथ।

तुराई (संज्ञा स्त्री.) गद्दा, ढुलाई, शीघ्रता, जल्दी।

तुराना (क्रि. अ.) घबराना, आतुर होना।

तुरीय *(वि.)* चतुर्थ, चौथा, तीनो गुणों (सत्व, रजस व तमस) से अतीत, वाणी के चार भेद: परा, पश्यंति, मध्यमों, और बैखरी (तुरीय, या उच्चारित वाणी)।

तुहिन *(संज्ञा पु.)* पाला, कोहरा, तुषार, हिम, चाँदनी, शीतलता, ठंडक, ओस।

तूल *(संज्ञा पु.)* रुई, आकाश, तूत या शहतूत। दीर्घता, खलु तूल= बड़ा या विशाल खल।

ते *(अव्य.)* से। (सर्व.) वे, वे लोग। तेऊ (सर्व.) वे भी।

तेइ *(सर्व.)* उसे, वे ही।

तेपि *(सर्व.)* वे लोग भी, तेऊ।

तेरहुत-तेरहूति *(संज्ञा पु.)* बिहार प्रांत का एक भाग।

तोपना *(क्रि. स.)* ढक देना-नीचे दबाना, ढाकना, छिपाना।

तोशक *(संज्ञा स्त्री.)* रुई भरा गद्दा।

त्रात *(वि.)* रक्षित।

त्राता *(संज्ञा पु.)* रक्षा करनेवाला।

त्रास *(संज्ञा स्त्री.)* डर, भय, कष्ट, तकलीफ।

त्राहि *(अव्य.)* सहायता के लिये, 'बचाओ, रक्षा करो' कह पुकारने वाला शब्द। त्राहि-त्राहि।

त्रिजग *(संज्ञा पु.)* आड़ा चलने वाला जंतु, पशु और कीड़े-मकोड़े। तिर्यक, तीनों लोक।

त्रिबिक्रम *(संज्ञा पु.)* वामन अवतार।

त्रीण *(संज्ञा पु.)* तरकस।

थ

थकित *(वि.)* थका हुआ, श्रांत, शिथिल, मोहित, मुग्ध।

थाती *(संज्ञा स्त्री.)* कठिन समय के लिये बचाकर रखी गई पूँजी या धन, जमा, धरोहर, अमानत।

थाना *(संज्ञा पु.)* ठहरने का स्थान, अड्डा, पुलिस विभाग की स्थानीय चौकी।

थापना *(क्रि. स.)* स्थापित करना।

थाह *(संज्ञा पु.)* ज्ञान, गहराई, महत्व आदि का अंत या सीमा। तल, तह, अधोभाग।

द

दंड *(संज्ञा पु.)* साठ पल भर का समय, घड़ी, डंडे जैसी कोई वस्तु, एक प्रकार की कसरत, जुरमाना, अर्थ दंड, शमन, दमन।

दमसील *(वि.)* इंद्रियों का दमन करनेवाला।

दर *(संज्ञा पु.)* शंख, गड्ढा, दरार।

दर्पना *(क्रि. अ.)* गर्वित होना।

दर्भ *(संज्ञा पु.)* कुश, दाभ, डाभ। दर्भ डसाना= कुछ बिछाना, अहं से दुःखी (घायल) होना।

दलमलना *(क्रि. स.)* कुचलना, मसल डालना।

दव *(संज्ञा पु.)* दावानल।

दवाना *(क्रि. अ.)* मुरझा जाना, जलना।

दशकंधर *(संज्ञा पु.)* दशग्रीव, रावण।

दसन *(दशन)* (संज्ञा पु.) दाँत, कवच, शिखर।

दसमौलि *(संज्ञा पु.)* दस चौटी, सिर या मस्तक वाला, रावण, किरीट, जूड़ा, सरदार, भूमि, जमीन।

दाप *(संज्ञा पु.)* क्लेष, गर्व, बल, उत्साह, रोब।

दाम *(संज्ञा पु.)* मोती, झालर, रस्सी माला, समूह, धन।

दारय *(संज्ञा पु.)* नाश करनेवाला, जलाने वाला।

दारिका *(संज्ञा स्त्री.)* लड़कियाँ, पुत्री, बालिका, बेटी, कन्या।

दारु *(संज्ञा स्त्री.)* काष्ट, काठ, लकड़ी, देवदारु।

दारु *(संज्ञा स्त्री.)* दवा, औषध। (संज्ञा पु.) मद्य, बारुद।

दावना *(क्रि. स.)* नष्ट करना, दमन करना।

दावनी *(संज्ञा स्त्री.)* महिलाओं के माथे की बिंदी, नष्ट करने वाली।

दिग *(संज्ञा स्त्री.)* दिक। दिशा ओर। दिगंत= दिशा का छोर।

दिग *(संज्ञा स्त्री.)* आँख, दृग। दिगंत= आँख का कोना।

दिगअंचल *(संज्ञा स्त्री.)* पलक। दिगांचल। दृग+अंचल।

दिनकर *(संज्ञा पु.)* सूर्य, सूर्यवंश।

दिसित्राता *(संज्ञा पु.)* दिगपाल।

दुंदुभी *(संज्ञा पु.)* नगाड़ा, धौंसा।

दुकाल *(संज्ञा पु.)* अकाल, दुर्भिक्ष।

दुरतिक्रम *(वि.)* जिसका अतिक्रमण न हो सके, जिसका पार पाना कठिन हो, प्रबल।

दुरना *(क्रि. अ.)* छिपना या छिपाना, आँख से दूर हट जाना।

दुरंत *(वि.)* बहुत भारी, भीषण, घोर, कठिन, जिसका अंत या परिणाम बुरा हो।

दुराघर्ष *(वि.)* अत्यंत प्रबल, जिसका दमन करना कठिन हो, उग्र, प्रचंड।

दुराना *(क्रि. अ.)* छिपना, आँख से दूर हट जाना।

दुराना *(क्रि. स.)* छिपाना, आँख से दूर हटाना, छोड़ना, त्यागना।

दुराव *(संज्ञा पु.)* छल, कपट, छुपाव।

दुर्गम *(वि.)* जहाँ जाना या पहुँचना कठिन हो, जिसे जानना कठिन हो, दुर्जेय।

दुष्टतर्क *(संज्ञा पु.)* कुतर्क।

दुस्तर *(वि.)* जिसे पार करना कठिन हो, विकट, कठिन।

दुहाई *(संज्ञा स्त्री.)* शपथ, सौगंध, कसम, घोषणा, पुकार। गाय, भैंस दोहने की क्रिया।

दैअ *(संज्ञा पु.)* देव, दैव, भाग्य।

ध

धन्वी *(संज्ञा पु.)* धनुर्धर।

धर *(वि.)* धारण करनेवाला, रक्षक। (संज्ञा पु.) पर्वत, कच्छप, शरीर। (संज्ञा स्त्री.) पकड़ने की क्रिया या भाव, पृथ्वी।

धरमादिक *(संज्ञा पु.)* पुरुषार्थ (अर्थ, धर्म, काम और मोक्ष)।

धरषना *(क्रि. स.)* मर्दन करना, चूर करना।

धरसना *(क्रि. अ.)* दब जाना, डर जाना, सहम जाना।

धर्मचरण *(संज्ञा पु.)* धर्म के चार चरण सत्य, दया, तप और दान।

धाता (*संज्ञा पु.*) विधाता, ब्रह्मा, विष्णु, शिव।

धानपान (*वि.*) दुबला-पतला, नाजुक (बाजारू)।

धामदा (*संज्ञा पु.*) धामधा। पालक, रक्षक।

धारि (*संज्ञा पु.*) सेना, फौज, समूह, झुंड। धार रु जोर की वर्षा का जल, उधार, कर्ज, लकीर, ओर।

धावन (*संज्ञा पु.*) दौड़कर चलने वाला हरकारा, दूत। एरेंड बोय।

धुआँ (*संज्ञा पु.*) सुलगती हुई आग से काली भाप। विनाश।

धुरीण (*संज्ञा पु.*) मुख्य, प्रधान, बोझ सँभालनेवाला, धुरंधर, जिसे कोई उत्तरदायित्व प्रदान किया जाए।

धुरीण (*वि.*) प्रमुख व्यक्ति, अग्रणी पुरुष, रथ आदि के घोड़े, कार्यभार सँभालने वाला व्यक्ति।

धूतना (*क्रि. स.*) छलना, धूर्तता करना।

धूताई (*संज्ञा स्त्री.*) धूर्तता।

धूर्त (*संज्ञा पु.*) छली, वंचक, चालबाजी से काम लेने वाला।

धौं (*अव्य.*) एक अवयव, जो ऐसे प्रश्नों के पहले आता है, जिनमें जिज्ञासा का भाव कम और संदेह का भाव अधिक होता है। विचिकित्सा सूचक एक शब्द, न जाने, कौन जाने।

ध्वज (*संज्ञा पु.*) चिह्न, निशान, झंडा, ध्वजा लेकर चलने वाला आदमी, शौडिक, लिंग, पुरुषेंद्रिय, दर्प, गर्व, घमंड, वह घर जिसकी स्थिति पूर्व की ओर हो, मदिरा का व्यवसायी, कलाल।

न

नक्र (*संज्ञा पु.*) घड़ियाल (नाक) मगर।

नक्रा (*संज्ञा स्त्री.*) नासिका, नांक।

नखत (*संज्ञा पु.*) नक्षत्र, तारे।

नतरु (*क्रि. वि.*) नहीं तो, नतर, अन्यथा।

नफीरि (*संज्ञा स्त्री.*) नफीरी। तुरही इत्यादि युद्ध के समय बजाने वाले वाद्य, शहनाई।

नभगेस (*संज्ञा पु.*) गरुड़।

नय *(संज्ञा पु.)* नीति, नम्रता, विष्णु। नयनागर=नीति निपुण। नयसानी= नीति से परिपूर्ण।

नयन *(संज्ञा पु.)* नेत्र, आँख। नयन अथिति= जिसे देखने से आनंद मिले।

नरनायक *(संज्ञा पु.)* राजा, भूपति, नरेश, जननायक।

नरनाह *(संज्ञा पु.)* राजा, प्रभु।

नर्म *(संज्ञा पु.)* परिहास, साहित्य में नायक को हँसाने वाला सखा, ठट्ठा, दिल्लगी। (वि.) नरम, कोमल।

नर्मद *(वि.)* प्रसन्न कारक, अल्हादक, आनंद देने वाला। (संज्ञा पु.) मसखरा।

नवसप्त *(संज्ञा पु.)* 16 की संख्या, सोलह श्रृंगार

नसाना *(क्रि. अ.)* नसना। बिगड़ जाना, खराब होना, नष्ट होना।

नाईं *(संज्ञा स्त्री)* एक सी गति, समान दशा, (अव्य.) समान, तुल्य, की तरह।

नाउँ *(संज्ञा पु.)* नाम।

नाउ *(संज्ञा स्त्री)* नाव।

नाक *(संज्ञा पु.)* स्वर्ग। *(संज्ञा स्त्री.)* प्रतिष्ठा।

नाग *(संज्ञा पु.)* हाथी, सर्प।

नागर, *(संज्ञा पु.)* चतुर, शिष्ट, देवर।

नागारि *(संज्ञा पु.)* नाग+अरि। गरुड़, मोर, सिंह।

नाना *(क्रि. स.)* नम्र करना, झुकाना।

नाराच *(संज्ञा पु.)* बाण।

नावरि *(संज्ञा स्त्री.)* नदी में खेलने का एक खेल, नाव, नौका।

नाह *(संज्ञा पु.)* नाथ, स्वामी, राजा, पति।

निकंदन *(संज्ञा पु.)* नाश, विनाश, वध।

निकर *(संज्ञा पु.)* समूह, झुंड, राशि, ढेर, निधि, कोष।

निकाम *(वि.)* बेकाम, दोषयुक्त, प्रचुर, बहुत अधिक। (क्रिया वि.) व्यर्थ, निष्प्रयोजन। (संज्ञा पु.) अभिलाषा, कामना। इच्छानुसार अत्यधिक।

निकाय *(संज्ञा पु.)* समूह, झुंड।

निगम *(संज्ञा पु.)* वेद, वेद का कोई अवतरण, मार्ग, पथ, बाजार, मैला, पैंठ, फेरीवाला सौदागर, कॉपरेशन, व्यवसाय, व्यापार।

निग्रह *(संज्ञा पु.)* रोक, अवरोध, बंभन।

नितांत (*वि.*) बहुत अधिक, एकदम, परम।

निदान (*संज्ञा पु.*) कारण, मूल कारण, रोग की डायग्नोसिस, रोगी का रोग निश्चय करना, अंत, अवसान, (वि.) अंतिम या निम्न श्रेणी का, बहुत ही गया बीता।

निधान (*संज्ञा पु.*) खजाना, आधार, आश्रय, निधि, कोष; वह जिसमें किसी गुण की परिपूर्णता हो। जैसे—कृपा निधान।

निनार (*वि.*) निनारा, निनरा। अलग, जुदा, पृथक, भिन्न, दूर, हटा हुआ।

निनारी (*वि.*) न्यारी।

निपातना (*क्रि. स.*) मार डालना, गिराना, नीचे गिरना।

निबिड़ (*वि.*) निविड़ अत्यंत घना, घोर, गहरा, चपटी या टेढ़ी नाक वाला।

निबुकना (*क्रि. अ.*) छुटकारा पाना, छूटना, बंधन से निकलना, बंधन आदि का खिसकना, समाप्त होना।

निबेरना (*क्रि. स.*) निबेड़ना। निवेरना, निबेहना। उन्मुक्त करना, मिली हुई वस्तु को अलग-अलग करना, छुटकारा पाना, चुनना, छाँटना, हटना, दूर करना, त्यागना, छोड़ना।

निमिष (*संज्ञा पु.*) क्षण, पल, आँख झपकने की क्रिया, आँख बंद करने की क्रिया, न्यूनतम समय।

निमेष (*संज्ञा पु.*) पलक झपकना या गिरना, पल, क्षण।

निमेषक (*संज्ञा पु.*) पलक, जुगनू।

नियोग (*संज्ञा पु.*) नियोजित करने का कार्य, तैनाती, काम में लगाना, प्रेरण, कमीशन, आज्ञा, निश्चय।

निरंजन (*वि.*) माया रहित, अंजन रहित, दोष रहित, माया से निर्लिप्त। (संज्ञा पु.) महादेव, परमात्मा।

निरंबु (*वि.*) निरम्बु। बिना जल का, निर्जल।

निरखना (*क्रि. अ.*) देखना, अवलोकन करना।

निरज (*संज्ञा पु.*) रजोगुण विहीन, विकार रहित, निर्मल।

निरजोसु (*संज्ञा पु.*) निरजोस। निश्चित सिद्धांत, निचोड़, निर्णय।

निरबहना (*क्रि. अ.*) निर्वाह होना। समय निर्बहना= समय गुजरजाना, समय जाता रहना।

निरवधि (*वि.*) निःसीम, जिसकी कोई सीमा न हो।

निरुअरना (*क्रि. अ.*) निरुवरना। छूटना, सुलझना।

निरुआरना *(क्रि. स.)* निरुवारना। सुलझाना, छुड़ाना, मुक्त करना, फँसी या गुथी हुई वस्तु को अलग करना, उलझन मिटाना, निबटाना।

निरूपण *(संज्ञा पु.)* निदर्शन, सोच-समझकर किया जाने वाला विचार या निर्णय, प्रकाश।

निर्गतना *(क्रि. अ.)* निकलना, उद्‍गम।

निर्दंभ *(वि.)* दंभ हीन, दंभ रहित।

निर्भर *(वि.)* पूर्ण, भरा हुआ, बहुत अधिक, तीव्र, गाढ़, अवलंबित आश्रित।

निवारना *(क्रि. स.)* नेवारना, रोकना, हटाना, दूर करना।

निविड़ *(वि.)* घना, घोर, गहरा, चपटी नाक वाला। निबिड़।

निषंग *(संज्ञा पु.)* तरकस, तूणीर, तूण, खंग।

निषँगी *(संज्ञा पु.)* आलिंगन करनेवाला, तरकस रखनेवाला।

निषगंथि *(संज्ञा पु.)* आलिंगन, धनुर्धर, सारथी, रथ।

निष्केवल *(वि.)* विशुद्ध, पूर्ण शुद्ध, खालिस, अनन्य।

निसरना *(क्रि. अ.)* निकालना, बाहर होना, आर-पार होना।

निसान *(संज्ञा पु.)* नगाड़ा, धौंसा।

निसित *(वि.)* तीक्ष्ण, तीव्र।

निसेनी *(संज्ञा स्त्री.)* नसेनी, सीढ़ी, जीना, सोपान।

निस्तार *(संज्ञा पु.)* छुटकारा, उद्धार, काम पूरा करके छुट्टी पाना, दोषमोचन।

निहार *(संज्ञा पु.)* कोहरा, पाला, ओस, हिम, बरफ।

निहोरना *(क्रि. स.)* प्रार्थना करना, विनय करना, मनाना, कृतज्ञ होना।

निहोरा *(संज्ञा पु.)* उपकार, अनुग्रह, एहसान, विनती, प्रार्थना, भरोसा, आसरा, आश्रय, आधार।

नीच *(वि.)* किसी बात में घटकर, गरीब।

नीति *(संज्ञा स्त्री.)* आचार पद्धति, समाज की भलाई के लिए निश्चित आचार- व्यवहार, नय, (एथिक्स), किसी कार्य को ठीक प्रकार से करने का ढंग (पॉलिसी)।

नेई *(संज्ञा पु.)* नींव, मकान की।

नेग *(संज्ञा पु.)* विवाहादि के अवसर पर संबंधियों और अतिथियों को भेंट देने की प्रथा या रीति।

नेगी *(संज्ञा पु.)* नेग पानेवाला या अधिकारी, प्रबंधक, सहायक। धर्म के नेगी= धर्म के सहायक।

प

पंक *(संज्ञा पु.)* कीचड़, दलदल।

पंचध्वनि *(संज्ञा स्त्री.)* वेदध्वनि, बंदिध्वनि, जयध्वनि, शंखध्वनि व हुल्ध्वनि।

पंचशब्द *(संज्ञा पु.)* तंत्री, ताल, तुरही, झाँझ व नगाड़ा।

पंचानन *(वि.)* पाँच सिरवाला, (संज्ञा पु.) शिव, शेर (चार पँजे+मुँह)।

पंजर *(संज्ञा पु.)* शरीर का ढाँचा, पिंजरा।

पखवाड़ा *(संज्ञा पु.)* पखवारा। दो-सप्ताह, 15 दिन।

पखारना *(क्रि. स.)* धोना।

पगिआना *(क्रि. स.)* पागने का काम करना, मग्न करना, अनुरक्त करना।

पचारना *(क्रि. स.)* लड़ने के लिए ललकारना, कोई कार्य करने के पूर्व लोगों के मध्य घोषणा करना, पचारी= ललकारा।

पटतर *(संज्ञा पु.)* समता, बराबरी, तुल्यता, उपमा, सादृश्य कथन।

पटतरना *(क्रि. अ.)* उपमा देना, सादृश्य कथन करना।

पटल *(संज्ञा पु.)* समूह, छत, छप्पर, आवरण।

पटली *(संज्ञा स्त्री.)* छान, छप्पर, छत, परदा, आवरण, घूँघट, बुरका, परिच्छेद।

पतंग *(संज्ञा पु.)* चिड़िया, पक्षी, सूर्य, टिड्डी, नाव, नौका, परवाना, भुनगा, फतिंगा।

पताका *(संज्ञा स्त्री.)* झंडा, ध्वजा, वह डंडा जिसमें झंडे का कपड़ा पहनाया रहता है।

पताकी *(संज्ञा पु.)* राज्य चिह्न, पताका उठाकर चलनेवाला व्यक्ति, ध्वजाधारी।

पति *(संज्ञा पु.)* मालिक, रक्षक, मर्यादा, प्रतिष्ठा, साख, स्त्री का विवाहित पुरुष।

पतिआना *(क्रि. अ.)* पतियाना। सच मानना, विश्वास करना।

पथ्य *(संज्ञा पु.)* जल्दी पचने वाला उपयुक्त भोजन, कल्याण, नमक।

पदज *(संज्ञा पु.)* पैर की अँगुलियाँ।

पदत्राण *(संज्ञा पु.)* पैरों की रक्षा करनेवाला, जूता।

पदिक *(संज्ञा पु.)* पैदल सेना, देवता के चरणांकित गले का गहना, हीरा, रत्न।

पदोदक *(संज्ञा पु.)* वह जल जिससे पैर धोया गया हो, चरणामृत।

पन (संज्ञा पु.) प्रण, प्रतिज्ञा, संकल्प। (प्रत्य.) जैसे लड़कपन।

पनवार (संज्ञा स्त्री.) पनवारा। पत्तल।

पनस (संज्ञा पु.) फनस, कटहल।

पन्नगरि (संज्ञा पु.) पन्नगाश्न। गारुड़। पन्नग+अरि=सर्प का शत्रु।

पबि (संज्ञा पु.) पवि। वज्र, बिजली, वाक्य, राह, मार्ग।

परचारना (क्रि. स.) ललकारना, प्रचार करना।

परछन (संज्ञा स्त्री.) वर की आगवानी पर पूजा।

परजरना (क्रि. अ.) अत्यधिक जलना।

परतीती (संज्ञा स्त्री.) प्रतीति। विश्वास, निश्चय, धारणा, ख्याति, प्रसिद्धि, आनंद, प्रसन्नता, आदर।

परदार (संज्ञा स्त्री.) परदारा। दूसरे की स्त्री।

परद्रोही (वि.) द्वेषी, बैरी, दूसरों का अनिष्ट करनेवाला, दूसरों से घृणा करनेवाला।

परनसाल (संज्ञा स्त्री.) पर्णशाला। पत्तों की झोपड़ी।

परमब्रह्मचारिणी (संज्ञा पु.) दुर्गा, परमेश्वरी।

परमायतनं (संज्ञा पु.) परम+आयतनं। परम स्थान।

परमार्थ (संज्ञा पु.) सर्वोत्कृष्ट सत्य, सत्य आत्मज्ञान, जीव और ब्रह्म संबंधी ज्ञान। उत्तम प्रकार की संपत्ति, परोपकार।

पयोध (संज्ञा पु.) बादल।

परवा (संज्ञा पु.) मिट्टी का कटोरा, पड़वा, परवाह।

परवान (संज्ञा पु.) प्रमाण, सबूत, सत्य, यथार्थ बात, हद, सीमा।

परस (संज्ञा पु.) छूने का भाव, स्पर्श, पारस पत्थर, स्पर्श मणि, फरसा।

परसना (क्रि. स.) परसाना। छूना, स्पर्श करना, छुवाना, किसी के सामने भोज्य पदार्थ रखना।

पराभव (संज्ञा पु.) हार, पराजय, नाश।

परावा (वि.) दूसरों से, पराया।

परास (संज्ञा पु.) ढाक, पलाश, टेसू, वह फासला जहाँ तक उस स्थान से फेंकी हुई वस्तु जा गिरे।

परिकर (संज्ञा पु.) कमर पट्टी, कमरबंद, नाड़ा, पटुका, अनुगत, सहचर।

परिघ (संज्ञा पु.) गंडासा, शूल, भाला, बरछी।

परिचरजा (संज्ञा स्त्री.) परिचर्या, सेवा-टहल।

परिचायक *(संज्ञा पु.)* सेवक, नौकर।

परितोष *(संज्ञा पु.)* तृप्ति, संतोष। सेटिसफेक्शन।

परिपालय *(वि.)* जो रक्षा या पालन करने योग्य हो।

परुष *(वि.)* कठोर, कर्कश, अप्रिय, निष्ठुर, उग, आलसी, मैला-कुचैला, (संज्ञा पु.) फासला, तीर, सरकंडा।

परुषवचन *(संज्ञा पु.)* कठोर वचन, कुवाच्य।

परुषता *(संज्ञा पु.)* कर्कशता, कठोरता, निर्दयता।

पल्लव *(संज्ञा पु.)* नए निकलते कोमल पत्ते।

पवन *(संज्ञा पु.)* वायु, हवा, कुम्हार का आँवा।

पवारना *(क्रि. स.)* फेंकना, डालना।

पविपात *(संज्ञा पु.)* वज्रपात।

पहुँनाई *(संज्ञा स्त्री.)* पहुनाई, पाहुने होने का भाव, मेहमानी।

पाँवड़ *(संज्ञा पु.)* पावँड। आगवानी के लिये बिछाया हुआ कपड़ा। रेड कार्पेट।

पाइक *(संज्ञा पु.)* पायक। धावक, दूत, हरकारा, पैदल सिपाही।

पाक *(संज्ञा पु.)* भोजन बनाने की क्रिया, पका हुआ अन्न, रसोई पकवान, मिश्री, चीनी या शहद में मिलाकर बनाई गई औषधि, पाचन, पका हुआ।

पाक *(वि.)* स्वल्प, लघु, बुद्धिमान, निष्कपट, अज्ञ, अनभिज्ञ, अप्राज्ञ।

पाक *(वि.)* पवित्र, शुद्ध, सुथरा।

पाकर *(संज्ञा पु.)* एक वृक्ष जो पंच वटों से माना जाता हे, रामअंजीर, पाखर, जंगली पिपली, एक फल।

पाकरिपु *(संज्ञा पु.)* इंद्र।

पाछना *(क्रि. स.)* चाकू से चीरना।

पाट *(संज्ञा पु.)* रेशम, सिंहासन, चौड़ाई, पीढा, शिला जैसे धोबी की।

पाटमय *(वि.)* रेशमी।

पाटल *(संज्ञा पु.)* पाढ़र का पेड, गुलाब। (वि.) गुलाबी रंग का।

पाथ *(संज्ञा पु.)* मार्ग, रास्ता, जल, पवन, भोजन, सूर्य, आकाश, वायु।

पाथोज *(संज्ञा पु.)* कमल।

पाथोद *(संज्ञा पु.)* जल युक्त मेघ, बादल।

पाथोध *(संज्ञा पु.)* मेघ, बादल।

पाथोधर *(संज्ञा पु.)* मेघ, बादल।

पाथोधि *(संज्ञा पु.)* सागर, समुद्र।

पाथ्य *(वि.)* आकाश में रहनेवाला, हवा में रहनेवाला, हृदयाकाश में रहनेवाला या बसनेवाला।

पादप *(संज्ञा पु.)* पेड़, वृक्ष। पादपतर=पेड़ के नीचे।

पायक *(संज्ञा पु.)* सेवक, अनुचर, पीने वाला।

पारावत *(संज्ञा पु.)* कबूतर, परेवा, पर्वत, बंदर।

पाषंड *(संज्ञा पु.)* माया, पाखंड।

पाहरु *(संज्ञा पु.)* पहरेदार।

पाहि *(क्रियापद)* बचाओ, रक्षा करो।

पाही *(अव्य.)* पाहिं। पास, निकट, समीप, ओर, तरफ, पास जाकर, संबोधन करके। किसी के प्रति।

पिऊष *(संज्ञा पु.)* पियूष, पीयूष, अमृत।.

पिरीत *(संज्ञा स्त्री.)* प्रीति, प्रार।

पिरीता *(वि.)* प्रारा।

पिसुन *(संज्ञा पु.)* चुगलखोर, पिशुन।

पिसुनता *(संज्ञा स्त्री.)* चुगलखोरी, पिशुनता।

पीन *(वि.)* मोटा, पुष्ट।

पीवर *(वि.)* मोटा, माँसल, स्थूल, तगड़ा, भारी।

पुट *(संज्ञा पु.)* दोना, कटोरा। जैसे श्रवणपुट= कान रूपी दोना, आच्छानद, ढाँकनेवाली वस्तु, जैसे रदपुट, नैत्रपुट, किसी वस्तु से तर करने या उसका हलका मेल करने के लिए डाला गया छींटा।

पुतोहू *(संज्ञा स्त्री.)* पुत्रवधू।

पुरंदर *(संज्ञा पु.)* पुर, नगर या घर को तोड़ने वाला, चोर, इंद्र, शिव अग्नि, विष्णु।

पुरइन *(संज्ञा पु.)* कमल का पत्ता, कमल।

पुरट *(संज्ञा पु.)* सोना, स्वर्ण, (संज्ञा स्त्री.) जरी।

पुरधारना *(क्रि. स.)* शहर में आना। पधारना।

पुरोडॉस *(संज्ञा पु.)* यज्ञ का अन्न, हवि।

पुहुमी *(संज्ञा स्त्री)* पृथ्वी।

पूग *(संज्ञा पु.)* समूह, कटहल, शहतूत का पेड़, सुपारी का वृक्ष या फल।

पूगफल *(संज्ञा पु.)* सुपाड़ी, सुपारी।

पूगसत *(वि.)* छूते हुए।

पूप *(संज्ञा पु.)* पुआ।

पेखन *(संज्ञा पु.)* देखने की क्रिया, प्रेक्षण, वह जो कुछ देखा जाए, दृश्य।

पेखना *(क्रि. स.)* देखना।

पेलना *(क्रि. स.)* कुछ कर्म करना, घुसेड़ना, अवज्ञा करना, जबरदस्ती करना।

पैरना *(क्रि. स.)* पानी के ऊपर हाथ पैर चलाना: तैरना। पैरा हुआ=निपुण, पारंगत।

पैहना *(क्रि. स.)* पाना।

पोच *(वि.)* तुच्छ, क्षुद्र, हीन, निर्बल।

पोचना *(क्रि. स.)* तुच्छता, क्षुद्रता, हीनता, निर्बलता का कर्म करना।

पोची *(संज्ञा स्त्री.)* हेठापन, नीचता, बुराई, ओछापन, निर्बलता।

पोत *(संज्ञा पु.)* किसी भी जीव या पशु-पक्षी का बच्चा, कपड़ा, जहाज, नौका।

पोसना *(क्रि. स.)* पालन-पोषण करना।

पोहना *(क्रि. स.)* पिरोना।

पौढ़ना *(क्रि. अ.)* लेटाना, सोना, झुलना।

पौढ़ाना *(क्रि. स.)* लेटाना, सुलाना, झुलना।

प्रक्रिया *(संज्ञा स्त्री.)* कार्य करने का तरीका, कार्य प्रणाली, विधि। प्रोसेस।

प्रगल्भ *(वि.)* चतुर, होशियार, प्रतिभाशाली, प्रत्युत्पन्नमति, हाजिरजावाब, तत्पर बुद्धिवाला। क्विक विट।

प्रघोर *(वि.)* भयंकर जोर से, अत्यंत घोर।

प्रचारना *(क्रि. स.)* सामने आकर लड़ने के लिए ललकारना, छेड़छाड़ करना।

प्रच्छन्न *(वि.)* लपेटा हुआ, ढका हुआ, छिपा हुआ, परिवेष्ठित।

प्रजंत *(अव्य.)* पर्यंत, पक, लौं। (संज्ञा पु.) परिधि, व्यास, सीमा, किनारा, पाश्व, बगल।

प्रजारना *(क्रि. स.)* अच्छी तरह जलाना।

प्रजासन *(संज्ञा पु.)* प्रजा+असन= प्रजा को खा डालने वाला या चूसने वाला।

प्रणत *(वि.)* नम्र, दीन, प्रणाम करता हुआ।

प्रणतपाल *(संज्ञा पु.)* दास या भक्तों का पालन करनेवाला।

प्रणतारित *(संज्ञा पु.)* प्रणतपाल, दास भक्तों का पालन करनेवाला, दीन रक्षक।

प्रति *(अव्य.)* एक उपसर्ग जो शब्दों के आरंभ में लगता है। मतलब: विरुद्ध, हरएक, जोड़ का, सामने का, सामने मुकाबले में, बदले में, समान, सदृश्य, ओर, तरफ।

प्रतिकार *(संज्ञा पु.)* बदला।

प्रतिकूल *(वि.)* विपरीत।

प्रतिक्रिया *(संज्ञा स्त्री.)* बदला, प्रतिकार, विरुद्ध अथवा विपरीत दिशा में होने वाली क्रिया अथवा गति। रिएक्शन।

प्रतिध्वनि *(संज्ञा स्त्री.)* वह ध्वनि जो (उत्पन्न होने पर) किसी बाधक वस्तु से टकराने के कारण अपने प्रारंभिक स्थान पर फिर से सुनाई पड़े। ECKO।

प्रतिपच्छ *(संज्ञा पु.)* प्रतिपक्ष। विपक्षी, विरोधी पक्ष, बैरी, शत्रु, समानता, बराबरी।

प्रतिपच्छिन्न *(संज्ञा पु.)* शत्रुता।

प्रतिपाद्य *(वि.)* समझाने योग्य, निरूपण करने योग्य।

प्रतिपालक *(संज्ञा पु.)* रक्षा करनेवाला।

प्रतिप्रभा *(संज्ञा स्त्री.)* परछाई, प्रतिबिंब।

प्रतिबोधक *(संज्ञा पु.)* जगाने वाला (ज्ञान), शिक्षा देनेवाला, तिरस्कार करनेवाला।

प्रतिभट *(संज्ञा पु.)* अपनी जोड़ी का योद्धा।

प्रतीति *(संज्ञा स्त्री.)* विश्वास, दृढ़ निश्चय, ख्याति, आनंद, आदर।

प्रत्युत्पन्न *(वि.)* जो फिर से उत्पन्न हो, जो ठीक समय पर उत्पन्न हुआ हो।

प्रत्युपकार *(संज्ञा पु.)* प्रति+उपकार। उपकार के बदले में किया गया उपकार। Requital of Obligation।

प्रत्यूष *(संज्ञा पु.)* प्रभात, सूर्य।

प्रत्यूक *(संज्ञा पु.)* प्रत्यूह। विघ्न, बाधा, रोक।

प्रद *(संज्ञा पु.)* प्रदाता। देने वाला।

प्रदोष *(संज्ञा स्त्री.)* संध्या।

प्रनत *(संज्ञा पु.)* प्र–नत। प्रणत। शरणागत।

प्रनतारित *(संज्ञा पु.)* प्रणतारित। शरणागत की लाज रखनेवाला।

प्रपंचु *(संज्ञा पु.) प्रपंची, छली, कपटी, ढोंगी।*

प्रभंजन *(संज्ञा पु.)* प्रचंड वायु, आँधी, अत्यधिक तोड़–फोड़, टुकड़े–टुकड़े कर डालना।

प्रभंजन (*वि.*) अत्यधिक तोड़-फोड़ करनेवाला, टुकड़े-टुकड़े कर डालनेवाला।

प्रमद (*संज्ञा पु.*) मतवालापन, हर्ष, आनंद।

प्रमदक (*संज्ञा पु.*) नास्तिक।

प्रमदा (*संज्ञा स्त्री.*) सुंदर स्त्री।

प्रमाद (*संज्ञा स्त्री.*) कर्तव्य कर्म में त्रुटि, भ्रम, भ्रांति।

प्रमोद (*संज्ञा पु.*) हर्ष, आनंद, सुख।

प्रलंब (*वि.*) लंबा, नीचे की ओर दूर तक लटकता हुआ, शिथिल, सुस्त।

प्रलंब (*संज्ञा पु.*) लटकाव, झुकाव, शाखा, टहनी, गले में पड़ी फूल माला, स्त्री के कुच, स्तन। सस्पेंशन।

प्रलंबन (*संज्ञा पु.*) अवलंबन, सहारा लेना, लटकना।

प्रवान (*संज्ञा पु.*) प्रमाण। सबूत, सत्यता, निश्चय, मूलधन, प्रमाणपत्र।

प्रवान (*वि.*) सत्य, प्रमाणित, मान्य।

प्रसून (*संज्ञा पु.*) फूल, पुष्प, कली, फल।

प्रसून (*वि.*) उत्पन्न हुआ, पैदा हुआ।

प्रहर्ष (*संज्ञा पु.*) अत्यधिक हर्ष या आनंद।

प्रहर्षना (*क्रि. अ.*) अत्यधिक हर्षित या आनंदित होना।

प्राबिट (*संज्ञा स्त्री.*) प्राविट। पावस, वर्षा ऋतु।

प्रेमातुर (*वि.*) प्रेम-आतुर। प्रेम के लिए आतुर (व्यग्र, अधीर, उत्सुक या उद्विग्न)।

फ

फनि (*संज्ञा पु.*) सर्प, फणि।

फराक (*संज्ञा पु.*) मैदान।

फराक (*वि.*) लंबा-चौड़ा, विस्तृत, फराख।

फलचारी फुर (*वि.*) सत्य, सच्चा।

फुरिबानी (*संज्ञा पु.*) सच्ची बात।

ब

बंका (वि.) बाँका, तिरछी, टेढ़ा, पराक्रमी, बलशाली।

बंगा (वि.) उद्‌दंड, टेढ़ा, मूर्ख।

बंचना (क्रि. स.) ठगना, छलना, पढ़ना।

बंचना (संज्ञा स्त्री.) ठगी, ठगाई, धूर्तता।

बंचनता (संज्ञा स्त्री.) ठगी, ठगाई, छल। पर बंचनताति= पर+बंचनता+अति= दूसरों को+ठगना+बहुत।

बंदिगन (संज्ञा पु.) वंदिगण, वंदना करने वाले, भाटगण।

बंध्या (संज्ञा स्त्री.) बाँझ।

बंसी (संज्ञा स्त्री.) बाँसुरी, मुरली, मछली पकड़ने का औजार। बंसी खेलना= मछली पकड़ना।

बगध्यानी (वि.) बकध्यानी। बगुला भगत।

बगमेल (क्रि वि.) पंक्तिबद्ध, बाग मिलाये हुए, साथ-साथ।

बगमेल (संज्ञा पु.) बराबरी, समानता, बराबर-बराबर चलना।

बगरना (क्रि अ.) फैलना, बिखरना, छितरना।

बज्र (संज्ञा पु.) *इंद्र का अस्त्र, हीरा, बिजली, भाला, अभ्रक, धात्री।*

बटु (संज्ञा पु.) ब्राह्मण।

बड़भागी (वि.) भाग्यशाली।

बतकही (संज्ञा स्त्री.) बातचीत, गप-शप, मन बहलाव के लिए बातचीत।

बतास (संज्ञा स्त्री.) वायु, हवा, वातरोग, गठिया।

बधिर (वि.) बहरा।

बधूटी (संज्ञा स्त्री.) पुत्रवधू, सुहागिनी स्त्री, नई आई हुई बहू।

बनज (संज्ञा पु.) कमल, वाणिज्य, व्यापार।

बनजात (संज्ञा पु.) कमल। बनजाता।

बनमाला (संज्ञा स्त्री.) वनमाला, तुलसी, कुंद, मदार, परजाता व कमल इन पाँच वस्तुओं की बनी माला।

बनिता (संज्ञा स्त्री.) स्त्री, औरत, पत्नी।

बपु (संज्ञा पु.) शरीर, देह, अवतार, रूप।

बपुरा (वि.) बपुर बेचारा, अशक्त, अनाथ, गरीब।

बपुष (*संज्ञा पु.*) वपुष। शरीर, देह।

बमन (*संज्ञा पु.*) मुँह से उगलना, कै-करना, आहुति, पीड़ा।

बयनी (*संज्ञा स्त्री.*) बोलने वाली।

बयार (*संज्ञा स्त्री.*) हवा, गरम हवा।

बर (*संज्ञा पु.*) बरगद, रेखा, लकीर, जबरदस्ती (वि.) अच्छा, उत्तम, ठीक, उपयुक्त।

बरजन (*संज्ञा पु.*) रोकने या मना करने का भाव।

बरजना (*क्रि. अ.*) रोकना, मना करना।

बरतोरू (*संज्ञा पु.*) बलतोड़, फोड़ा।

बरना (*क्रि. स.*) वर या वधू के रूप में वरण करना, चुनना, नियुक्त करना।

बरना (*क्रि. स.*) वारना। मना करना, रोकना।

बरना (*क्रि. अ.*) जलना।

बरना (*अव्य.*) अन्यथा, नहीं तो, वरना।

बरिआना (*क्रि. स.*) जबरदस्ती करना। बरियाना।

बरिआर (*वि.*) बलवान, मजबूत।

बरिबंड (*वि.*) बरबंड। प्रचंड बली।

बरिया (*वि.*) बलवान, शक्तिशाली।

बरियाई (*क्रि. वि.*) जबरदस्ती, बरिआई।

बरियाई (*संज्ञा स्त्री.*) बलवान होने का भाव, बलशालिता, बलप्रयोग, जबरदस्ती।

बरु (*अव्य.*) भले ही परवा नहीं, बल्कि, मगर।

बरुथ (*संज्ञा पु.*) वरुथ, समूह, झुंड।

बर्बर (*संज्ञा पु.*) असभ्य या जंगली व्यक्ति, घुँघराले बाल, जंगली, अशिष्ट।

बलकना (*क्रि. अ.*) आपे से बाहर होना, उबलना, खोलना, आवेश में आना।

बलाहक (*संज्ञा पु.*) बादल, मेघ, बगुला, सारस।

बलि (*संज्ञा पु.*) देवता पर चढ़ाया गया खाद्य पदार्थ, उपहार, भेंट। चँवर का दंड।

बलि (*संज्ञा पु.*) भोग।

बस (*वि.*) पर्याप्त, भरपूर, प्रयोजन के लिए पूरा।

बस (*संज्ञा पु.*) बल, शक्ति, काबू, वश। (अव्य.) ठहरो, रुको।

बसकरी (*संज्ञा स्त्री.*) वशकरी। वश में करने वाली स्त्री।

बसबर्ती *(वि.)* अधीन, बसका।

बसीठ *(संज्ञा पु.)* दूत, संदेसा ले जाने का काम करनेवाला।

बसीठना *(क्रि. अ.)* दूत का काम करना।

बसीठी *(संज्ञा स्त्री.)* दूत का काम, दौत्य।

बहँगा *(संज्ञा पु.)* बड़ी काँवर, बड़ी बहँगी।

बहँगी *(संज्ञा स्त्री.)* काँवर।

बहोरि *(अव्य.)* बार-बार, फिर, पुनः।

बहोरी *(वि.)* बहुत प्रकार से।

बहुरना *(क्रि. स.)* बहोरना। लोटना, वापस आना।

बाँकुरा *(वि.)* बाँका, टेढा, पैना, चतुर, कुशल।

बाऊ *(संज्ञा पु.)* वायु, हवा, पवन।

बाग *(संज्ञा पु.)* उद्यान, वाटिका। (संज्ञा स्त्री.) लगाम।

बाग *(संज्ञा पु.)* वाक। वाणी, वाक्य, सरस्वती, बोलने की इंद्रिय, कथन।

बागीचा *(संज्ञा पु.)* (वागीचा) वाणी। छोटा बगीचा, वाटिका।

बागीसा *(संज्ञा स्त्री.)* सरस्वती। (संज्ञा पु.) वाक+ईश= वागीश= वाणी के पति, ब्रह्मा, बृहस्पति, अच्छा बोलने वाला, कवि।

बागुर *(संज्ञा पु.)* फंदा, मृग या पक्षी फँसाने का जाल।

बाचाल *(वि.)* बकवादी, बोलने मे तेज, बहुत बोलने वाला।

बाजनिआ *(संज्ञा पु.)* बाजेवाले।

बाज *(संज्ञा पु.)* बाजा, घोड़ा। बाजिमेध= बाजमेध= अश्वमेध।

बाट *(संज्ञा पु.)* रास्ता, पथ। बाटपारना (क्रि.स.) डाका डालना।

बात *(संज्ञा पु.)* बात, हवा।

बात *(संज्ञा स्त्री.)* सार्थक शब्द या वाक्य, वाणी, बोल, वचन, कथन।

बादना *(क्रि. अ.)* विवाद करना, बकवास करना।

बादि *(संज्ञा पु.)* बेकार, व्यर्थ, फिजूल, निष्प्रयोजन।

बाधा *(संज्ञा स्त्री.)* भय, रुकावट, अड़चन, विघ्न, संकट, कष्ट, दुःख।

बाना *(संज्ञा. पु.)* स्वभाव, रीति, चाल, भेस, पहनावा, वस्त्र, पोशाक, वेश-विन्यास, बुनावट, बुनाई।

बाना *(क्रि.स.)* फैलाना, सिकोड़ना। जैसे: मुँहबाना।

बानैत *(संज्ञा पु.)* भेश (भेस) या बाना धारण करनेवाला, योद्धा या सैनिक।

बापिका *(संज्ञा स्त्री.)* बावड़ी।

बापुरा *(वि.)* बेचारा, दीनहीन, गरीब, तुच्छ; जिसकी कोई गिनती न हो।
बाबूड़ा *(संज्ञा पु.)* हास्यप्रद बाबू।
बाम *(वि.)* टेढ़ा।
बायस *(संज्ञा पु.)* कौआ। बायस तन= कौए जैसा मुंह।
बार *(संज्ञा स्त्री.)* काल, समय, विलंब, देर, बाढ़, किनारा, धार, मरतबा, दफा, बेर,
बार *(संज्ञा पु.)* द्वार, आश्रय, घर।
बारक *(क्रि. वि.)* एक बार।
बारा *(वि.)* बाला, बालक उम्र का।
बारि *(संज्ञा स्त्री.)* वारि। जल, पानी, वर्षा।
बारिज *(संज्ञा पु.)* वारिज। कमल।
बारिधि *(संज्ञा पु.)* समुद्र।
बारीस *(संज्ञा पु.)* समुद्र।
बास *(संज्ञा पु.)* डेरा, निवास स्थान।
बासर *(संज्ञा पु.)* दिन, समय।
बाहिज *(क्रि. वि.)* ऊपर से, बाहर से।
बिंदक *(वि.)* ज्ञाता, जाननेवाला, पाने या प्राप्त करनेवाला।
बिकटानन *(वि.)* विकटानन= विकट+आनन। विकट भयंकर मुँह वाला।
बिखंडन *(वि.)* नाश करनेवाला।
बिगत *(संज्ञा पु.)* विगत। बीता हुआ, व्यतीत, ब्योरा, विवरण।
बिगसत *(वि.)* विकसत, विकसित, जिसका विकास हो चुका हो, खिला।
बिगोना *(क्रि. स.)* नष्ट करना, बिगाड़ना, दुर्दशा करना, तंग करना, बिताना।
बिचच्छन *(वि.)* विचक्षण। चमकता हुआ, जो स्पष्ट दिखाई दे, निपुण, चतुर, ज्ञाता, भारी विद्वान्।
बिटप *(संज्ञा पु.)* विटप, वृक्ष।
बिड़ई *(संज्ञा स्त्री.)* गेंडुरी, कुंडली, गोल चक्कर।
बिडारना *(क्रि. स.)* तितर-बितर करना।
बितान *(संज्ञा पु.)* मंडप।
बिद्रुम *(संज्ञा पु.)* मूंगा।
बिधि *(संज्ञा पु.)* ब्रह्मा, भाग्य, विष्णु, अग्नि।
बिधु *(संज्ञा पु.)* चंद्रमा, वायु, कपूर, विष्णु, आयुध।

बिनसाना *(क्रि. स.)* नष्ट या चौपट करना, नष्ट या चौपट होना, फटना (जैसे दूध का)

बिपिन *(संज्ञा पु.)* विपिन। वन, वाटिका, उपवन, जंगल।

बिबर *(संज्ञा पु.)* विवर, विविर। खोह, गुफा, कंदरा, बिल, दरार।

बिबर्धन *(संज्ञा पु.)* विवर्धन=विवर्द्धन। बढ़ाने या वृद्धि करने की क्रिया। वृद्धि, बढ़ती, उन्नति, विभाजन, विखंडन।

बिबरना *(क्रि. अ.)* बिवरना। सुलझना।

बिबराना *(क्रि. स.)* बिवराना। बालों को खुलवाकर सुलझाना, बाल सुलझाना।

बिबुध *(संज्ञा पु.)* देवता।

बिबुधतरु *(संज्ञा पु.)* कल्प वृक्ष।

बिमात्र *(वि.)* सौतेला या सौतेली।

बिरंच *(संज्ञा पु.)* बिरंचि। ब्रह्मा।

बिरचना *(क्रि. स.)* रचना, बनाना।

बिरंज *(संज्ञा पु.)* चावल, भात।

बिरति *(संज्ञा स्त्री.)* विरत्ति। वैराग्य।

बिरथ *(वि.)* बिना रथ या वाहन के।

बिरद *(संज्ञा पु.)* बड़ाई, यश।

बिरदु *(संज्ञा पु.)* बिरद।

बिरदैत *(संज्ञा पु.)* प्रसिद्ध वीर या योद्धा। (वि.) नामी, प्रसिद्ध।

बिरवा *(संज्ञा पु.)* वृक्ष, पौधा।

बिरिदि *(संज्ञा स्त्री.)* विरिदावली, प्रशंसा के गीत, यश या कीर्ति की गाथा।

बिरुज *(वि.)* बिना रोग का, रोग हीन, निरोग।

बिलसना *(क्रि. अ.)* शोभा देना, बहुत भला जान पड़ना। (क्रि.स.) भोगना, विलास करना।

बिलाई *(संज्ञा स्त्री.)* बिल्ली, किवाड़ बंद करने की सिटकनी, कुएँ से रस्सी या सामान निकालने का काँटा।

बिलाना *(क्रि. अ.)* विलायन। नष्ट होना, अदृष्य होना, गायब होना।

बिलास *(संज्ञा पु.)* विलास। प्रसन्न या प्रफुल्लित करने की क्रिया, सुखभोग, आनंद, हर्ष, हाव-भाव, नाज-नखरा, किसी चीज का हिलना-डुलना। भुकुटिबिलास= भौंहों के इशारे।

बिलोकनि *(संज्ञा स्त्री.)* दृष्टि, निगाह, चितवन, देखने की क्रिया या भाव।

बिषम माया *(संज्ञा स्त्री.)* विषम माया। दुस्तर माया।

बिसद *(वि.)* विशद। स्वच्छ, साफ, उज्ज्वल।

बिसमउ *(संज्ञा पु.)* विस्मय, बिसमय, आश्चर्य, ताज्जुब, विषमय, गर्व, संदेह।

बिसमरना *(संज्ञा पु.)* भूलना।

बिसिख *(संज्ञा पु.)* बाण।

बिसूरना *(क्रि. अ.)* मन में विलाप करना, दुख मनाना।

बिसेष *(वि.)* विशेष। विस्तार, अधिक, प्रचुर, असाधारण, असामान्य।

बिसेष *(संज्ञा पु.)* विशेष। भेद, अंतर, फरक, प्रकार, तरह, नियम, कायदा, व्यक्ति, सार, निचोड़।

बिसोक *(वि.)* शोक रहित।

बिस्वेस *(संज्ञा पु.)* विष्वनाथ, बिसेस्वर।

बिहंगपति *(संज्ञा पु.)* गरुड़।

बिहँसना *(क्रि. अ.)* मंद-मंद मुसकाना।

बिहगेस *(संज्ञा पु.)* बिहग-ईस= पक्षीराज, गरुड़।

बिहरना *(क्रि. अ.)* टहलना, घूमना-फिरना।

बिहरना *(क्रि. स.)* फटना, विदीर्ण होना, बात टाल देना।

बिहान *(संज्ञा पु.)* प्रभात, सुबह, भोर।

बिहाना *(क्रि. स.)* छोड़ना, त्यागना। (क्रि.अ.) गुजरना, बीतना, व्यतीत होना।

बिहाल *(वि.)* बेहाल। जिसकी दशा अच्छी न हो, व्याकुल, विकल।

बीचि *(संज्ञा स्त्री.)* लहर, विचि, तरंग। अंदर में दरमियान।

बीचु *(संज्ञा पु.)* मौका, अवसर, अंतर, फरक। बीचु पाइ=मौका पाकर

बीणा *(संज्ञा स्त्री.)* वीणा।

बीथ *(संज्ञा स्त्री.)* बीथि, वीथि। गली, मार्ग, आकाश मार्ग। आकाश में नक्षत्रों के रहने का स्थान।

बीथी *(संज्ञा स्त्री.)* गली, मार्ग, आकाश मार्ग। वीथि।

बुझाना *(क्रि. स.)* समझाना, बोध कराना, अग्नि या आग शांत करना, मन के आवेग को शांत

बुताना *(क्रि. अ.)* बुझना; (क्रि.स.) बुझाना।

बूड़ना *(क्रि. स.)* डुबना, निमज्जित होना, गर्क होना।

बृंद *(संज्ञा पु.)* वृंदे। झुंड, राशि, ढेर।

बृक *(संज्ञा पु.)* भेड़िया, गीदड़, कौआ, क्षत्रिय, चोर, लुटेरा।

बृषल	*(संज्ञा पु.)* वृषल। वह जिसे धर्म आदि का कुछ भी ज्ञान न हो, पाप और दुष्कर्म करनेवाला, शूद्र।
वृषली	*(संज्ञा स्त्री.)* वृषली। नीच जाति की व्यभचारिणी स्त्री, अविवाहित रजस्वला कन्या।
बेचक	*(संज्ञा पु.)* बेचने वाला।
बेड़ा	*(संज्ञा पु.)* (नाव की तरह) नदी पार करने के लिये बनाया गया लट्ठों का ढाँचा, जहाज।
बेरे	*(संज्ञा पु.)* बेड़े। जहाज, पोत। बेरा या बेड़ा का बहुवचन।
बेतस	*(संज्ञा पु.)* वेतस। बेंत, जलबेंत, समुद्र के भीतर की आग या ताप, बड़वाग्नि, बड़वानल।
बेदबिदूशक	*(संज्ञा पु.)* वेदों की निंदा करनेवाला या मजाक उड़ाने वाला।
बेनु	*(संज्ञा पु.)* बाँस, मुरली, बंशी। बेनु मूल= बाँस की जड़।
बेर	*(संज्ञा पु.)* देर, विलंब, एक झाड़ी का फल। (संज्ञा स्त्री.) बार (संख्या)।
बेसर	*(संज्ञा पु.)* खच्चर।
बेसाहना	*(क्रि. स.)* खरीदना, जानबूझ कर अपने सर लेना (बैर, विरोध, संकट या झंझट आदि)।
बैखानस	*(संज्ञा पु.)* वह जो वानप्रस्थ आश्रम में हो।
बैन	*(संज्ञा पु.)* वचन, बात।
बैनतेय	*(संज्ञा पु.)* गरुड़।
बोरना	*(क्रि. स.)* जल या किसी पदार्थ में निमग्न कर देना, डुबोना, डुबाकर भिगोना, कलंकित करना।
बोहित	*(संज्ञा पु.)* जहाज, बड़ी नाव।
ब्यजन	*(संज्ञा पु.)* पंखा।
ब्यलीक	*(वि.)* झूठा, अप्रिय, कष्टदायक, अपरिचित, डाँट-डपट, फटकार, विलक्षण, छल-कपट।
ब्याज	*(संज्ञा पु.)* वृद्धि, सूद, व्याज का अपभ्रंश, बहाना, छल, मिस, बाधा, विघ्न, विलंब।
ब्याज-निंदा	*(संज्ञा पु.)* व्याज-निंदा, निंदा, जो निंदा न जान पड़े।
ब्याज-स्तुति	*(संज्ञा पु.)* ब्याज-स्तुति, स्तुति जो स्तुति न जान पड़े।
ब्याप्त	*(वि.)* पूरित, भरा हुआ, फैला हुआ, व्याप्त, सर्वरूप।

ब्यालारि (*संज्ञा पु.*) साँप का शत्रु, गरुड़।

ब्यास (*संज्ञा पु.*) फैलाव, विस्तार।

ब्यास-समास (*संज्ञा पु.*) घटाना-बढ़ाना, काट-छाँट।

ब्रन (*संज्ञा पु.*) घाव, फोड़ा।

ब्रात (*वि.*) व्रात्य, वृत संबंधी। (संज्ञा पु.) वह जिसके दस संस्कार न हुए हो, संस्साकरहीन, वह जिसका उपनयन न हुआ हो, वर्णसंकर, दोगला।

ब्राता (*संज्ञा पु.*) व्रात। वह परिश्रम जो जीविका के लिये किया जाए, दल, समूह, मनुष्य, बराती, दैनिक मजदूरी, यदा-कदा कार्य में नियुक्ति।

ब्रीड़ा (*संज्ञा स्त्री.*) लज्जा।

ब्रीड़ना (*क्रि. अ.*) लजाना, लज्जित होना।

भ

भगवान् (*वि.*) धन संपति या ऐश्वर्य वाला, पूज्य। (संज्ञा पु.) पूज्य और आदरणीय व्यक्ति, ईश्वर।

भजना (*क्रि. अ.*) भजन करना, सेवन करना।

भटभेरना (*क्रि. स.*) ठुकरा देना।

भटमानी (*वि.*) वीरता के अभिमान वाले।

भड़िहाई (*संज्ञा स्त्री.*) चोरी, तस्करी।

भड़िहाई (*क्रि. वि.*) सूना देख कुत्ते का बरतन-भाड़ों में मुँह डालना, चोरों की तरह छुपकर।

भनक (*संज्ञा स्त्री.*) धीमा शब्द, ध्वनि, उड़ती हुई खबर।

भनना (*क्रि. स.*) कहना, बोलना। भणना।

भयाकुल (*वि.*) भय+आकुल= भय से व्याकुल, दुखी, व्यग्र या व्यथित।

भवंत (*वि.*) भवत् का बहुवचन, आपका, आप लोगों का।

भव (*संज्ञा पु.*) संसार, शिव, जन्म, उत्पत्ति, मेघ, बादल, कारण, हेतु, कामदेव।

भवखेद (*संज्ञा पु.*) जन्म मरण का श्रम।

भवत् (*संज्ञा पु.*) भूमि, जमीन, विष्णु। (वि.) मान्य, पूज्य।

भवमोचन (*वि.*) संसार के बंधनों से छुड़ाने वाले, भगवान्।

भवाना *(क्रि. स.)* घुमाना, चक्कर देना (जैसे भौंरे को)।

भाऊ *(संज्ञा पु.)* भावना, प्रेम भाव।

भाजन *(संज्ञा स्त्री.)* बड़ाई, आधार, पात्र, जैसे किसी का प्रेमभाजन होना, बरतन।

भाजनता *(संज्ञा स्त्री.)* योग्यता, पात्रता।

भाथा *(संज्ञा पु.)* तूणीर, तरकस।

भानना *(क्रि. स.)* तोड़ना, भंग करना।

भानना *(क्रि. स.)* समझना, प्रतीति होना, अनुमान करना, जानना, आभास होना

भानस *(संज्ञा पु.)* भोजन बंनानेवाला, रसोइया।

भामिनि *(संज्ञा स्त्री.)* क्रोध करनेवाली स्त्री, स्त्री, औरत।

भारती *(संज्ञा स्त्री.)* वचन, वाणी, सरस्वती।

भायप *(संज्ञा पु.)* भाईचारा।

भिंदिपाल *(संज्ञा पु.)* भिंडपाल, एक प्रकार का डंडा (अस्त्र), जो फेंक कर मारा जाता है।

भिनुसार *(संज्ञा पु.)* प्रात:काल, सुबह।

भिन्नसेतु *(वि.)* जिसने मर्यादा, व्यवस्था, नियम या प्रतिबंध तोड़ दिए हों।

भीर्ति *(संज्ञा पु.)* भय, डर, खौफ। सभीत=सभीति=भयभीत हुआ।

भीर *(संज्ञा स्त्री.)* भीड़।

भुजंग *(संज्ञा पु.)* साँप, सर्प

भुज *(संज्ञा पु.)* भुजा। दच्छिन भुजा= दाईं भुजा।

भुआल *(संज्ञा पु.)* राजा।

भूत *(संज्ञा पु.)* प्राणी, चर-अचर, वे मूल द्रव्य जिनकी सहायता से सृष्टि रचना हुई है सत्य, वृत, कार्तिकेय, कृष्णपक्ष, योगींद्र, मृत प्राणी। भूत-दया= चर-अचर पर दया।

भूधर *(संज्ञा पु.)* पहाड़, शेषनाग, राजा, विष्णु।

भूपाल *(संज्ञा पु.)* राजा।

भूमिनाग *(संज्ञा पु.)* केंचुआ।

भूरि *(वि.)* अधिक, प्रचुर, बड़ा भारी। (संज्ञा पु.) ब्रह्मा, विष्णु, स्वर्ण, इंद्र।

भूरिभाग *(वि.)* भाग्यशाली।

भूर्ज *(संज्ञा पु.)* भोज का पेड़।

भूसुर *(संज्ञा पु.)* ब्राह्मण।

भेक *(संज्ञा पु.)* मेढक।

भेद *(संज्ञा पु.)* रहस्य, मर्म, तात्पर्य, अंतर, फर्क, भेदन, दुराव, छिपाव, सुर–ताल का अंतर। जाति। गत–भेद=भेद शून्य, भेद–भक्ति=मार्मिक भक्ति। भेदबुद्धि=एकता का अभाव।

भेषज *(संज्ञा पु.)* दवा, औषधि, विष्णु, जल, सुख।

भेषना *(क्रि. स.)* भेसना। भेष बनाना।

भोराना *(क्रि. स.)* भ्रम में डालना, धोखे में डालना, धोखा देना।

भोराना *(क्रि. अ.)* भ्रम में आना, धोखे में आना।

भौंराना *(क्रि.स.)* घूमना, चक्कर खाना।

भौंराना *(क्रि. अ.)* घुमाना, चक्कर दिलाना, विवाह के फेरे दिलाना।

भ्रकुटि *(संज्ञा स्त्री.)* भ्रकुटि। भौंह, भ्रकुटि विलास=भौंहों के इशारे।

भ्राजना *(क्रि. अ.)* सुशोभित होना।

भ्रूविलास *(क्रि. वि.)* भ्रकुटि के इशारे पर।

म

मंगन *(संज्ञा पु.)* भिखारी, माँगनेवाला। (संज्ञा स्त्री.) शुभ निर्माण, शुभ कृत्य।

मंजीर *(संज्ञा पु.)* नुपूर, घुंघरू, पाजेब।

मंडन *(संज्ञा पु.)* सजाना, प्रमाण द्वारा सिद्ध करना, भरना, भूषण।

मंडना *(क्रि. स.)* सजाना, प्रमाण द्वारा, सिद्ध करना, दलित करना।

मंडल *(संज्ञा पु.)* परिधि, घेरा, गोलाई, विस्तार, वृत, घेरा, समूह, समाज, समुदाय, जैसे मित्रमंडल।

मंद *(वि.)* धीमा, सुस्त, आलसी, मूर्ख, खल, दुष्ट।

मंद *(संज्ञा पु.)* शनि, यम, अभाग्य।

मंदिर *(संज्ञा पु.)* घर, देवालय, नगर, शिविर।

मंदिरा *(संज्ञा पु.)* अश्वशाला।

मंदिरपशु *(संज्ञा स्त्री.)* बिल्ली।

मकर *(संज्ञा पु.)* मगर, मछली।

मख *(संज्ञा पु.)* यज्ञ।

मज्जा *(संज्ञा पु.)* हड्डी के अंदर का गूदा।

मत्सर *(संज्ञा पु.)* डाह।

मदार *(संज्ञा पु.)* आक का पौधा, हाथी, धूर्त, सूअर।

मदार *(संज्ञा पु.)* धूरी, कीली, आधार। दार-मदार=संबल।

मधुकर *(संज्ञा पु.)* भ्रमर, कामी पुरुष।

मनजात *(संज्ञा पु.)* कामदेव।

मनसंभव *(वि.)* मन से उत्पन्न।

मनसा *(संज्ञा स्त्री.) कामना, इच्छा, संकल्प, अध्यवसाय, इरादा, अभिलाषा, मनोरथ, मन, बुद्धि, अभिप्राय, तात्पर्य।*

मनसा *(वि.)* मन से उत्पन्न, मन का।

मनसिज *(संज्ञा पु.)* कामदेव।

मनामयम *(वि.)* निर्विकार।

मनिआरा *(वि.)* मणि जड़ित।

मनुजाद *(संज्ञा पु.)* राक्षस, (वि.) मनुष्य को खाने वाला, नरभक्षक, मनुजादा।

मनुसाई *(संज्ञा स्त्री.)* मनुषाई, मनुष्यता, पुरुषार्थ, बहादुरी।

मनोगुप्ति *(संज्ञा स्त्री.)* मन को अशुभ प्रवृत्तियों से हटाने का भाव या क्रिया।

मनोज्ञा *(संज्ञा पु.)* कलौंजी, मदिरा, राजपुत्री।

मनोदंड *(संज्ञा पु.)* मन का निग्रह, चित्त का एकाग्र करना।

मनोरथ *(संज्ञा पु.)* इच्छा, अभिलाषा।

मनोव्यापार *(संज्ञा पु.)* मन की क्रिया, संकल्प-विकल्प, विचार।

ममताहन *(वि.)* ममता का हनन करनेवाला, ममता को मारने वाला।

मयूख *(संज्ञा पु.)* किरण चंद्रमा की, रश्मि, शोभा, प्रकाश।

मरकत *(संज्ञा पु.)* एक प्रकार का फूल, पन्ना।

मराल *(संज्ञा पु.)* हंस।

मर्दन *(संज्ञा पु.)* कुचलना, मसलना, रौंदना, नाश करना, शरीर में मालिश करना।

मर्दना *(क्रि. स.)* मर्दन करना, मसलना, कुचलना, मार डालना, नष्ट करना।

मर्मवचन *(संज्ञा पु.)* चुभनेवाली बात।

मलाकर *(संज्ञा पु.)* पाप की खान।

मलायतन	*(संज्ञा पु.)* पापों का घर।
मलिन	*(वि.)* मैला, गंदा, दूषित, बदरंग, फीका, म्लान।
मष्ट	*(संज्ञा पु.)* संस्कारशून्य, उदासीन, मौन, चुप।
मष्ट करना	*(क्रि. स.)* चुप करना। मष्ट मारना या मष्ट धारना= मौन धारण करना।
मसक	*(संज्ञा पु.)* मच्छर, डाँस।
महागद	*(संज्ञा पु.)* विशेष औषध, महा+कद=महारोग, कठिन रोग।
महानल	*(संज्ञा स्त्री.)* प्रचंड अग्नि।
महिष	*(संज्ञा पु.)* भैंसा।
महिषि	*(संज्ञा स्त्री.)* महिषी। भैस, रानी या पटरानी, व्यभचारिणी स्त्री।
माँजा	*(संज्ञा पु.)* पहली वर्षा का फेन जो मछलियों के लिये मादक होता है।
माँझ	*(अव्य.)* अंदर, भीतर, में, बीच।
माख	*(संज्ञा स्त्री)* अप्रसन्नता, नाराजगी, घमंड, अपने दोष को ढकना, पछतावा।
माखना	*(क्रि. अ.)* अप्रसन्न या नाराज होना, तमतमाना।
मातहि	*(संज्ञा पु.)* मातुल, मामा, धतूरा।
मानस	*(संज्ञा पु.)* मन, हृदय, मानसरोवर, कामदेव, संकल्प विकल्प, दूत, चर, विष्णु का एक रूप, एक प्रकार का नमक।
मानस	*(वि.)* मन से उत्पन्न, मनोभव, मन का विचारा हुआ।
मानस	*(क्रि. वि.)* मन के द्वारा।
मानस	*(संज्ञा पु.)* मनुष्य, आदमी।
मानस	*(संज्ञा पु.)* दूसरों को मान देनेवाला।
मापना	*(क्रि.स.)* नापना, (क्रि.अ.) मतवाला होना, जैसे शराब पीकर।
मार	*(संज्ञा पु.)* कामदेव, विष, विघ्न। (संज्ञा स्त्री.) पीटने की क्रिया, आघात, लक्ष, निशाना, लड़ाई, माला। (अव्य.) अत्यंत, बहुत।
मारगन	*(संज्ञा पु.)* बाण, तीर, भिक्षुक, याचक, भिखमंगा।
मारादि	*(संज्ञा पु.)* मार+आदि= काम, क्रोध और लोभ।
मारुत	*(संज्ञा पु.)* पवन, हवा, वायु, देवता। मारुत ग्रासना= वातग्रस्त होना, भयभीत होना।
मार्मिक	*(वि.)* प्रभावशाली, मनुष्य के कोमल स्थानों को छूनेवाली।
मायाछन्न	*(वि.)* मायाच्छन्न। माया से ढका हुआ।

माहुर *(संज्ञा पु.)* विष, जहर।

मिति *(संज्ञा स्त्री.)* मान, परिमाण, माप-तोल, सीमा, हद, काल की अवधि।

मिथ्या *(वि.)* असत्स, झूठ, बेकार, व्यर्थ। यौगिक शब्द : मिथ्याकोप, मिथ्याग्रह, मिथ्याचार, मिथ्यात्व, मिथ्यादृष्य, मिथ्यादृष्टि, मिथ्यामति, मिथ्यायोग, मिथ्याहार, मिथ्योपचार, मिथ्योत्तर।

मिस *(संज्ञा पु.)* बहाने, हीला, पाखंड, आडंबर।

मीचु *(संज्ञा स्त्री.)* मृत्यु।

मुकुंद *(संज्ञा पु.)* मोक्षदाता, विष्णु, पारा, कुंदरु, सफेद कनार।

मुखर *(संज्ञा पु.)* कौआ, शंख।

मुखर *(वि.)* जो अप्रिय बोलता हो, कटुभाषी, अधिक बोलने वाला, बकवादी, प्रधान, अगण्य।

मुखागर *(संज्ञा पु.)* मुखाग्र। ओंठ। किसी वस्तु का अग्र भाग। (वि.) कंठस्थ, जो जबानी याद हो।

मुखाग्नि *(संज्ञा स्त्री.)* दावानल, मृत व्यक्ति को चिता पर रखकर पहले उसके मुँह में आग लगाने की क्रिया।

मुठिका *(संज्ञा स्त्री.)* मुट्ठी, मुक्का।

मुद *(संज्ञा पु.)* हर्ष, आनंद।

मुदा *(अव्य.)* तात्पर्य यह है कि; मगर, लेकिन, परंतु।

मुदित *(वि.)* प्रसन्न, खुश।

मुधा *(क्रि. वि.)* व्यर्थ, बेफायदा। (वि.) व्यर्थ, निष्प्रयोजन। (संज्ञा पु.) मिथ्या, झूठ।

मुराना *(क्रि. स.)* चुभलाना, चबाना, मोड़ना।

मूरि *(संज्ञा स्त्री.)* जड़, जड़ी-बूटी, मूल, वनस्पति।

मृगया *(संज्ञा पु.)* शिकार, आखेट।

मृग्य *(संज्ञा पु.)* गीदड़, शिकार, ब्रह्मा।

मृतक *(संज्ञा पु.)* मरा हुआ।

मृतकधूम *(संज्ञा पु.)* राख, भस्म।

मृषा *(अव्य.)* झुठ-मूठ, व्यर्थ।

मृषा *(वि.)* मिथ्या, झूठ।

मेखला *(संज्ञा पु.)* करधनी, वह कपड़ा जो साधू लोग गले में डाले रहते हैं, कमर में तलवार बाँधनेवाली पेटी।

मेघडंबर (*संज्ञा पु.*) बादल की गरजन, बड़ा शामियाना।

मेचक (*संज्ञा पु.*) अंधकार, अँधेरा। श्यामल, काला।

मेचकताई (*संज्ञा स्त्री.*) कालापन।

मेलना (*क्रि. स.*) भेजना, डालना, कर लेना।

मेलना (*क्रि. अ.*) इकट्ठा होना, एकत्र होना, जुटना।

मोचन (*संज्ञा पु.*) बंधन आदि खोलकर मुक्त करना, दूर करना, हटाना, छीन लेना।

मोचना (*क्रि. स.*) छोड़ना, गिराना, बहाना, छुड़ाना, मुक्त करना।

मौलि (*संज्ञा पु.*) सिर, चोटी, सिरा, किरीट, जूड़ा, सरदार, भूमि। मौलिमणि= शिरोमणि।

य

यूथ (*संज्ञा पु.*) समूह, झुंड, टोलियाँ, सेना, फौज।

योगिनि (*संज्ञा पु.*) रण पिशाचिनी, योग साधन करनेवाली तपस्विनी, योगमाया।

र

रंगभूमि (*संज्ञा पु.*) उत्सव का स्थान, रण क्षेत्र, नाट्यशाला, अखाड़ा।

रजायस (*संज्ञा पु.*) आज्ञा

रतनार (*वि.*) लाल, सुर्खी लिये हुए लाल।

रद (*संज्ञा पु.*) दाँत

रवन (*संज्ञा पु.*) पति। जैसे सीतारवन= सीतापति, राम।

रवनि (*संज्ञा पु.*) स्त्री, पत्नी, भार्या, सुंदरी, रमणी।

रस (*संज्ञा पु.*) (मुँह का स्वाद) छः मधुर, अम्ल, लवण, कटु, तिक्त (तीखा), व कषाय। साहित्य के नौ रस।

रसना (*संज्ञा स्त्री.*) जीभ।

रसाल (*संज्ञा पु.*) रसल। आम, ऊख, गन्ना।

रहसना (*क्रि. अ.*) प्रसन्न होना, हँसना।

रहसि (*संज्ञा स्त्री.*) रहस्य, एकांत, गुप्त स्थान, लीला, क्रीड़ा।

राउर (*वि.*) आपका, श्रीमान का।

राका (*संज्ञा स्त्री.*) पूर्णिमा की रात, चंद्रमा, खुजली का रोग।

राकापति (*संज्ञा पु.*) चंद्रमा।

रिषय (*संज्ञा पु.*) ऋषि

रुंड (*संज्ञा पु.*) धड़।

रुख (*संज्ञा पु.*) कपोल, गाल, मुख, आकृति, चेष्टा, कृपादृष्टि।

रुचिरकर (*वि.*) सुंदर, मनोहर।

रुज (*संज्ञा पु.*) रोग। भूरि रुजा= भयंकर कष्ट। भंग, भाँग, वेदना, कष्ट

रुख (*संज्ञा पु.*) वृक्ष, पेड़, रुखा।

रेखा (*संज्ञा स्त्री.*) रुप, आकार, गणना, गिनती।

रेणु (*संज्ञा स्त्री.*) रज, धूल। रेनु, पृथ्वी।

रोपना (*क्रि. स.*) पैर जमाना, बीज रखना या बोना, कुछ लेने के लिये हाथ पसारना, हाथ रोपना।

रोम (*वि.*) देह का बाल, रोयाँ, ऊन।

रौरे (*सर्व.*) आप।

ल

लंगूर (*संज्ञा स्त्री.*) पूँछ। (संज्ञा पु.) बंदर।

लकुट (*संज्ञा स्त्री.*) लाठी, डंडा।

लग्न (*संज्ञा स्त्री.*) शुभ समय, शुभ घड़ी, अवसर, विवाह के दिन, सहालग।

लच्छा (*संज्ञा पु.*) लक्ष। लाख की संख्या।

लटना (*क्रि. अ.*) थककर गिर जाना, लड़खड़ाना, अशक्त होना, श्रम, रोग आदि से शिथिल होना, श्रम से निकम्मा होना, अधिक काम करने योग्य न रह जाना, ढीला पड़ना, व्याकुल होना।

लटना (*क्रि. अ.*) ललचाना, लेने के लिये लपकना, अनुरक्त होना, प्रेमपूर्वक तत्पर होना।

लबार (*वि.*) झूठ बोलनेवाला, गप्पी, प्रपंची।

ललन (*संज्ञा पु.*) बच्चा, बालक, प्यारा बालक, दुलारा लड़का, क्रीड़ा, केलि।

ललना (*संज्ञा स्त्री.*) स्त्री, कामिनी, जिव्हा, जीभ, विलासिनी या कामुक औरत, स्वैरिणी।

ललाम (*वि.*) रमणीय, सुंदर, बढ़िया, श्रेष्ठ, शिरोमणि। (नारी) ललामी।

ललामी (*संज्ञा स्त्री.*) सुदंरता, लालिमा, लाली, सुर्खी।

लव (*संज्ञा पु.*) बहुत छोटी मात्रा, काल का एक मान या माप।

लवलेश (*संज्ञा पु.*) अंश मात्र भी, अत्यंत अल्प मात्रा।

लवा (*संज्ञा स्त्री.*) बटेर, भुने हुए धान या ज्वारा की खील। पोपकोर्न।

लवाई (*संज्ञा स्त्री.*) हाल की ब्याई गाय, फसल कटाई की मजूरी।

लहना (*क्रि. स.*) *प्राप्त करना, पाना, काटना, छीलना।*

लहना (*संज्ञा पु.*) किसी को दिया हुआ धन, जो वसूल करना हो, उधार दिया हुआ पैसा।

लागना (*क्रि. अ.*) लगना। दो पदार्थों का तल आपस में मिलाना, जान पड़ना, अनुभव होना, मालूम होना, जैसे अच्छा लगना, मोह लगना।

लागना (*संज्ञा पु.*) लगना। वह किसी की टोह में लगा रहता हो, शिकार करनेवाला, अहेरी इत्यादि।

लाघव (*संज्ञा पु.*) लघुता, कमी, न्यूनता, हाथ की सफाई, तेजी, आरोग्यता, नपुसंकता।

लाघवी (*संज्ञा पु.*) फुरती, शीघ्रता।

लाटी (*संज्ञा स्त्री.*) अवस्था जिसमें मुँह का थूक सूख जाता है।

लाधना (*क्रि. स.*) प्राप्त करना, पाना।

लावक (*संज्ञा पु.*) लवा पक्षी, बटेर।

लाहू (*संज्ञा पु.*) लाहु। नफा, फायदा, प्राप्ति, लाभ।

लिलार (*संज्ञा पु.*) ललाट, माथा।

लूक (*संज्ञा पु.*) टूटा हुआ तारा, उल्का (संज्ञा स्त्री.) लू, आग की लपट।

लेखना (*क्रि. स.*) गणना करना, समझना, मन ही मन ठहराना, विचार करना।

लेसना (*क्रि. स.*) जलाना।

लोल (*वि.*) चंचल, हिलता-डुलता, क्षीणक, उत्सुक।

लौनाई (*संज्ञा स्त्री.*) लावण्य, सुंदरता, सौंदर्य।

व

वक्रोक्ति *(संज्ञा स्त्री.)* वह काव्यालंकार जिसमें काकु या श्लेष से वाक्य का कुछ और अर्थ निकलता है, काकूक्ति (काकुवाद, गिड़गिड़ाकर कही हुई बात) चमत्कार पूर्ण उक्ति।

वमन *(संज्ञा पु.)* उलटी। बमन।

वमना *(क्रि. स.)* उलटी करना।

वर्म *(संज्ञा पु.)* कवच, घर, मकान।

वर्मा *(संज्ञा पु.)* क्षत्रियों की एक जाति।

वल्कल *(संज्ञा पु.)* वृक्ष की छाल या छाल का वस्त्र

वर्षासन *(संज्ञा पु.)* वर्षासन। वर्ष भर के लिये दिया जानेवाला अन्न का दान।

वाग्विलास *(संज्ञा पु.)* आनंद पूर्वक परस्पर संभाषण, व्यर्थ का वागांडबर, डींग।

वाणी *(संज्ञा स्त्री.)* आवाज, सरस्वती मुँह से निकले सार्थक शब्द, वचन, जीभ।

वात *(संज्ञा पु.)* वात, हवा।

वातगाती *(संज्ञा पु.)* पक्षी, चिड़िया।

वाला *(प्रत्य.) कर्तव्य, स्वामित्व, संबंध आदि का सूचक प्रत्यय।*

वाहनी *(संज्ञा पु.)* अनी, सेना, सेना का एक भेद, जिनमें निश्चित गणना में हाथी, घोड़े, रथ, और पैदल सैनिक हों।

विघटन *(संज्ञा पु.)* संयोजक अंगों को अलग-अलग करना। डिजोल्यूशन, बिगड़ना, नष्ट करना।

विडंबना *(संज्ञा स्त्री.)* किसी को चिढ़ाने के लिये नकल करना, उपहास करना। जैसे : लोभ ने किसकी विडंबना मिट्टी पलीद नहीं की है।

विथकि *(वि.)* विथकित, थकित, स्तब्ध।

विदिश *(संज्ञा स्त्री.)* दो दिशाओं के बीच का कोना।

विपुल *(वि.)* बड़े, भारी, अधिक संख्या में, अगाध।

विभव *(संज्ञा पु.)* धन, संपत्ति, ऐश्वर्य, शक्ति, मोक्ष, पद, प्रतिष्ठा, पालन, रक्षण।

विभेद *(संज्ञा पु.)* विभिन्नता, अंतर, विशेष रूप किया गया भेद या अलगाव। पार्शियेलिटी।

विभु	*(संज्ञा पु.)* ब्रह्मा, आत्मा, जीवात्मा, ईश्वर, स्वामी।
विमोचन	*(संज्ञा पु.)* बंधन आदि से मुक्त होना, बंधन से छुड़ाना। सोच विमोचन= चिंता से मुक्त करानेवाला।
विमोह	*(संज्ञा पु.)* मोह, अज्ञान, बेहोशी।
विमोही	*(वि.)* मोहित करनेवाला, निष्ठुर, कठोर, भ्रम में डालने वाला।
विरद	*(संज्ञा पु.)* बड़ा नाम, ख्याति, प्रसिद्धि, यश, कीर्ति।
विरदावलि	*(संज्ञा स्त्री.)* विरुदावलि। प्रशस्तिगान, यशगान, कीर्ति गान।
विलास	*(संज्ञा पु.)* प्रसन्न या प्रफुल्लित करने की क्रिया, सुखभोग, आनंद क्रीड़ा, मनोरंजन, आनंद, हर्ष, प्रेम सूचक क्रियाएँ जिनसे स्त्रियाँ पुरुषों को अपनी ओर अनुरक्त करती हैं। किसी अंग की मनोहर चेष्टा : जैसे, भ्रूविलास, करविलास, प्रफुल्लता, उत्साहशीलता, तेजस्विता जैसे, मति विलास = बुद्धि की तेजस्विता।
विलासना	*(क्रि. अ.)* भोगना, बरतना।
विशद	*(वि.)* निर्मल, स्वच्छ, साफ, उज्ज्वल। (संज्ञा. पु.) अतिविषा, हीरा कसीस, बादल, सफेद रंग।
विषम	*(वि.)* असमान, कठिन, बहुत, तीव्र, भीषण, विकट।
विषाण	*(स्त्री.) (संज्ञा पु.)* सींग, हाथी दाँत, सूअर का दाँत, इमली।
विष्ठा	*(संज्ञा)* मल, गू, पाखाना, पेट, मध्यभाग।
विसमयवंत	*(वि.)* आश्चर्य चकित।
विसूरन	*(संज्ञा पु.)* दु:ख, रंज, शोक, चिंता, विरक्ति, वैराग्य
विसूरना	*(क्रि. स.)* दु:खी करना।
विहंग	*(संज्ञा पु.)* पक्षी, मेघ, बादल, चंद्रमा, सूर्य।
वृंद	*(संज्ञा पु.)* बृंद। झुंड।
व्याजोक्ति	*(संज्ञा स्त्री.)* कपट भरी बात।
व्यासगद्दी	*(संज्ञा पु.)* धार्मिक कथा कहने वाले के लिये ऊँचा स्थान।
व्रज	*(संज्ञा पु.)* जाना, चलना, व्रजन, गमन, समूह, झुंड, मथुरा के पास कृष्ण का लीला क्षेत्र
व्राज	*(संज्ञा पु.)* कुत्ता, कुक्कट, मुर्गा, जाना, चलना, व्रजन, गमन, समूह, झुंड।

श

शम *(संज्ञा पु.)* शांति, मोक्ष, कर, हस्त, उपचार, रोगमुक्ति, इंद्रियाँ वश में करना।

शमक *(वि.)* शांति कारक।

शमन *(संज्ञा पु.)* यज्ञ के लिये होनेवाले पशुओ का बलिदान, यम, समन। मिटाना, शम, शांति, जैसे रोग का शमन, दोष, विकार, उपद्रव इत्यादि दबाना।

शमनी *(संज्ञा स्त्री.)* रात्रि, रात।

शावक *(संज्ञा पु.)* किसी पशु या पक्षी का बच्चा।

शुक *(संज्ञा पु.)* सुग्गा, तोता, व्यास के पुत्र, रावण के दूत का नाम।

श्रमखोना *(क्रि. अ.)* थकावट दूर होना।

श्रवण *(संज्ञा पु.)* कान। श्रवण करने की क्रिया, सुनना (भाव)।

श्रवणपूर *(संज्ञा पु.)* श्रवणफूल। कर्णफूल।

श्रीखंड *(संज्ञा पु.)* शीतल चंदन सा (मलयागिरी चंदन), एक पेय पदार्थ, शिखरण।

श्रीरंग *(संज्ञा पु.)* लक्ष्मी पति, विष्णु।

श्रीवत्स *(संज्ञा पु.)* विष्णु, भगवान् विष्णु की छाती का चिह्न, जो कि भ्रगु ऋषि के लात मारने के कारण हुआ था।

श्रेणि *(संज्ञा स्त्री.)* कतार, पंक्ति, पाँती, अवली, शृंखला, परंपरा, सिलसिला, दल, समूह, सेना, सीढ़ी, जीना, सिकड़ी, जंजीर।

श्रेणी *(संज्ञा स्त्री.)* समान व्यवसायियों का दल। कोरपोरेशन।

ष

षट्रस *(संज्ञा पु.)* छः प्रकार के रसः 1. मधुर (मीठा), 2. लवण (नमकीन), 3. तित्त (तीखा, तीता), 4. कटु (कडुआ), 5. कषाय (कसैला) और 6. अमल खट्टा।

षट्विकार *(संज्ञा पु.)* प्राणियों के छः विकार या परिणाम, काम, क्रोध, लोभ,

मोह, मद, और मत्सर, पाँचों ज्ञानेंद्रियाँ व मन, इनके छः विकार, क्षुधा, पिपास, हर्ष, शोक, जन्म, मरण।

षडानन *(वि.)* छः मुखवाला, कातिकेय।

षड्गुण *(संज्ञा पु.)* छः गुणों का समूह, राजनीति की छह बातें : संधि, विग्रह, यान/या चढ़ाई, आसन या विराम, द्वैधभाव, और संश्रय।

स

संकल *(संज्ञा पु.)* संकलन, मिलाना। (संज्ञा पु.) साँकल।

संकुल *(विं.)* भरा, परिपूर्ण, संकुलित, संकीर्ण, घना, (संज्ञा पु.) युद्ध, लड़ाई। परस्पर विरोधी वाक्य, असंगत वाक्य, समूह, झुंड।

संघर्षण *(संज्ञा पु.)* संघर्षण। रगड़ना, घिसना, (संज्ञा पु.) संघर्ष। होड़, प्रतियोगिता, रगड़, दो दलों में दबाव डालने के लिये विरोध। कॉनफिक्ट।

संजम *(संज्ञा पु.)* संयम।

संजुग *(संज्ञा पु.)* (युद्ध में जाकर) लड़ाई, संग्राम।

संजुत *(वि.)* संयुक्त।

संडसी *(संज्ञा स्त्री.)* धातु का बना बरतन पकड़ने का औजार।

संतत *(अव्य.)* सतत। सदा, सर्वदा, हमेशा, निरंतर लगातार। (वि.) विस्त्रत, फैलाया हुआ, हमेशा रहनेवाला, बहुत, अधिक, अविकल, अटूट।

संदोह *(संज्ञा पु.)* समूह, झुंड, घन।

संधानना *(क्रि. स.)* धनुष इत्यादि साधना, निशाना, लगाना, तीर चलाना, चलाने के लिये अस्त्र ठीक करना।

संधि *(संज्ञा स्त्री.)* मेल, संयोग, जोड़, सेंध, छेद।

संपुट *(संज्ञा पु.)* खप्पर, पात्र के आकार की वस्तु, दोना।

संभव *(संज्ञा पु.)* उत्पत्ति, संयोग, सहवास, हेतु, शोभा, हो सकने के योग्य होना, ध्वंस, नाश, युक्ति। जो हो सकता हो। पोसिबल।

संभारना *(क्रि. स्र.)* सँभालना।

संभारी *(वि.)* भरा हुआ, पूर्ण। स्त्री संभारिणी।

संभ्रम *(संज्ञा पु.)* आतुरता, उतावली, झूमना, चक्कर लागाना, व्याकुलता,

हलचल, धूम, मोह, भ्रम, भ्राँति।

संभ्रम *(क्रि. वि.)* उतावली में, आतुरता के साथ।

संवतु *(संज्ञा पु.)* वर्ष, संवत्।

संसृति *(संज्ञा स्त्री.)* संसार, जगत्, भवचक्र। संसृति सरि= जन्म मृत्यु रूपी नदी।

सकाना *(क्रि. अ.)* शंका करना, संदेह करना, डर जाना, भय के कारण संकोच करना।

सकाना *(क्रि. स.)* सकना का प्रेरणात्मक रूप।

सकुचना *(क्रि. अ.)* सकुचाना। संकोच करना, शरमाना, लज्जा करना, (फूलों का) बंद होना।

सकुचाना *(क्रि. स.)* किसी को संकोच में डाल देना।

सक्र *(संज्ञा पु.)* इंद्र।

सजन *(संज्ञा पु.)* स्वजन, अपने लोग, प्रिय व्यक्ति, भला आदमी, सज्जन, शरीफ।

सतत *(अव्य.)* लगातार, सदा, सर्वदा, निरंत। संतत।

सत्यसंध *(वि.)* सत्य प्रतिज्ञ, अपने वचन का पालन करनेवाला।

सद्य *(अव्य.)* बहुत शीघ्र ही, आज ही, अभी इसी समय, तुरंत शीघ्र, तत्काल, शिव। सद्यपाक= जिसका फल तुरंत मिले।

सन *(प्रत्य.)* करण कारक का चिह्न, साथ, से। (संज्ञा पु.) रस्सी बनाने का अवयव।

सनाल *(वि.)* नाल या डंठल से युक्त, डंडियों सहित।

सनाथ *(वि.)* सुरक्षित, जिसका कोई रक्षक हो।

सनेमा *(वि.)* नियमपूर्वक किया गया।

सन्यपात *(संज्ञा पु.)* सन्निपात रोग, जिसमें वात, कफ और पित्त तीनों बिगड़ जाते हैं।

सपच्छ *(संज्ञा स्त्री.)* स+पच्छ। पंख धारी, जो अपने पक्ष में हो, सपक्ष।

सपदि *(अव्य.)* जल्दी, उसी समय, तुरंत।

सपेला *(संज्ञा पु.)* साँप+ऐला। साँप का छोटा बच्चा, सर्प।

समन *(संज्ञा पु.)* शमन। यमराज।

समय *(संज्ञा पु.)* वक्त, काल, अवसर, मौका, अवकाश, फुरसत, कौल करार, रिवाज, प्रथा, सामान्य रीति-रस्म।

समयाचार *(संज्ञा पु.)* धर्म।

समर *(संज्ञा पु.)* स्मर, कामदेव।

समर *(संज्ञा पु.)* अच्छे कामों का सुफल, सत्कर्म का फल, सुंदर फल, मेवा आदि।

समर *(संज्ञा पु.)* युद्ध, संग्राम, लड़ाई।

समागम *(संज्ञा पु.)* आगमन, आना, मिलन, स्त्री के साथ संभोग, मैथुन, संघ, समूह, समुदाय। लोगों का किसी उद्‌देश्य के लिये संबद्ध होना। एसोसिएशन। जैसे : संत समागम।

समास *(संज्ञा पु.)* संक्षिप्त, संग्रह, समर्थन, दो शब्दों का मिलकर एक होना (व्याकरण)।

समिटना *(क्रि. स.)* एकत्र होना, पास-पास आना।

समीर *(संज्ञा पु.)* पवन, हवा, वायु। समीर कुमार= पवन पुत्र, हनुमान।

समीहा *(संज्ञा स्त्री.)* प्रयत्न, उद्योग, चेष्टा, इच्छा, जाँच-पड़ताल।

समुहाना *(क्रि. अ.)* सामने आना।

सम्मुख *(अव्य.)* सामने, आगे, समक्ष।

सम्मुख *(वि.)* आगे आनेवाला, सामने आनेवाला, आँखें मिलानेवाला, मुकाबला करने या भिड़नेवाला, जो अनुकूल हो, ठीक, उचित उपयुक्त।

सम्यक् *(वि.)* यथार्थ=यथा+अर्थ। शुद्ध, सत्य, सही, युक्त, ठीक।

सय *(संज्ञा पु.)* सौ। सयगुन (संज्ञा पु.) सौगुना।

सयन *(संज्ञा पु.)* इशारा। सयन बुझाना=इशारा करना।

सर *(संज्ञा पु.)* जलाशय, तालाब, सिर, सिरा, चोटी, तीर, शर। (संज्ञा स्त्री.) चिता।

सरना *(क्रि. अ.)* चलना, सरकना, काम चलना, पूरा होना।

सरसिज *(संज्ञा पु.)* वह जो तालाब में पैदा हो। कमल, सारस पक्षी।

सरसिरुह *(संज्ञा पु.)* कमल। सरसीरुह।

सरासन *(संज्ञा पु.)* धनुष। शरासन।

सरासुर *(संज्ञा पु.)* बाणासुर।

सरिस *(वि.)* समान, सदृश्य।

सरुज *(संज्ञा पु.)* रोगी।

सरोरुह *(संज्ञा पु.)* कमल।

सर्वगत *(वि.)* सर्व व्यापक। (संज्ञा पु.) जल, पानी, आत्मा, ब्रह्मा, शिव।

सलभ *(संज्ञा पु.)* पतंगा।

सवति *(संज्ञा स्त्री.)* सौत।

ससंक *(वि.)* सशंक। जिसे शंका हो, भयभीत, शंका उत्पन्न करनेवाला।

सस *(संज्ञा पु.)* ससक। खरगोश, चंद्रमा।

ससि *(संज्ञा पु.)* अन्न, खेती, शशि, चंद्रमा।

सहिदान *(संज्ञा पु.)* चिह्न, निशान, पहचान, स्मृति के लिये किसी को दी हुई कोई वस्तु।

सहिदानी *(संज्ञा स्त्री.)* निशानी, पहचान, स्मृति के लिये किसी को दी हुई कोई वस्तु।

सहोदर *(वि.)* एक ही उदर से। सहोदर भाई= सगा भाई। पर्याय= अपरोदर।

साँगी *(संज्ञा स्त्री.)* बरछी, शक्ति।

साका *(संज्ञा पु.)* संवत्, शाका, ख्याति, प्रसिद्धि, शोहरत।

साखामृग *(संज्ञा पु.)* शाखामृग। बंदर।

साखि *(संज्ञा पु.)* साखी, साक्षी, देखनेवाला, गवाह, ज्ञान संबंधी दोहे। (संज्ञा स्त्री.) गवाही।

साथरी *(संज्ञा पु.)* चटाई, बिस्तर, बिछौना।

सानना *(क्रि. स.)* दो वस्तुओं को आपस में मिलाना, खास करके किसी तरल पदार्थ में, गूँधना, मिलाना, लपेटना, सम्मिलित करना।

सायक *(संज्ञा पु.)* तीर, बाण,

सायुज्य *(संज्ञा पु.) योग, मिलन, एक प्रकार की मुक्ति।*

सायुज्य *मुक्ति (संज्ञा पु.)* पाँच प्रकार की मुक्तियों में से एक।

सारना *(क्रि. स.)* पूर्ण या समाप्त करना, साधना, बनाना, सुंदर या सुशोभित करना, सँभालना, अस्त्र-शस्त्र चलाना, प्रहार करना।

सारा *(संज्ञा स्त्री.)* दूब, दूर्वा, कुश, कुशा।

सारिखा *(वि.)* सरीखा।

साल *(संज्ञा स्त्री.)* पीड़ा।

सालक *संज्ञा पु.)* दंड देनेवाला।

सालना *(क्रि. स.)* दंड देना।

सावक *(संज्ञा पु.)* श्रावक। सुननेवाला, दूर का शब्द, शिष्य, छात्र।

सावकाश *(संज्ञा पु.)* अवकाश, छुट्टी, अवसर। फुर्सत या सुभीते से।

सावकाश *(वि.)* जिसे फुरसत हो, अवकाशयुक्त, अनुकूल, उचित योग्य।

साहनी *(संज्ञा पु.)* सेना, फौज, साथी, संगी, परिषद्, मध्य कालीन भारत में एक प्रकार के कर्मचारी, घुड़साल का अध्यक्ष।

सिंधुरगामिनी *(संज्ञा स्त्री.)* सौभाग्यवती स्त्री, गजगमिनी।

सिकता *(संज्ञा स्त्री.)* बालू, रेत, एक प्रकार का प्रमेह, चीनी, शर्करा, लोणि साग।

सिख *(संज्ञा पु.)* सिक्ख, शिष्य, चेला, गुरुनानक के अनुयायी। (संज्ञा स्त्री.) सीख, शिखा, चोटी।

सित *(वि.)* श्वेत, स्वच्छ, उज्ज्वल, निर्मल,

सित *(संज्ञा पु.)* चीनी, मूली, चंदन, चाँदी, सफेद तिल, शुक्र ग्रह।

सितासित *(वि.)* श्वेत व श्याम, सफेद और काला।

सिबिका *(संज्ञा स्त्री.)* पालकी।

सियनाहू *(संज्ञा पु.)* सीतापति, राम।

सिरजना *(क्रि. स.)* रचना, बनाना, निर्माण करना, उत्पन्न करना, सृजना।

सिराना *(क्रि. अ.)* शीतल या ठंडा होना, समाप्त होना, मंद पड़ना, मिटना, दूर होना, बीत जाना। (क्रिया स.) ठंडा करना, समाप्त करना, बिताना।

सिलीमुख *(संज्ञा पु.)* शिलीमुख। भ्रमर, बाण, तीर, युद्ध, लड़ाई, मूर्ख।

सिस्नोदर *(संज्ञा पु.)* पुरुष की उपेंद्रिय, लिंग।

सिहाना *(क्रि. अ.)* ईर्ष्या करना।

सिहाना *(क्रि. स.)* ललचना। ईर्ष्या भरी दृष्टि से देखना।

सींव *(संज्ञा पु.)* सीमा, हद, मर्यादा।

सीकर *(संज्ञा पु.)* जलकण, पानी की बूँद, छींटा, पसीना, स्वेदकण।

सीधा *(संज्ञा पु.)* बिना पका हुआ अन्न, जैसे दाल, चावल, आटा, ब्राह्मण को दिया जानेवाला बिना पका हुआ अन्न।

सुअन *(संज्ञा पु.)* आत्मज, पुत्र, बेटा।

सुआर *(संज्ञा पु.)* रसोइया, सूपकार।

सुकुति *(संज्ञा पु.)* सींप, शुक्ति।

सुखेन *(क्रि. वि.)* सुख पूर्वक।

सुजान *(वि.)* ज्ञानी, चतुर, समझदार। पति या प्रेमी, परमात्मा, ईश्वर।

सुठि *(वि.)* सुंदर, बढ़िया, अतिशय या बहुत अच्छा। अत्यंत, पूरा,

बिलकुल।

सुतंत्र *(वि.)* स्वतंत्र, जिसका तंत्र, सेना आदि ठीक हो। तंत्र का ज्ञाता, जानकार।

सुतीक्ष्ण *(वि.)* बहुत तीक्ष्ण या तेज।

सुतीछी *(वि.)* तीखी, अप्रिय।

सुधाई *(संज्ञा स्त्री.)* (संज्ञा पु.) सीधापन।

सुधि *(संज्ञा पु.)* सुध, स्मरण, याद, चेत, समाचार।

सुनासीर *(संज्ञा पु.)* इंद्र, देवता।

सुपास *(संज्ञा पु.)* सुख, आराम।

सुपेंती *(संज्ञा पु.)* चादरें।

सुबट्ट *(संज्ञा पु.)* सुंदर मार्ग, बींथी, गलियाँ।

सुबुइ *(संज्ञा पु.)* समान।

सुबेल *(संज्ञा स्त्री.)* मर्यादा।

सुभग *(वि.)* सुंदर।

सुरति *(संज्ञा स्त्री.)* याद, चेत, सुधि, स्मृति, सूरत, काम के लिये, संभोग।

सुरतिय *(संज्ञा स्त्री.)* देवताओं की स्त्रियाँ, देवांगनाएँ।

सुरनायक *(संज्ञा पु.)* इंद्र।

सुरबासा *(संज्ञा पु.)* देवालय।

सुराई *(संज्ञा स्त्री.)* शूरता, वीरता।

सुलभ *(संज्ञा पु.)* पतंगा, सहज, सरल।

सुहृद *(वि.)* मित्र, सखा, दोस्त। स्नेहयुक्त हृदय वाला।

सुहृदय *(वि.)* स्नेहयुक्त हृदय वाला, सहृदय।

सूतना *(क्रि. अ.)* सोना, शयन कराना। (संज्ञा पु.) पाजामा।

सून *(वि.)* सूना, सुनसान, निर्जन, रहित, हीन। (संज्ञा पु.) प्रसव, जनन, पुत्र, बेटा, फूल की कली, शून्य।

सूनी *(संज्ञा पु.)* मांस बेचनेवाला, शिकारी।

सूनू *(संज्ञा स्त्री.)* कन्या, पुत्र, बेटी।

सूप *(संज्ञा पु.)* मूँग, मसूर, अरहर आदि की पकी हुई दाल। दाल का जूस, रसा, रसे की तरकारी आदि मसालेदार व्यंजन।

सूपक *(संज्ञा पु.)* रसोइया।

सूपकार *(संज्ञा पु.)* भोजन पकाने वाला, रसोइया, पाचक।

सूपोदन *(संज्ञा पु.)* दाल-भात।

सूरि *(संज्ञा पु.)* यज्ञ करानेवाला, पंडित, आचार्य, बृहस्पति का एक नाम, कृष्ण का एक नाम, सूर्य।

सूरी *(संज्ञा पु.)* सूली, भाला, विद्वान्, पंडित।

सृंग *(संज्ञा पु.)* श्रृंग, सृगानि। शिखर (पर्वत का)।

सृंगन्ह *(संज्ञा पु.)* श्रृंग, सृगनि। शिखर।

सेतु *(संज्ञा पु.)* पुल, सीमा, हद, बंधन, प्रतिबंध, प्रणव, ओंकार, मर्यादा।

सेव *(संज्ञा स्त्री.)* सेवा, दूसरे को आराम पहुचाने की क्रिया, नौकरी, चाकरी, आराधना, उपासना, आश्रय, शरण, रक्षा, संभोग, जैसे स्त्री सेवा, व्यवहार, चापलूसी।

सेवन *(संज्ञा पु.)* परिचर्या, खिदमत, उपासना, आराधना, उपभोग।

सैल *(संज्ञा पु.)* शैल, पर्वत, (संज्ञा स्त्री.) बाढ़, जलप्लावन। स्रोत, बहाव।

सोच विमोचन *(संज्ञा पु.)* सोच (चिंता) से छुड़ाने वाले।

सोध *(संज्ञा पु.)* शोध, खोज, खबर।

सोन *(वि.)* शोन। लाल, अरुण।

सोनित *(वि.)* लाल, अरुण। (संज्ञा पु.) रक्त, लहू, केसर।

सोपि *(सर्व.)* सः + अपि = वही, वह भी।

सोम *(संज्ञा पु.)* चंद्रमा, यम, वायु, अमृत, जल, प्राचीन काल की एक लता का एक नाम, जिसका रस पीला और मादक होता था।

सौंध *(संज्ञा स्त्री.)* सुगंध, खुशबू। (संज्ञा पु.) सौध। महल, प्रासाद।

सौंधा *(वि.)* रुचिकर, अच्छा, उत्तम, ठीक।

सौंधाई *(वि.)* अधिकता, बहुतायत, सस्तापन।

स्पृहा *(संज्ञा स्त्री.)* इच्छा, किसी वस्तु प्राप्ति की इच्छा जो धर्मानुकूल हो।

स्फटिक *(संज्ञा पु.)* एक प्रकार का बहुमूल्य या पारदर्शी पत्थर, सूर्यकांत मणि, शीश, काँच, कपूर, फिटकरी।

स्फटिक शिला *(संज्ञा स्त्री.)* स्फटिक की शिला, बिल्लौर।

स्यंदन *(संज्ञा पु.)* रथ।

स्रुवा *(संज्ञा स्त्री.)* घी आदि की आहुति देने की काठ, छोटी करछी।

स्वजन *(संज्ञा पु.)* सजन। अपने लोग, बंधु-बाँधव।

स्वपच *(संज्ञा पु.)* श्वपच। चांडाल, कुत्ते का मांस पकाकर खाने वाला।

स्वल्प *(वि.)* बहुत छोटा।

स्वामी *(संज्ञा पु.)* चार स्वामी, तेजस, प्रांग्य और ब्रह्मा/वह जिसे किसी वस्तु पर पूर्ण रूप से सब प्रकार से अधिकार प्राप्त हो।

ह

हँकारना *(क्रि. स.)* हाँक देकर बुलाना, बुलाना, पुकारना, हँकरावा = बुलावा, बुलावट।

हँकारना *(क्रि. अ.)* ऊँचे स्वर में बुलाना, टेरना, पुकारना, ललकारना।

हटकना *(क्रि. स.)* रोकना, मना करना (बल पूर्वक, बिना आधार के)।

हठ *(संज्ञा स्त्री) (संज्ञा पु.)* किसी बात के लिये होने वाली अड़, दुराग्रह, जबरदस्ती अवश्य होने की क्रिया या भाव हठ मारना=हठ पूर्वक करना।

हत *(वि.)* मारा हुआ, ताड़ित, रहित, विहीन, पीड़ित। हतभागी = भाग्यहीन।

हनन *(संज्ञा पु.)* आघात, जान से मारा।

हनना *(क्रि. स.)* चोट लगाना, आघात करना, जान से मारना।